WHICH WAY GOES CAPITALISM?

WHICH WAY GOES CAPITALISM?

In Search of Adequate Policies
in a Dramatically Changing World

DANIEL DĂIANU

A partnership between American Library Association
and FINRA Investor Education Foundation

FINRA is proud to support the American Library Association

Central European University Press
Budapest New York

©2009 by Daniel Dăianu

Published in 2009 by
CENTRAL EUROPEAN UNIVERSITY PRESS

An imprint of the
Central European University Share Company
Nádor utca 11, H-1051 Budapest, Hungary
Tel: +36-1-327-3138 or 327-3000
Fax: +36-1-327-3183
E-mail: ceupress@ceu.hu
Website: www.ceupress.com

400 West 59th Street, New York NY 10019, USA
Tel: +1-212-547-6932
Fax: +1-646-557-2416
E-mail: mgreenwald@sorosny.org

In cooperation with
CENTER FOR EU ENLARGEMENT STUDIES
Central European University
Nádor u. 9, H-1051 Budapest, Hungary

ISBN 978-963-9776-47-0

This publication was sponsored by

Alliance of Liberals and Democrats for **Europe**
Alliance des Démocrates et des Libéraux pour l'**Europe**

LIBRARY OF CONGRESS CATALOGING-IN-PUBLICATION DATA

Daianu, Daniel.
    Which way goes capitalism?: In Search of Adequate Policies in a Dramatically
Changing World / Daniel Daianu.
    p. cm.
    Includes bibliographical references and index.
    ISBN 978-9639776470 (cloth : alk. paper)
    1. European Union countries—Economic policy. 2. European Union countries—
Foreign economic relations. 3. Capitalism—European Union countries. 4. Inter-
national trade. 5. International finance. I. Title.

HC240.D25 2009
337.1'42--dc22

2009014861

Printed in Hungary by
Akadémiai Nyomda, Martonvásár

To my son, Matei Alexandru,
with the hope of a better world

Table of Contents

Foreword

This book goes to press as the world is in the middle of the most severe financial crisis since the Great Depression. It is not only timely but extremely relevant for the message it delivers. As leaders struggle to face the crisis with short-term responses and begin to tackle the severe recession that the financial crisis has triggered, a deeper and more relevant challenge is facing the international policy community: to define the basic features of a new sustainable model of the world economy in ways that can draw the best lessons from the crisis. Daniel Dăianu sends a very strong and important warning. The main lesson from the crisis is that to deliver their best results in terms of growth, employment and fight against poverty, markets must be embedded in the right set of principles and rules. Without appropriate rules there will always be market failures. Without sound and timely implementation of rules there will always be policy failures. And this crisis is definitely the result of both market and policy failures.

There is another very important message that this book contains. The definition of new rules, of a new framework for global markets, requires the active participation of all major players, including the emerging economies. The new global system will be larger and more diverse. Making it work better and in ways that benefits are shared equally will be a great challenge that cannot be left only to a specific group of participants. In this respect the author also reminds us of the key role that Europe should play in shaping a new global economy.

PIER CARLO PADOAN
Deputy Secretary-General of the OECD

Acknowledgements

This volume illustrates a train of thought which has shaped my profile as an economist and policymaker, for many years now. It also reflects part of my activity in the European Parliament. My work on the Lamfalussy Report (see Appendix 1), which deals with the financial crisis and the supervision of financial markets in the EU, involved a very intense dialogue with MEPs. First and foremost I have to mention Ieke van den Burg, the other co-rapporteur, among them. Pervenche Berès, Sharon Bowles, Wolf Klinz, Piia-Noora Kauppi, John Purvis, Poul Nyrup Rasmunssen, Michel Rocard, Dariusz Rosati, Olle Schmitt, Margarita Starkevičiūtė, and other MEPs were journey fellows on the way of drawing up the report which was passed by the European Parliament in October 2008. With some of them I have disagreed, with others I have empathized, more or less. I am indebted to a few individuals with whom I worked closely during the past decade. With Radu Vrânceanu, from ESSEC (Paris), I co-edited *Ethical Boundaries of Capitalism*. Laurian Lungu, from Cardiff Business School, co-authored with me the study on the financial crisis and the one on the Monetary Union, which are contained in this volume. I thank also Alina Ujupan, Cătălin Păuna and Liviu Voinea for their collaboration in working out the study on the EU Budget. I am grateful to Governor Mugur Isărescu and to the National Bank of Romania, which hosted events where I presented my views on the reform of the regulatory and supervison framework of financial markets, on euro adoption by New Member States and prospects for the Monetary Union. I thank *Ashgate*, *European Voice*, *OECD Publishing*, *Europe's World*, and the *European Journal for Comparative Economics* for the permission to bring together some of my texts in this volume. I thank also Jennifer Doran, Sonja Schröder and Liviu Ştirbăţ for their support in preparing this manuscript for publication.

Introduction

Return to Common Sense Is Needed

I write these words at a time of a deepening financial crisis which is ricocheting worldwide and causing tremendous anguish and tremors, a spreading economic downturn. It is also not a long while after the European Parliament passed a report which I worked out together with a Dutch colleague, Ieke van de Burg, in which we argue in favour of an overhaul of the regulatory and supervision frameworks of financial markets in the EU.[1] I should underline that the paradigmatic underpinnings of our report were not dawned upon us by a growing financial mess engulfing western economies; for a longer period of time both of us, though belonging to two different political groups in the European Parliament, had harboured similar views on what has been wrong with the dynamics of world finance.

Economic freedom and entrepreneurship, which lie at the root of innovation and economic advance, rely on and feed on free markets; this explains why communist economies collapsed, eventually, during the last century. But it is misleading to argue that free markets are synonymous with non-regulated markets, with the practical extinction of public sectors and public policies. Modern economies and societies do need regulations and public policies so that public goods be in adequate supply and negative externalities be prevented or constrained; this implies the functioning of public sectors against the backdrop of a free allocation of resources (at market prices) and vibrant economic

---

[1] Ieke van den Burg and Daniel Dăianu, "Report with recommendations to the Commission on Lamfalussy follow up: future structure of supervision," Rule 39 of the Rules of Procedures, European Parliament, 2008 (see Appendix 1). I am glad that the main recommendations of the de Larosière Group Report are in consonance with the spirit and the letter of our report. The same can be said of the recommendations made by the Turner Report in the UK.

competition. That one needs to streamline public sectors and make them run efficiently so that public resources be not wasted goes without saying. And there is also need of a moral compass, without which everything else gets bogged down, sooner or later.

I was chief economist of Romania's central bank when I was asked by some IMF officials whether I would support the opening of its capital account; that dialogue happened in 1996, about one year before the eruption of the Asian financial crisis. I responded that such a move would be highly risky in the Romanian environment, a dangerous course of action, which I would not recommend to my country's political leaders. Fortunately, Romanian policy-makers took the right course of action during those years. As many accept nowadays, the Asian crisis was caused, primarily, by a premature opening of the capital account in the economies of that region. I always felt that the rush to privatise public utilities is not warranted. As Joseph Stiglitz[2] and others have highlighted, institutional contexts are essential for companies which are turned private to perform well. In addition, there are public utilities which should rather stay in public hands. One has to add here that institutional change is time-consuming and time cannot be compressed at will.

The oversimplification of "good practices" in governance and, not least, the hypocrisy which has, in not a few instances, accompanied their propounding by major industrialized countries around the world is more than obvious nowadays.[3] The deep financial crisis, the failed Doha trade round (with the controversy between free and fair trade), the lack of results wherever development policies have been simplistically encapsulated in the ideological mantra of neo-liberalism are quite telling. Having said that, I do not overlook the corruption, lack of clarity of property rights, waste and stealth of public resources in many poor countries, a terrible misallocation of resources, all of

---

[2] Joseph Stiglitz, *Making Globalization Work*, New York, Allen Lane, 2006. See also Narcis Serra and Joseph Stiglitz (ed.), *The Washington Consensus Reconsidered*, New York, Oxford University Press, 2008.

[3] The World Bank has been concerned with "good practices" (good governance) for a long time and disseminates information on this topic around the world regularly. I wonder why hasn't this institution paid attention to malpractice in the financial industry in advanced economies, which are not of recent vintage, as well.

which impede economic growth.[4] But such structural weaknesses do not make up a convincing argument in favour of accepting, without qualifications, policy remedies which are too general and, sometimes, in divorce of concrete local conditions. Market-oriented reforms have unfettered entrepreneurship and have stimulated economic growth in China after 1978, and in India during the last decade, but those reforms have been implemented in a pragmatic way, with a close attention paid to social issues and rural development problems, while financial markets have not been liberalised recklessly. In these two very complex cases big policy trade-offs and dilemmas remain, though economic progress has been extraordinary. Dani Rodrik,[5] Paul Krugman[6] and other clairvoyant economists have constantly asked for open-mindedness in examining the major problems afflicting poor countries; they have rejected oversimplifications and asked for policy variety depending on local circumstances. Although their academic credentials are exceptional, their voices were not sufficiently listened to.

I lived for a substantial part of my life under communism and I value economic and political freedom in ways which those who were fortunate to live in liberal democracies (to use Fareed Zakaria's concept) may not understand fully. But I am not blind to the bads which can plague market economies, especially those that are not adequately regulated and do not offer a decent amount of public goods to their citizens. For me, liberal values (in the European sense) undergird, essentially, liberal democracies; in a democracy liberal creeds, arguably, underlie various political inclinations—be they more social-democratic or of the "people's party" brand, along the European political spectrum. I espouse a type of liberalism which owes a lot to Karl Popper and his concept of an "open society."[7] For me individual liberties

---

[4] See for instance William Easterly, *The Elusive Quest for Growth*, Cambridge, MIT Press, 2001.

[5] Dani Rodrik, *One Economics, Many Recipes*, Princeton, Princeton University Press, 2007. See also his *The New Global Economy and Developing Economies. Making Openness Work*, Washington DEC, Overseas Development Council, 1998.

[6] Paul Krugman got his Nobel Prize for having shown the effects of economies scale on trade patterns and on the location of economic activity. He was prescient in foreboding the pitfalls of the new financial system; see his *The Return of Depression Economics*, New York, Norton, 1999.

[7] Karl Popper, *The Open Society and Its Enemies*, London, Routledge, 1945.

coexist with concepts of social solidarity, social equity,[8] public goods and moral values (trust, honesty, trustworthiness, sense of responsibility and accountability, etc). The German notion of "social market economy" (*soziale Marktwirtschaft*)[9] illustrates pretty well my way of thinking in this regard. I mention moral values because, frequently, I hear people (in the European Parliament, too) who claim that morality is meaningless in business. I would argue that it is so for those who choose to disregard moral values and for whom society is quite meaningless. I also think that ruthless competition in the global economy does strain European societies and their social model. But measures which focus on boosting competitiveness, while ignoring social cohesion and the social contract between state and citizens, can be equally damaging to society as it is a policy *status quo*. In the European Union the experience of Scandinavian countries with undertaking reforms that enhance competitiveness without disregarding the social fabric of society is quite relevant in this regard.

The financial crisis which has struck the core of the world financial industry is, in my opinion, a decisive refutation of the paradigm that glorifies total deregulation in economies, be they wealthy or poor.[10] The repeal in 1999 of the Glass-Steagall Act that limited ownership of financial companies operating in other market segments, like the decision in 2004 to exempt the brokerage operations of Wall Street investment banks from limits on the amount of debt they could take

---

[8] See John Rawls, *A Theory of Justice*, Cambridge, Harvard University Press, 1971.

[9] A main theorist of the social market economy was Wilhelm Roepke and a leading practioner in Germany was Chancellor Ludwig Erhard.

[10] In a letter published by the leading French daily *Le Monde*, 22 May 2008, one can read: "Some are tempted to see the ongoing financial crisis as a recurrent accident, albeit more severe, along an economic cycle and following worldwide very cheap credit for years in a row. But a careful reading would go at its structural roots. Globalisation of markets and financial engineering, with precarious and, frequently, missing regulations, highly skewed incentive schemes, and numerous conflicts of interest, have created the milieu for the current crisis." The letter was signed by Helmut Schmidt, Otto Graf Lambsdorff, Lionel Jospin, Jacques Delors, Michel Rocard, Romano Prodi, Jacques Santer, Göran Persson, Pär Nuder, Massimo d'Alema, Hans Eichel, Poul Nyrup Rasmussen, Daniel Dăianu, Paavo Lipponen, Ruairi Quinn, Laurent Fabius, Anneli Jaatteenmaki. The full text of the letter can be read in Appendix 2.

on, have proved to be historic blunders.[11] The root cause of this crisis is an inadequately and under-regulated financial system. The waves of deregulation in the financial industry brought to the market a plethora of fancy products whose risks were poorly understood. Mortgages are not toxic *per se*; badly constructed securities based on them are toxic. The packaging and repackaging of financial products are toxic, making their valuations increasingly unclear and reducing their tradability. Reward schemes that shape the decisions of managers and agents in markets and that make their behaviour irresponsible—that is toxic. Misleading quantitative models are toxic. The trigger for this financial crisis may have been in the housing industry, but housing is not the structural cause of the crisis.

What this crisis should make plain to everyone is that not all financial innovation is benign. It is baffling to hear the argument that fresh regulation is bad because it would stifle financial innovation. Fresh regulation is necessary because there has been a lack of proper regulation and supervision. The enormous mistakes that have been made by allowing finance to develop its own, highly risky *raisons d'être* must be undone. But are we capable of learning that lesson? Why is it that we fail to learn from previous crises? Alexander Lamfalussy issued warnings almost a decade ago; the financier Warren Buffett, Lyle Gramlich and the former Federal Reserve chairman Paul Volcker are among those important figures who fired off warnings years ago. Nouriel Roubini did the same, including at Davos Forum meetings. How is it that their predictions of a major crisis have not been listened to?

As traffic needs rules and lights in order to protect people's lives, so market economies need regulations to limit collateral damage and enhance the production of public goods. A lax monetary policy can lead to higher inflation and, ultimately, to a recession, but cannot, by itself, cause the meltdown of a financial system. This is the crux of the matter: the features of the financial system that have brought the threat of collapse are structural features of the "new" financial system, including a breakdown of due diligence.

---

[11] Alan Greenspan, the long-serving president of the Fed is quoted by the *International Herald Tribune* to have acknowledged that something has been wrong with the free market theory he has upheld (Brian Knowltoon and Michael Greenbaum, "Greenspan makes rare admission of fallibility," 24 October 2008, p. 1). Greenspan is well known for having been a staunch opponent of regulating derivatives, the "new banking sector."

Vested interests can have a long arm and try to influence regulations and supervision. But vested interests must be strongly resisted, using all means available. Regulators and supervisors should know that financial markets are volatile and prone to instability, and that the *efficient-markets hypothesis*—that prices reflect all known information—is a fantasy.[12]

The huge bail outs underway (in the financial sectors) are going to introduce, or reinforce, elements of state capitalism in numerous industrialized countries, including the US. The impact on national budgets would be burdensome for years to come. In order to mitigate the pains and reduce dependency on external borrowings, saving ratios would have to go up in all economies where bank recapitalization will be very serious. A legitimate question arises: can rich societies become, almost all of a sudden, much more economizing and forward looking? This very much hinges on social cohesion (solidarity) and the capacity of politicians to lead in times of distress. If one adds here the implications of aging and strained welfare states, climate change, as well as the competitiveness challenges posed by emerging global powers, the contours of very complicated public policy agenda in the decades to come are not hard to delineate.

The effects of the current financial crisis have hit the western world at a time when tectonic shifts in the global economy had been taking place for more then a decade. The rise of China, India, Brazil, the resuscitation of a capitalist Russia (that benefits on huge natural resources) are ushering in an increasingly multi-polar world, with growing reverberations economically and geopolitically. The struggle for the control of exhaustible resources (oil and gas in particular) epitomises this phenomenon. The financial crisis has given more salience to the inherent weaknesses of policies which are not pragmatic and which succumb to fundamentalist tenets.

The fall of communism, which was equated by some with the *End of History*,[13] has favoured immensely the advance of neo-liberal ideas. In the western world this advance has fuelled the ascendancy of the so-called Anglo-Saxon type of capitalism—with its Third Way[14]

---

[12] For a strong indictment of the *efficient markets hypothesis* see also Benôit B. Mandelbrot and Richard L. Hudson, *The (Mis)behaviour of Markets: A Fractal View of Risk, Ruin and Reward,* London, Profile Books Ltd., 2004.

[13] Francis Fukuyama, *The End of History*, New York, Free Press, 1990.

[14] Anthony Giddens, *The Third Way*, Cambridge, Polity Press, 1998.

reflex on the left side of the political spectrum. Needless to say that the overwhelming superiority of the US on all fronts (economic, military, technological), offered a sort of a *sui generis Pax Americana* and created prerequisites for an *international regime*. The latter was supposed to order the world by providing international public goods and resolving/preventing possibly major conflicts. Neo-liberalism (market fundamentalism) has revealed its serious flaws over time and is, currently, willy-nilly, put on the shelf for the sake of salvaging the functioning of market economies. Because what is happening now is not a dismissal of market forces as an essential mechanism for resource allocation and stimulating entrepreneurship, but an invalidation of a grossly misinterpretation of what it takes for a modern economy to perform economically and socially over the long run.

Fragments of state capitalism are being put in place and we will see what will remain out of them over time. Probably, substantial chunks of the new state sectors in the making will turn private at one point in time. Monetary policies have been geared now, primarily, toward avoiding financial meltdown and have acquired a sort of flexibility that is reminiscent of the injunctions of John Maynard Keynes, the great British advocate of the value of government intervention, regarding ways of avoiding bad equilibria (the Great Depression was a terribly bad "equilibrium"). The very concern of governments and central banks with radically overhauling the regulation and supervision of financial markets, so that "Minsky moments"—moments at which, according to the now deceased economist Hyman Minsky, financiers lay waste to the economy[15]—are averted, is a strong validation of Keynes' intellectual legacy and of his sense of realism in understanding the functioning of markets in general.

The crux of the matter is that the reshaped mixed economies have to function in such a way that extravagant policies be avoided for the benefit of democracy and the welfare of most citizens. Cycles cannot be eliminated, and crises will pop up again. But a financial meltdown, with its very dire effects on the real economy, can be prevented by adopting proper policies and regulations; and very severe crises can also be averted.

---

[15] Hyman Minsky, *Stabilizing an Unstable Economy* (first edition, 1986), New York, McGraw Hill, 2008.

The EU and the US will come out of this crisis with reshaped economies (with larger public sectors) and will, very likely, continue to be, fundamentally, liberal democracies. But the financial crisis has already weakened them, whereas the ascendancy of the new global powers is hard to stop, although an economic slowdown will be felt worldwide. I see the future as being driven by a competition between liberal democracy and authoritarian forms of capitalisms—the latter being represented by China and the Russian Federation, principally.

For the European Union the aims of the Lisbon Agenda are not diminished by this financial crisis. But they have to be pursued while momentous changes are occurring in the *Zeitgeist* and the frame of policy-making.

Liberal democracies will have to come to grips with their weakened relative status in the world economy and shed much of their hubris in dealing with the rest of the world, for their own sake.[16] This would apply to the reform of the International Financial Institutions and a new architecture for tackling global governance issues, which would have to involve the emerging global powers. As some say, a new Bretton Woods is needed.

This period, the years to come, mark the prominent return of Keynes and the idea of government intervention. We need common sense and pragmatism in economic policy-making, not fundamentalism. As some aptly observe: "History proves the importance of policies for preserving the social fabric."[17]

This volume brings together pieces of analysis which I did write, alone or with colleagues of mine, during this decade. These studies focus on the prerequisites of economic development (Chapter 1), including the role of ethics (Chapter 2), the current financial crisis (Chapter 3 and 4), the European model and challenges facing the EU (Chapter 5, 6 and 7), the crisis of the international regime against the backdrop of the diminishing power of the West, tectonic shifts in the world economy and a looming "clash of capitalisms" (Chapter 8). As a matter of fact, the competition among models of capitalism is a silver-line of this volume.

---

[16] To see how "others" view the US and the EU in the 21st century, read Kishore Mahbubani, *The New Asian Hemisphere*, New York, Public Affairs, 2008.

[17] Robert Shiller, *The Subprime Solution*, Princeton, Princeton University Press, 2008, p. 2.

CHAPTER 1

Institutional and Policy Diversity as an Engine of Economic Development[1]

Diversity, or variety, is the essence of economic life in the sense of underlying choice; economic calculation gives numerical substance to how people make choices in their daily endeavours, either as consumers or entrepreneurs.[2] As Kevin Lancaster pointed out years ago, *variety* has value in itself,[3] for we enjoy a wider range of choices instead of a smaller one. How does diversity/variety take shape in the realm of institutions and policy making? Is the range of choices open-ended? How does institution competition operate in the real world?

The last couple of decades have revealed an overwhelming offensive of the neo-liberal paradigm in terms of defining "best practices" and spreading the gospel of its policies throughout the world; this offensive was carried out by IFIs as well. Even language was shaped accordingly with market reforms being seen in a quasi-single theoretical and policy framework. Are we heading towards increasing uniformity—according to the logic of this paradigm—with regard to institutional and policy set-ups, worldwide? An affirmative answer would underline the successful market-based transformation of series of command economies, some of which are going to join the European Union in 2004.[4] Likewise, some convergence between institutional patterns in

---

[1] This text was published by the *European Journal of Comparative Economics*, Vol. 1, No. 1, pp. 33–58, 2004. Comments made by Michael Keren, Jacques Pelkmans, Tsumeaki Sato and Radu Vrânceanu are highly appreciated. I bear sole responsibility for the content of the paper.

[2] As Rosen (2002, p. 1) says, *Diversity is the stuff of economics*.

[3] Lancaster (1979).

[4] Albeit notable differences among reform policies have existed at the same time, China provides a glaring example of successful market based gradualistic transformation.

the USA and the EU economies might be alluded to in the same vein. A supportive argument for this line of reasoning could be that what matters for individual achievement, in the end, are equal opportunities. But this argument can be turned around when debating the merits of various institutional set-ups in terms of creating fair chances for people.

A sceptical answer would highlight the mounting challenges which confront societies, whether rich and poor, and the international community in general—in spite of the high hopes of not long ago. The demise of the "New Economy"—the almost metaphysical notion of the 90s—the corporate scandals across the Atlantic (and not only there) and the subsequent recourse to new regulatory legislation, recurrent financial and currency crises throughout the world (which evince major flaws of the international financial system), the controversies surrounding the activity of IFIs should compel "ideologues," of all sorts, to be more humble in their prescriptions. In this context one can mention the partial counter-offensive represented by the so-called "Third Way" paradigm,[5] the new vigor found by neo-Keynesian ideas, the powerful insights of the "New Theories," as Robert Gilpin calls them, and last, but not least, the rising ambivalence triggered by unmanaged globalisation.

This essay argues that there is substantial scope for institutional and policy diversity to operate as a means to foster economic development; that there might be paradigmatic cyclicity in the dynamic of economic policies.

I. What Influences Institutional and Policy Diversity?

Institutional and policy diversity falls, arguably, under the impact of an array of factors and circumstances; some of these are enumerated briefly below.

---

[5] The guru is Anthony Giddens. The "new social democrats" talk about a worldwide political movement which should embrace their ideas.

1 Institution and Policy Competition

Competition rewards better performance, which is revealed at both micro and macro/societal level.[6] The adoption of best practices illustrates the power of better ideas and institutions. But best practices have their own dynamic and are shaped by local conditions, which further imply that institutions evolve over time—some decay, some advance, some transform themselves.[7]

2 Ideology

John Maynard Keynes remarked that economists are intellectual prisoners of famous ideas. But ideas do not operate in a social vacuum. This is why, where democracy exists, it is not hard to detect linkages between the dynamic of political life (which is influenced by ideas/doctrines) and changes in economic policies. This is because the constellation of interests in society, which are articulated politically, drives policy formulation. When circumstances modify the texture of interests and entail also variations in the power (relevance) of ideas (some decay while others are resuscitated...), policies change and this can change institutions as well.

3 Values (Culture) and Institutions

Values influence individual and corporate behaviour, policies; they also modulate public intervention in the economy (society). Thence the debate on the merits and weaknesses of various brands of capitalism is not irrelevant.[8] But whatever cultural and social differences exist, people prize highly trust, honesty and loyalty. As J.K. Arrow[9] said in a beautiful essay, these moral values have economic value, are basic institutions that oil the economic machinery and make it function better.

---

[6] Although some (like Paul Krugman) would argue that nations do not compete, I still believe that nations, when seen as economic spaces (clusters of economic activities), compete. Otherwise, why would we care about national laws and norms and local networks?

[7] For a sharp analysis of evolving institutions in capitalism, see Mancur Olson (1982). See also North (1981).

[8] In spite of convergence tendencies there are still important differences between American-type and European-type capitalisms. Asian capitalism has its own peculiar traits, as Latin-American economies also reveal specificities.

[9] Arrow (1970).

4 Complexity

Complexity does affect the ability of policy to influence economic out-comes. Undoubtedly, growing complexity magnified the costs of com-mand-type planning in the former communist states and speeded up their collapse. Another example is provided by the European Union. Thus, the EU encounters mounting difficulties in its quest for institu-tional reforms (the Common Agricultural Policy included) due to its growing size and complexity. And it is clear that *enlargement* would not make this task easier. Japan achieved an economic miracle during the last century, especially after the Second World War; her success was fuelled by an ingenious combination of market-based economic struc-tures and state intervention. Nonetheless, the increasing complexity and export orientation of the Japanese economy has entailed changes in its functioning and is forcing policy-makers to rethink their policy tools in order to cope with new policy dilemmas[10] (I refer here, in par-ticular, to the decade long stagnation, and not, necessarily, to the con-sequences of the crisis in the banking system). And the late corporate scandals in the USA show the proliferation of conflicts of interest and the dangers of excessive market deregulation against the background of increasingly complex financial innovations.[11]

5 Economic Openness

The more open and smaller is an economy, the more severely con-strained is its national policy by external stimuli (phenomena). This is why open macroeconomics are quite different from macroeconomics in a relatively closed economy. Size matters considerably in explaining the intensity of transmitted effects, the power of interdependencies.

6 International Agreements

International agreements operate as a constraining factor, unless a country's policy-makers obtain derogations or enter into special ar-rangements with partners.

---

[10] For an excellent presentation of Japan's economic pains and travails, see Gao (2001).
[11] One can see here some bad effects of the repeal of the Glass-Steagall Legisla-tion.

7 The Rules Imposed by the Functioning of the Economic and Monetary Bloc

For example, the EU accession countries have to comply with the so called *Acquis Communautaire*. However, there is room for bargaining and the EU itself should be interested in better policy venues—in view of its own reform pains and the need to help accession countries catch up economically.

8 Policy Conditionality

In a world of growing interdependencies, the effectiveness (performance) of policy-making hinges on local expertise and the bargaining power of local negotiators in dealing with IFIs and other entities (such as the EU). Policy conditionality is to be linked to *policy ownership*. Lately, the IFIs have increased their concern for enhanced policy ownership, although, sometimes, this smells more of a rhetorical exercise or an attempt to diffuse the responsibility for failed programs.

9 Special Circumstances

Powerful adverse shocks force policy-makers to change their views and entrenched habits. Think about the rescue package mounted by the Republican Administration in the USA in order to help airline companies (following the tragedy of September 11) together with the possibility (as aired by Ben Bernanke, who is a member of the Board of FED) of combating deflation by buying T-bills, or the credits granted by the central bank of Brazil to firms which were badly affected by credit lines withdrawn by foreign banks (during late 2002), etc.

II. An Historical Perspective

A. THE HIGH AGE OF POLICY DIVERSITY

Institutional and policy variety was quite obvious in the aftermath of the Second World War. I am not referring to the philosophical and practical underpinnings of command (communist systems). What I have in mind is the wide spectrum of views with regard to economic development, the macro-management of capitalist economy, trade policy arrangements, foreign exchange regimes for dealing with capital movements, etc. One can argue that a national economy-cantered view dominated policy-making, as against the nowadays' conception of a "borderless world."[12]

That was a period in which Keynesianism seemed to be hardly assailable in the realm of macroeconomic policy; structuralism got a high profile in relation with key problems afflicting developing countries, while the theory of the developmental state was embodied by Asian accomplishments. Trade policy, too, was used by various countries in order to acquire new competitive advantages, or protect domestic markets.

There was much confidence in the regulatory power of the state and in its ability to make the markets function better, a vision which had roots in the Great Depression. This vision may have been reinforced by the tasks of post-war economic reconstruction and post-colonialism. But these policies were frequently abused during that period and wishful thinking influenced policy-making often. Arguably, this policy thrust did undermine the vigour of market forces.

Nonetheless, the record showed positive results: there was economic reconstruction in Western Europe, a string of economic miracles in Asia, Brazil's impressive economic growth in the 1950s and the 1960s (however fractured and skewed that was...), etc.

B. The Neo-liberal Zeitgeist of the Last Couple of Decades

I would submit that globalisation is driven by both technological and institutional (policy) factors. Therefore, it can be seen as a facet, too, of the neo-liberal offensive which started a couple of decades ago.[13] But one should make a distinction between technological change (progress), which has economic and institutional consequences and which is, historically, of inscrutable vintage, and the range of policies initiated in the framework of wide-ranging financial and trade liberalisation, as well as of massive privatisation.

---

[12] See Ohmae (1995).
[13] Soros (2002), among others, calls it "market fundamentalism."

During this period one meets the retreat of Keynesianism (against the background of rising inflation in several advanced economies and setbacks of profligate welfarism) together with a belief in the preponderance of government failures in macro and micro-managing economies; market coordination failures are largely dismissed. Likewise, the poor record of economic progress in large areas of the world speeded up the sunset of development economics. As a matter of fact, mainstream (neoclassical) economics was seen as providing a valid toolbox for any circumstances. Thence emerged a policy framework—supported by the IFIs (the so called Washington Consensus)—which supplanted the much wider conceptual policy approach of the 1950s and the 1960s.

In the 1980s there was much talk about a clash of models: the Anglo-American model vs. a so-called continental model, and an Asian model. Nonetheless, trade liberalisation, market deregulation and privatisation contained ideological fervour and were pushed by the IFIs unrelentlessly. The collapse of communism gave a further impetus to this vision and policy orientation.

The complete independence of central banks, fiscal conservatism and neutrality, rejection of macro-management of the economy, downsizing of the public sector and market deregulation were seen as epitomes of sound economics and policy, to be generalised worldwide. And globalisation supplied the world arena for thinking that there is "one way, and only one way" in order to achieve economic progress and, eventually, catching-up.

The natural inference would be that policy diversity in policy-making is senseless in a world which appears to have discovered the ultimate best practices, either at the macro, or the micro level.

III. Examining the Record

There are numerous facts which invalidate the rosy outlines of the picture sketched above and invite intellectual soul searching and honest debate.

The Washington Consensus[14] has performed much below expectations in not a few cases, and there are a significant number of top

---

[14] The Washington Consensus, as a name, was concocted by John Williamson,

notch economists who question some of its working hypotheses; some theoretical premises have been severely questioned[15] and the work of the IMF and the World Bank has come under fire.[16]

Policies aimed at fostering growth in developing countries seem to have fared quite poorly, in many respects, in the last couple of decades—at a time of widespread application of the main tenets of the Washington Consensus. According to a foremost development economist, William Easterly (who, for many years, was among the World Bank staff), during 1980–1998, average per capita income growth in developing countries was practically 0.0% (!), as compared to 2.5% during 1960–1979.[17] I would add that this discrepancy becomes even larger when singling out the economic performance of some Asian countries—which, as an increasing number of economists would concede, did pursue export orientation, but also implemented measures which, often, were at odds with the "orthodox" policies[18]; these countries shaped their own, particular, strategies. As Easterly also points out, "the increase in world interest rates, the increased debt burden of developing countries, the growth slowdown in the industrial world, and skill-biased technical change may have contributed" to this stagnation.[19] Easterly also stresses the inability of governments' policies

---

with reference to the essence of IMF and World Bank's policies pursued in the last couple of decades.

[15] Stiglitz (1994, 2002) is the most notorious critic, and the list includes Paul Krugman, Jeffrey Sachs, Jagdish Bhagwati and others.

[16] James Wolfensohn himself has indicated that he is not insensitive to what is wrong with the World Bank.

[17] Easterly's (2001a) results seem to contradict one of the main conclusions of the World Bank's Global Economic Prospects for Developing Countries 2001, which asserts that "Developing countries as a group enjoyed accelerated economic growth over the past decade..." (World Bank Policy and Research Bulletin, April–June 2001, p. 1). It is fair to say, however, that Easterly refers to per capita income growth.

[18] These countries achieved macroeconomic stabilization via low budget deficits and tight monetary policies, but did nor refrain from targeting potential "winners," through industrial and trade polices. A normal question arises whether such policies can be effective under the pressure of globalisation and when public administration is weak, or captured by vested interests, as is the case in many transition economies.

[19] Easterly (2001a). See also his *The Elusive Quest for Growth* (2001b).

worldwide to make good use of incentives for growth. This state of affairs begs a simple question: why is it so difficult to use incentives in order to foster sustained growth?[20] Easterly goes on, "We economists who work on poor countries should leave aside some of our past arrogance. The problem of making poor countries rich was much more difficult than we thought."

Mainstream (neoclassical) theory has still to explain why divergence is so much prevalent in the world economy.[21] Moreover, endogenous growth models[22] and economic geography models have reinforced misgivings about the unqualified optimism on the distribution of benefits of free trade and free capital movements. Hence, a natural question arises: is opening (integration) to the outer economy advantageous, irrespective of circumstances?

There has been an insufficient attention paid to the reality of asymmetries and informational problems in the functioning of both domestic and international markets, and to the key role of institutions. Partially, this is mirrored by the talk regarding "second-generation reforms," "good governance" and "reinvigorating the state's capabilities." But as Dani Rodrik remarked, "the bad news is that the operational implications of this for the design of development strategy are not that clear," and "there are many different models of a mixed economy. The major challenge facing developing nations is to fashion their own particular brands of mixed economy."[23] In this respect, he stresses the key role of institutions of property rights, conflict management and law and order. This search for country-specific solutions does not clash with the

---

[20] *Op. cit.*, p. 291.

[21] See The World Bank's Annual Conference on Development Economics, proceedings of 1999 and 2000 meetings. As the World Bank economist P. Richard Agenor (2000, p. 392) put it, "the conventional neoclassical theory has proved incapable of explaining in a satisfactory manner the wide disparities in the rates of per capita output growth across countries."

[22] Pioneered by Paul Romer and Robert Lucas. Lucas (1988, pp. 3–42) explains why divergence, instead of convergence, does happen.

[23] Rodrik (2000b). Rodrik emphasizes five functions that public institutions must serve for markets to work properly: protection of property rights, market regulation, macroeconomic stabilization, social insurance, and conflict management. He also underlines that "there is in principle a large variety of institutional setups that could fulfill these functions" (p. 3).

need to use so called "best practices," but one should equally acknowledge that "best practices" are not always clear. In this context, one has to give a fair hearing to Mauro Guillen, who argues that globalisation should not be understood as encouraging "convergence toward a single organizational pattern" and that "organizational outcomes in the global economy are contingent on country-specific trajectories."[24] The implication is that diversity does matter and adds value.

The issue of asymmetries acquires particular salience in the international economy, where there is increasing disenchantment with the distribution of trade gains[25] and the functioning of financial markets. In this respect, one has to stress both the distribution aspect of trade (which relates to the rules of the game and to the way in which industrial countries defend their own markets),[26] as well as the institutional dimension.

Prominent voices argue that the world community needs new arrangements, new institutions, which should be capable of addressing the problems of world governance.[27] For instance, it is disconcerting to see that the efforts initiated in the field of financial markets reform, by the Financial Stability Forum, in 1998, subsided. As Larry Summers astutely pointed out, world integration demands financial integration, but, as the 20s and the 30s of the last century prove, recurrent financial crises can lead to world disintegration.[28]

Post-communist economic transition has had very mixed results and the mantra of quick privatisation and liberalisation has clearly indicated its limits and simplicity. Under the term "the second wave of reforms" there has been an attempt to renew transformation economics by acknowledging the role of institutional change (and its

---

[24] Guillen (2001).

[25] As the World Bank's Global Economic Prospects and the Developing Countries 2001 Report says, "trade barriers in industrial countries represent a major roadblock for developing countries" (*Ibid.*, p. 2).

[26] The preparations for the Doha WTO conference were quite telling in this respect, with the USA, the EU and Japan having basically set the agenda. The failure of the Cancum meeting (in October 2003) point at the same policy attitude.

[27] This is the message of George Soros' book (2002). Lord Dahrendorf is also very critical of the way in which the existing international institutions address these issues (for instance, in his lecture delivered at the New Europe College, Bucharest, October, 2001).

[28] Summers (2000, p. 1).

consuming nature), the importance of competition and structures of governance (in the public and the private sectors), the need of public goods (which cannot be supplied by the private sector), etc.

The backlash against globalisation is a stark reminder of the perils of succumbing to a simplistic economic cosmology. Growing economic gaps in the world,[29] increasingly unstable financial markets and recurrent crises, the deterioration of the environment and the challenge of sustainable development in the world, spreading diseases, etc. have brought home many pieces of bad news. There is now talk of the need to manage (correct) globalisation and reform the international financial system.

The fading away of the myth of the "New Paradigm" and "the New Economy" in the USA, the spate of corporate scandals across the Atlantic[30] and the plunging bourses worldwide (during 2001–2002), the rocky recovery in the USA together with poor growth in the EU are not without policy consequences. In the USA, the Bush Administration has resorted to a heavy dose of Keynesian economics in order to stem recession, whereas the heavyweight economies in the EU are flouting the Stability Pact provisions on budget deficits.

The discrepancy between preaching and practice, particularly in the case of advanced economies,[31] should give much food for thought, apart from its hypocritical undertones.

IV. Where Do We Stand?

A. BASIC RULES AND CONTENTIOUS ISSUES

One can hardly question basic rules of the economic game which underlie a sound functioning of economies. Such rules are: free prices are essential for proper resource allocation; there is need for clearly

---

[29] The 2002 Annual Report of the World Bank furthers the debate on the inadequacies of current policies for dealing with poverty reduction (*Financial Times*, 23 August 2002).

[30] Following these scandals, the Anglo-American model has lost some of its lustre (see also Eric Orts, "Law is never enough to guarantee fair practice," *Financial Times*, 23 August 2002).

[31] Think only about farm subsidies provided by both the USA and the EU and steel protectionism on the part of the USA.

defined and protected property rights in order to foster entrepreneurship and commercial transactions; hard budget constraints need to operate ubiquitously in order to have financial stability; over the longer
term low budget deficits are better than large ones; money printing is
bad for monetary stability, outward-orientation of the economy is essential for making good use of comparative advantages.

These basic rules, however, do not extinguish the battle of paradigms and resulting advocated policies. Moreover, intellectual bigotry
and doctrinal fundamentalism are detrimental to good policy-making,
for the latter needs to be pragmatic and not skewed to vested interests.

At the start of the new century the jury is still out on central issues, which have divided economists over the decades. This ambiguous
reality and theoretical situation should trigger more candid debate in
the places where policy is formulated or among those instances which
advise governments. Let me single out some of these central issues, as
they relate, particularly, to emerging economies.

1 The Macroeconomic Policy-Mix

The Asian crises of the late 90s have revealed the shortcomings of
using budget retrenchment as the primary means for balance of payments adjustment at a time when the main source of high external in-
debtedness is the private sector. Likewise, overly restrictive monetary
policies for supporting the local currencies proved to be quite damaging to the corporate and the banking sectors, since they entailed lasting
sharp rises in real interest rates—which accentuated *adverse selection*
and, often, made things worse. For this reason some form of financial
repression may be necessary in exceptional circumstances, as it is the
imposition of smart capital controls. These insights get more salience
against the backdrop of the revival of Keynesian-type policies in not a
few places (when inflation is very low, or deflation turns threatening).

2 Trade

Although free trade is deemed desirable by most economists (as a
weapon of satisfying consumers and making good use of comparative
advantages), the existence of big asymmetries and dynamic effects (including increasing returns in ascending industries) provide a rationale
for developing countries to seek some protection—in this respect some
distinguish between free and fair trade. As Dani Rodrik put it, free

trade is not always conducive to economic growth.[32] One has to stress also here the discrepancy between what some rich countries preach and what they practice. Let us think about trade in agricultural products and not only.

3 Capital Movements

Free capital flows have revealed to be quite threatening for emerging markets and the IMF no longer recommends the opening of the capital (KAL) account unless proper regulatory and institutional prerequisites exist. KAL was strongly recommended by the IMF to developing countries in the 90s, following the logic of free capital flows and the creation of a "level playing field" in a, supposedly, increasingly globalised world economy. It is fair to acknowledge that capital account liberalisation has exposed many institutional and policy weaknesses in various countries; but it is also correct—for those who advocated this policy drive—to acknowledge that KAL was, frequently, a mistake in view of the turbulence it caused in many countries and the contagion effects it entailed.[33] Nowadays, the IMF admits, both explicitly and implicitly, this mistake when it links KAL with sound macroeconomic policy, proper institutions (including the banking/financial system) and solid prudential regulations.

4 Exchange Rate Policy

The financial debacle in Argentina and the demise of its currency board question another tenet of the late 1990s (following the financial crises): that the corner solutions are inescapable exchange rate regimes in a world of free capital flows. Life shows again its complexity and the danger of oversimplifications.

5 Provision of Domestic Public Goods

The role of government in dealing with market coordination failures is widely debated and there is acknowledgment that there is scope for public intervention in the economy; the proliferation of financial and

---

[32] Paul Krugman developed the concept of "strategic trade," which is rooted in the behavior of large enterprises.

[33] For an illuminating account of this issue, see Eichengreen (2003). For the case of transition countries, see Dăianu and Vranceanu (2003).

currency crises, gross irregularities in the function of other markets (energy trading, for example) are making a compelling case for strengthening regulatory frameworks and law enforcement by the state.[34]

6 Tax Policy

Fiscal neutrality can be deceptive in a world of huge asymmetries. Developed countries used a different level and structure of taxes when they were at an inferior level of economic development. How does this fact bear on the suggestion—which some make—to use their current taxation systems as signposts for tax reform in developing/transition countries? Several questions can be raised in this respect: a) Which *best practices* do one have in mind? Can an economy leapfrog development stages by just trying to imitate (import) institutions? b) Do *best practices* mean uniform rates? c) Does it make sense to look at the experience of economies, be they very few, which scored remarkable economic progress during the last decades (the successful catching-up stories), too? d) To what extent globalisation and the rules and regulations of the international economic system (WTO, etc) allow an economy room for using fiscal devices with the aim of fostering growth—the case of Ireland is conspicuous in Western Europe; and among transition countries, the Visegrad group, which attracted most of the FDI by fiscal incentives as well, is pretty well known. But one can broaden the discussion and look at Asian economies, too. The developmental challenge may be less relevant for the accession countries (albeit, they, themselves, have to close major gaps *vis-à-vis* the West), but it is certainly becoming of paramount importance for South east Europe. The conventional wisdom (and the advice provided by the IFIs) stresses the need for fiscal neutrality. But how can least distortionary effects of taxes be judged in a world in which there are numerous externalities, asymmetries, adverse external shocks, multiple equilibria, etc? How can one deal most effectively with the frequency of second-best situations? And what are policy implications, in general, and for taxation, in particular?

Policy conditionality was mentioned already as a high profile issue. The IFIs seem to be ambivalent in this respect; on one hand they seem to concede to the need for allowing governments more room in

---

[34] As Prof. Tsumeaki Sato argued at a Zagreb conference, the "market oriented regulatory state" gets an increasing profile.

formulating their own national policies; on the other hand, the IFIs have a hard time in devising new procedures to this end and, also, show a sort of organisational/intellectual inertia in absorbing new ideas. Thence comes out a major challenge for the IFIs when they are seen as a repository of knowledge and providers of sound advice. The IFIs would have to engage in a more candid debate on the policy challenges facing the developing world (the World Bank is, apparently, more open in this respect…) and explore new policy venues by assimilating what Robert Gilpin called the "New Theories." As a matter of fact, these new insights hook up with some of the main ideas of classical development economics.

7 International Public Goods

Who is accountable for the provision of public goods in the world economy? Do the major economies have a moral and operational responsibility in this respect, including the coordination of various policies in order to avert bad equilibria? Most of the time the IFIs and officials of rich economies talk about the need of good governance in developing economies as a means to foster development and avert major crises. But what can small open economies do when confronted with large upswings in capital flows and other adverse external shocks? As some contend, big changes in the flow of international liquidity may be more responsible for understanding financial crises in emerging economies than other causes.[35]

8 The Role of IFIs

What about the IFIs? Perfection does not exist in life and criticism is part and parcel of what prods progress. This reality does apply to the activity of large organisations as well, including the IFIs; the latter are supposed to provide public goods to the world community and, for this reason their endeavours is constantly examined by governments, NGOs and citizens at large—in a world increasingly under the pressure of globalisation. The activity of IFIs has been surrounded by rising controversies starting with the late 90s. The recurrent financial and currency crises worldwide, the disappointments of trade liberali-

---

[35] See Pettis (2001) and Desai (2003).

sation (particularly in developing countries),[36] the record of economic development in poor countries, the ambiguous effects of globalisation, have brought the IFIs more under the scrutiny of public debate in academic, policy and wider circles.

The IFIs and other international organisations would have to come to grips with the issue of "global governance"; this involves their own operations as well as some substantive institutional reform—as in the case of the international financial system. But here one meets the vested interests of the main players in the international economic system, which may delay changes unless a major event (as a major crisis) forces a radical shift in their policy propensity.

B. VALUES, INSTITUTIONS AND POLICY

Lately, the issues of ethical behaviour and social responsibility of firms and individuals have come prominently to the forefront of public debate. Widespread corruption and unethical behaviour are primarily seen as features of institutional fragility and lack of democratic credentials, which are to be found in the developing world, in particular. Nonetheless, the late spate of corporate scandals across the Atlantic and similar cases in the rich part of Europe illustrate a more complex reality. One should remember that a similar wave of scandals gripped the USA in the 80s. Is there a cyclical pattern in advanced economies, linked with unavoidable behavioural excesses during periods of exuberance, which would subside over time following policy and institutional adjustments? Or, can one establish institutional circumstances and peculiar policies which enhance unethical behaviour, and which do not trigger adequate/counter-acting responses automatically? Can one link social and economic dynamics of capitalism to apparent shifts in some of the values which drive entrepreneurs' behaviour? Is the profit motive similar to greed, or to use Alan Greenspan's famous words, to "irrational exuberance"? What is the role of norms (formal and informal) in constraining socially irresponsible behaviour?

---

[36] The way rich economies have attempted to link trade issues with the so-called Singapore issues (on investment policies) has also disappointed the developing world.

Post-communist transition is replete with cases of corruption and unethical behaviour. The handy answer to explain them would be the very institutional weakness of post-communist societies, a precarious functioning of checks and balances and a corrupted judiciary together with very feeble law enforcement capacity. In an optimistic vein, the same reasoning would highlight the advance of structural and institutional reforms, which would allow these societies to diminish considerably malign (unethical) behaviour gradually. Joining the European Union can be seen through the lenses of this upbeat logic. A more broadly defined answer would look at the issue of governance in both the public and the private spheres and scrutinise lessons worldwide, both in rich and poor countries. Differently, a pessimistic answer would talk about a bad "path dependency" and point at the persistence of widespread corruption, precarious institutions and malfunctioning markets in large parts of the world.

In transition societies the prospects of joining the EU has operated as a catalyst for reforms and a strong support for dealing with the pains and frustrations of social change. But not a few citizens are disappointed by the results of reforms, and the widespread corruption and unethical behaviour incense most of the population; some citizens relate these phenomena to market reforms, and this perception shows up unabashedly in the polls. Once the first wave of accession would take place benefits would accrue to many citizens, but disappointments, too, are likely to become more intense. Such likely outcomes beg a candid discussion on the linkage between values, morality and the dynamic of capitalism and what it takes to make it more fulfilling for most of the population. This is why the public debate on effective regulations (law enforcement/institutions), which should strengthen the ability of markets to deliver for the satisfaction of most citizens (consumers) and avoid massive social exclusion, has not lost any relevance. The scope of the state in providing public goods should be judged in the same vein, albeit this role should be judged in conjunction with the need for a streamlined and more efficient public sector, which should not crowd out (undermine) the proficiency of the private sector.

The public debate on ethics and economy acquires new overtones when looking at the world under the impact of globalisation and other forces at work. Aside from international terrorism, one can point at the dark side of globalisation: inability to cope with global issues (such as global warming), massive illegal immigration, increasing poverty in many areas of the world, poor functioning of international financial markets, etc. In this context, the issues of governance, both in the public and private spheres, get more salience. And governance cannot be dissociated from the values, mindsets of those who make decisions.

The years following the Great Depression brought about new regulations, aimed at restraining excesses and unethical behaviour in markets' functioning. An example was the Glass-Steagall Act in the USA, which split investment banking from commercial banking. The recent scandals in corporate America and on Wall Street raise questions on the wisdom of wide deregulation which occurred in the banking industry in the late 90s. Institutional adjustments followed the end of the Second World War as well. History seems to indicate a cycle of policies and institutional adjustments following large economic dynamics. It may be that after the "deregulation euphoria" which featured so highly on the agenda of governments, especially in the Anglo-Saxon world, during the last couple of decades, a new phase is about to set in; this phase would underline the need for effective market regulations and a more enlightened working together between the public and the private sphere. This logic would have to apply to the international economy as well, which needs public goods so badly, which further demand reshaped international institutions—capable of ensuring global governance. The latter, clearly, asks for more international cooperation and a common vision on how to tackle the major challenges confronting mankind. These challenges cannot be dealt with unless economic rationality blends with social and moral values,[37] which should preserve the necessary social cement of societies.[38]

C. REINTERPRETING GLOBALISATION

There can hardly be a concept in international life that has triggered more controversy than globalisation in recent years. Some, particularly in the rich countries, see in it a *deus ex machina* for doing away with

---

[37] In order to "reinvent" capitalism or its soul by Greider (2003). See also Bebear (2003).

[38] Lal talks about the importance of shame-based and guilt-based cement in explaining cultural traits of long run economic performance (1999).

misery and conflict in the world. Others, especially in the poor countries, see it at the roots of mounting tensions in the world. Why is it so? What lies behind this stark cognitive dissonance? There can be two ways to look at this dispute: one is to examine facts which, directly or indirectly, rightly or wrongly, are related to *globalisation*; another is to judge the concept itself, its very content.

Facts give highly conflicting signals. Technological change has reduced transportation and transaction (information) costs and speeded up the transfer of know-how, albeit in a highly skewed manner, among regions of the world; the internet connects instantaneously hundreds of millions of people; the world trade has expanded tremendously and broadened the scope of choice for individuals throughout the world. The collapse of communism has expanded the work of market forces and democracy in a large area of the globe. And the very dynamic of the European Union can be seen as an *alter ego* of globalisation on a regional scale. But, at the same time, the distribution of wealth in the world seems to be more unequal nowadays than, let's say, twenty years ago[39]; the myth of the "new economy" has dissipated and corporate scandals in the affluent world shows that cronyism and bad governance are a more complex phenomenon that is usually assumed and ascribed geographically; financial and currency crises have been recurrent in emerging markets and have produced economic and social havoc in not a few countries; trade liberalisation has favored primarily rich countries, which, most of the time, preach what they do not practice; social fragmentation and exclusion have been rising both in rich and poor countries; there is sense of disorder and a rising tide of discontent and frustration in many parts of the world; non-conventional threats, the use of mass destruction in particular, are looming menacingly.

Arguably, to make sense of the facts is to look at the conceptual underpinnings of globalisation. And here there is an interpretation of globalisation, which is pretty much overloaded ideologically. I refer to the paradigm which extols the virtues of unbridled markets, privatisation and extreme downsizing of the public sector (state intervention

---

[39] Stanley Fischer (2003, p. 23), the former deputy managing Director of the IMF and a leading macroeconomist, says that "The overall challenge to economic globalisation is to make the global system deliver economic growth more consistently and more equitably."

in the economy); this philosophy widened to international markets—finance and trade and, often, the IFIs did champion it. This paradigm has retreated, somewhat, in recent years following disappointing economic performances around the world and the nefarious functioning of financial (and energy) markets; but its resilience is powerful and is visible even in how it shapes the language used by some media (I was always puzzled by the use made of the term "market-friendly": is a neo-Keynesian a foe of the market economy?).

I submit that globalisation can be understood in a different vein, which looks at the functioning of real markets—with their goods and bads—and which takes into account insights of advanced economic theory such as: informational asymmetries, increasing returns (while technological progress is intense), agglomeration effects (clusters), multiple (bad) equilibria, the role of economic geography, etc. This causes important lessons to come to the fore: the need for effective regulation of markets, the role of the state in providing public goods, the role of institutions (structures of governance), the need of public goods and good governance in the world economy, the importance of diversity and policy-ownership in policy-making, etc. To some, this interpretation may sow seeds of confusion. But, in this way, one can dispel a biased interpretation of globalisation. Moreover, globalisation would no longer be assigned an ideological mantra and one-sided policy implications. Instead, it becomes an open-ended concept, which purports to define the mutual "opening" of societies, under the impetus of technological change and the manifold quest for economic progress. Moreover, it rids itself of a perceived western-centered origin. Such an unconstrained interpretation of globalisation would have major repercussions for national public policies and international politics.

Thus, national public policies could be fairly pragmatic and varied (not succumbing to fundamentalism) and geared towards the traditional goals of economic growth, price stability and social justice. Markets would have to be properly regulated and the state would have to provide essential public goods, which crowd in private output. As the rigged financial and energy markets in the USA have shown, these theses are valid for rich and poor countries alike. Dani Rodrik aptly observed that there is no modern economy which does not blend the public and the private spheres. An inference would be that going to the extreme with privatisation can be more than deleterious, which is particularly valid in the case of public utilities.

The international economy is replete with problems which beg adequate answers. Financial markets—under the pressure of volatile capital flows—function precariously, and the system needs repair. It appears that one of Keynes' intellectual legacies, which is enshrined in the Bretton Woods arrangements (namely, that highly volatile capital flows are inimical to trade and prosperity), has not lost relevance. Those who say that it is hard to fetter capital movements in our times make a strong point, but do not solve the issue. The volatility of financial flows imparts a deflationary bias to policies worldwide, enhances trade protectionism and competitive exchange rate devaluations. Ultimately, the international financial system would have to undergo substantive changes in order to avert lethal crises.

Free trade cannot benefit poor countries when rich economies subsidise heavily their agriculture and use trade barriers whenever they feel like being "injured"; double talk and hypocrisy make a mockery of the virtues of free trade and give moral ammunition to advocates of *fair trade*. Likewise, the diminishing aid to the very poor countries is hard to justify when acknowledging the huge asymmetries in the world. And a keen sense of urgency and pragmatism would demand a different policy in order to deal with the threats of spreading epidemics, massive illegal migration, abject poverty, and environmental disasters. Not to mention the scourge of international terrorism. All these challenges make up an agenda, which can be assumed by an enlightened interpretation of globalisation.

D. WOULD DEVELOPMENTAL ECONOMICS STAGE A COMEBACK?

Can the neo-liberal framework foster economic development, irrespective of circumstances? In certain respects it can, as is the case of stimulating entrepreneurship and fighting excessive welfarism and central regulation. But, as some argue, this framework is far from sufficient in enabling policy-makers to deal with the complexity of development efforts in a world which is replete with asymmetries, market imperfections, and precarious equilibria.

Table 1. Annual GDP growth rates in CEECs, % on previous year

Country	1990	1991	1992	1993	1994	1995	1996	1997	1998	1999	2000	2001
Bulgaria	-9.10	-8.40	-7.25	-1.48	1.82	2.86	-10.14	-6.94	3.50	2.51	5.8	5.0
Czech R.	-1.22	-11.49	-3.29	0.57	3.21	6.36	3.91	0.98	-2.50	-0.21	3.1	3.5
Estonia	-8.10	-10.01	-14.15	-8.51	-2.00	4.29	3.98	10.53	4.06	-1.39	6.9	4.7
Hungary	-3.50	-11.90	-3.06	-0.58	2.95	1.50	1.34	4.57	5.07	4.27	5.2	3.8
Latvia	2.90	-10.41	-34.86	-14.87	0.65	-0.81	3.34	8.61	3.56	0.47	6.6	7.5
Lithuania	-3.30	-5.68	-21.26	-16.23	-9.77	3.29	4.71	7.28	5.15	-3.07	3.9	4.7
Poland	-11.60	-7.00	2.63	3.80	5.20	7.01	6.05	6.85	4.80	4.04	4.0	1.1
Romania	-5.58	-12.92	-8.77	1.53	3.93	7.14	3.95	-6.07	-5.43	-3.19	1.8	5.3
Slovakia	-2.47	-14.57	-6.45	-3.70	4.90	6.91	6.58	6.54	4.42	1.90	2.2	3.1
Slovenia	n.a	-9.0	-5.0	2.8	5.3	4.1	3.5	4.5	4.0	4.8	4.6	3.0

Source: Based on Economic Survey of Europe, 2000, vol. 2, UN-ECE, Geneva; WIIW Research Report 283/2002.

Economists, nowadays, while underlining the pre-eminence of markets in resource allocation and rewarding of entrepreneurship, debate fiercely about the economic role of governments. This debate has been fuelled by theoretical insights brought about by the "New Theories":[40] the theory of multiple equilibria, which posits the possibility of persistent bad equilibria; the theory of *endogenous growth*, which undermines some basic constructs of neoclassical economics (such as "the law of diminishing returns"); the thesis of "path dependency" (the role of history), the importance of geography; the role of information costs and asymmetries, the importance of *clusters* for achieving competitive advantages,[41] etc.

The "New Theories" rely, or bring back to the limelight, theses of the old development economics. For Albert Hirschman, Paul Rosenstein Rodan, Ragnar Nurkse, Gunar Myrdal, Harvey Leibenstein, all of them highlighted the role of institutions, structural features of poor countries, which keep them hostage to various types of traps, the need for assistance (what Rodan termed as the "Big Push" in a famous article written in 1943[42]).

To sum up: the current debate on development economics has rediscovered several of its old issues and, in this context, it reemphasizes the existence of externalities, multiple equilibria, bad path-dependencies, vicious circles and "underdevelopment traps," all of which pose numerous challenges to public policy. For it is increasingly obvious that public policy (at the national and the international level) has a role to play in order to address market coordination failures. This is because "[t]here may be a social equilibrium in which forces are balanced in a way that is Pareto improving relative to one in which the government's hands are completely tied—and certainly better than one in which the private sector's hands are completely tied."[43] In this context, one needs to underline the importance of good institutions, of proper structures for public and corporate governance, which condition the overall performance of the economy.

---

[40] Gilpin (2001).

[41] Michael Porter's use of clusters in explaining competitive advantages makes a link with Gunar Myrdal's concept of cumulative causation.

[42] Rosenstein-Rodan (1943).

[43] Hoff (2000, p. 170).

It is increasingly clear that the wide variety of economic performance in transition (post-communist) countries has to be related to the different functioning of institutional set-ups and policy diversity.

It may be that we are on the verge of a new age of development economics against the backdrop of the very disappointing record of economic advance in most of the developing world (if one excludes China and parts of India), transition failures and in many post-communist countries, and the backlash against globalisation. Olivier Blanchard, Paul Krugman, Dani Rodrik, Joseph Stiglitz and others form a remarkable platoon of brilliant economists who can inject more realism and creativity into development policy-making.

V. Transition Economies and Institutional and Policy Diversity

A. PERFORMANCE DIFFERENCES

For most of the past decade, policy makers in transition countries, have been concerned with the construction of the main building blocks of the new economic system. Institutional disarray (disorganization[44]), and the effects of the collapse of the former COMECON trade area, brought about the first transformational recession and high inflation in the early 90s. Macroeconomic stabilization, privatization, opening, formed their main policy thrust in the early years of transition. Table 1 illustrates the collapse of output in these economies at the start of transition period.

But even so, one can easily discern a major difference between macroeconomic dynamics in CEECs (Central and Eastern Europe) and in the CIS (Community of Independent States) countries. In Central and Eastern Europe, inflation was brought down much more rapidly and output recovery started earlier. What lies behind this difference? A World Bank study remarks that "while initial conditions are the dominant factor in explaining the output decline at the start of transition, the intensity of reform policies explains the variability in

---

[44] Concept used by Blanchard (1997).

output recovery thereafter."[45] I would argue that initial conditions and geography played a major role during all this period, and that bad path dependencies have evolved in the meantime.

The World Bank study mentioned above highlights four major lessons of transition, namely the key role of the entry and growth of new firms (the strategy of encouragement and discipline); the need to develop and strengthen legal and regulatory institutions; the need for more aggressive use of the budget during a reform program in order to protect the most vulnerable social groups; the recognition that initial winners may oppose later stage reforms.

However, what seems to be underplayed in this enumeration is the time consuming nature of institutional development, which is at the root of various path dependencies. In this regard, one needs to highlight the relationship between precarious institutions and the persistence of bad equilibria, which hamper long-term economic growth. Likewise, the World Bank study seems to underplay the very severe budget retrenchment in most transition economies (due to collapsing revenues), which badly impaired the ability to protect low income population against the pains of transformation. But not the whole of the CEE area has had similar macroeconomic dynamics. A salient feature is the boom and bust dynamic of Romania and Bulgaria during the 90s; both countries have been undergoing economic recovery in recent years.

Over time, and in conjunction with reform consolidation, new concerns have emerged for the CEECs. Thus, economic growth has become of paramount importance in the quest to join the European Union, and also, as a means to solve increasingly sensitive social difficulties—at a time of rising unemployment. The main features of economic dynamics in the CEECs, which have relevance for the debate on catching-up, are summarized below:

– Steady high growth rates have proved to be quite an elusive goal for CEECs;

– In all CEECs, there have been substantial fluctuations of GDP growth rates, besides the impact of the first transformation recession;

– Moderate (not high) growth rates seem to be characteristic for the better performing CEECs;

---

[45] Mitra and Selowsky (2001).

– Boom and bust cycles did appear in a few cases, and this type of dynamics may appear again unless severe balance of payments crises are avoided. Arguably, for the countries which are likely to join the EU in the near future this danger would largely disappear. However, looming fiscal crises (in view of the EU requirements) would pose a new danger and hamper growth;

– Saving and investment ratios are not impressive, whereas the inflows of FDI were concentrated in a few countries;

– All CEECs trade extensively with the EU; for all of them, the EU is by far the largest trading partner. Arguably, therefore, output dynamics in the CEECs has benefited from increased openness and integration with the EU;

– Substantial inflows of FDI foster growth, but they need favourable accompanying circumstances;

– Persistent large current account deficits cause balance of payments crises and harm sustainable growth.

The features highlighted above cast some doubt on the thesis that catching up is looming at the horizon, or that it is likely to happen as an automatic outcome of current policies.[46] This inference should

Table 2. Per capita income levels in Europe
(1998, in PPP terms as % of EU average)

Country	Per Capita income level	Country	Per Capita income level
Greece	66	Latvia	27
Ireland	101	Lithuania	31
Bulgaria	23	Poland	36
Czech Republic	59	Romania	27
Estonia	37	Slovakia	46
Hungary	49	Slovenia	68

Source: "Progress Towards the Unification of Europe," World Bank Report, 2000, p. 40.

---

[46] For a thorough analysis of catching up prospects of transition economies, see Kolodko (2002) as well.

sober us, particularly in view of the kind of growth rates that CEECs need in order to catch up with the EU area. It may well be that what is realistic to achieve are more moderate rates of income per capita growth; however, even such moderate growth rates require heavy advances in structural and institutional reforms. Higher growth rates may occur if steady FDI flows are substantial (and profits are reinvested), investment ratios stay around 30%, and there is constant upgrading of production. But, at the same time, the CEECs would have to avoid, as much as possible, adverse external shocks.

B. The EU Factor

In the above context, a related question appears: are the current negotiations and the efforts to adopt the *Acquis Communautaire* the equivalent of an effective strategy for economic *catching-up*? In many domains, they may well be so, to the extent that good institutions are smoothly "imported" and function effectively, and to the extent that technology transfer and upgrading of production (via FDIs) occur intensely, for the benefit of a majority of the citizens (and *social cohesion* is not impaired).

The EU, as a phenomenon, is exceptional in a historical perspective; it is unique both economically and politically in modern history. This is why one can hardly establish an analogy between NAFTA and the Europe Agreements, which the accession countries have with the EU. As a matter of fact, the accession countries see in the EU enlargement an historical chance to speed up their economic development and modernization. Can integration into the EU be viewed as a Grand Strategy for economic catching-up (*beta*-convergence) and modernization—for the "Big Push," which most of CEECs have been seeking during the last century?[47] It is worthwhile reminding what Paul Rosenstein-Rodan had in mind when he wrote his famous article in 1943. In that article, he referred to key inter-dependencies in an economy, which may preclude its development, unless there is effective coordination among its constituent parts (industries); development asks for complementary changes of action and resources. And such simultaneous endeavours may not be possible in the absence of a strong

---

[47] Rosenstein-Rodan (1943, 1961).

stimulus, of a "Big Push." This is a crucial question to be addressed by policy makers.

Central and Eastern European societies do not look poor in important respects (e.g. the literacy rate of the population and general educational standards, behavioural patterns), but most of them face a set of challenges, which are specific to poor countries: still fragile institutions, perturbing growing inequality[48] (precarious social cohesion), incompetent governments (political elites), endemic corruption, which distorts and taxes business, etc. Therefore, these countries need to formulate policies which should tackle poor countries-type problems as well; they need development (catching-up) strategies

Empirical analyses show that the opening of the economy and integration with the outside world have better chances to foster economic growth when there is an intense inflow of foreign direct investment which upgrades the capital stock and human capital of the recipient countries—while it does not crowd out domestic investment. It is no surprise, therefore, that the frontrunner accession countries have received a disproportionate share of FDI.

Equally, a strategy of economic development (catching-up) requires policy ownership, which refers to both domestic intellectual capabilities (expertise), as well as to the capacity to formulate policies. This is the lesson of the most impressive cases of catching-up of the last century (whether one thinks of Japan, South Korea, Singapore, and more recently, Ireland).

It may be that the EU arrangements could supplant partially the need for domestic policy capabilities. But, as the reports of the European Commission consistently document, particularly in the case of the less performing accession countries, public administration reform is critical for development, which is a clear indication of the essential tasks of domestic policy. It is true, however, that, within the constraints of the institutional functioning of the EU, domestic policy formulation acquires a new connotation. But the problem remains as such, since Brussels cannot be a substitute for key decisions at the national level.

---

[48] It should be acknowledged, nonetheless, that much of this growing inequality is unavoidable, as a result of the change from a command (highly equalitarian) to a market-based economic system.

Here is a caveat about the linkage between EU integration and convergence. Some of CEECs' premises for catching-up may clash with the strict conditionality of the Maastricht Treaty criteria, in case the accession countries intend to join the Exchange Rate Mechanism (ERM) and, later on, the Monetary Union. A related situation is entailed by the implications of the Balassa-Samuelson Effect, which may make it impossible for accession countries to comply with the requirement of a low inflation rate in order to fit the EU (ERM) area.[49] And, should they try to attain a very low inflation rate, this may undermine growth and, therefore, catching-up. If this is the case, should some of the accession criteria be made more flexible?[50] How would the EU member countries view such a weakening of criteria? To what extent can the logic of a "variable geometry" play a role in this context? Would such a variable geometry process of enlargement be manageable?

For the EU candidate countries, the low inflation criteria (and, further, the Maastricht Treaty provisions) and the negotiations with Brussels raise two main sets of questions: one regards trade links and, more specifically, the capacity of accession countries to withstand competitive pressures when trade protection asymmetries and other adjustment instruments disappear; the other issue regards the possibility for the candidate countries to accommodate the stern exigencies of a very low inflation environment, even if they do not adopt the single currency.

It should be also highlighted that, against the backdrop of vagaries in an increasingly uncertain world environment, the EU can provide a shelter, which should be seen in the context of attempts, worldwide, to form economic and monetary blocks.

---

[49] Rosati (2001). See also Halpern and Wyplosz (2001).

[50] One can make an analogy with the current debate on the adequacy of some of the provisions of the Stability Act of the European Union—the 3% budget deficit upper limit at a time of very slow growth in the Eurozone.

C. A Few Thoughts on South East Europe[51]

The tragedy of September 11 has reignited the debate on the linkage between poverty, social destitution and what breeds deep resentments, inter-ethnic conflicts, terrorism. Europe, too, is not devoid of dismaying events, with the Balkans' last decade epitomizing much of what is evil in the contemporary world.

What can puzzle an observer of Western Balkans,[52] in particular, is a visible clash of perceptions on the recent social, political and economic dynamics of this area. There has been, thus, a series of positive developments, which are hardly questionable and which do influence perceptions in an optimistic vein: wars and violent inter-ethnic clashes have stopped, democratically organised elections took place region wide, inflation was brought under control, and some economic recovery has occurred lately, just to name just a few such developments. As a matter of fact, South East Europe, which includes the Western Balkans, overstripped Central Europe in terms of GDP growth in 2001, and would do the same, apparently, this year. Such tendencies are frequently highlighted by not a few local politicians, by international representatives. It would be foolish to underestimate these positive tendencies and not try to capitalise on them. On the other hand, it would be equally foolish to ignore the dark side of the story and the tensions which continue to strain the Region.

The Western Balkans, as a whole, is plagued by huge unemployment, which reaches about 40% of the entire active population in Bosnia-Herzegovina and over 70% in Kosovo; this unemployment breeds the underground economy and criminality. There is an increasing addiction to foreign aid, which is of a debilitating sort to the extent external assistance does not focus on the creation of viable economies and it finances mostly consumption. Migration of young and skilled labour is gathering pace, which is depleting the most valuable asset of the region. Low saving and investment ratios throughout the area indicate

---

[51] For more on economic policy in the Balkans, see also my paper (2001). I do not address herein Turkey's situation, which is highly complex and overloaded with geopolitical content.

[52] This excludes Bulgaria and Romania, which were invited to start accession negotiations with EU and, at the Copenhagen Summit of December 2002, were set 2007 as a possible entry date.

that current economic recovery has a low chance of turning into sustainable economic growth. In addition, the region is rife with organised crime, and criminality often reaches the upper layers of government. Many citizens are disappointed with the results of reforms and this shows up in the polls; there is growing apathy among the electorate and nationalistic parties are staging a comeback. And not least, constitutional and status issues and continuing inter-ethnic strife could easily unleash new crises. Against this still very complicated background it does make sense to keep policy makers in the region and abroad alert to the danger of complacency and underestimation of what maintains the region as Europe's hotbed.

Some pundits are tempted to make an analogy with the end of the Second World War in evaluating the Balkans. Even putting forward the idea of a new Marshall Plan for the region sources part of its justification in such an analogy. But one should rather be cautious in making such a comparison, in over-stretching the relevance of history. There are several motives in adopting a cautious approach. Firstly, at that time there was no process of state-formation (state dissolution) and, thence, no ensuing conflicts; this fact favoured, in a few years time, the start of the process of economic integration by the setting up of the Coal and Steel European Communities. Secondly, there was a clear distinction between victor and loser in the war, which did not involve revision of borders.[53] This is not the case in the Western Balkans nowadays, where borders have been and, still are questioned by some. Thirdly, the Marshall Plan meant, primarily, an infusion of funds for energizing economic reconstruction in an area which did possess the institutional ingredients of a market economy. This is clearly not the case with large parts of the Balkans, in spite of the decades of market experience of many of the inhabitants of the states, which previously made up Yugoslavia. Fourthly, there was, at that time, a big common enemy: communism, external and internal. Who is the big common enemy of the peoples in the Balkans, at the start of the new century? The prime candidate would be poverty, underdevelopment and criminality in an area which, yet, belongs to a prosperous Continent. But

---

[53] Certainly, the division of Germany could be mentioned as a counterexample, but it does not change the thrust of the assertion.

this is an imprecise enemy and not easy to deal with by looking at worldwide experience.

Assistance is badly needed in the Balkans; whereas it needs to be considerable, it should also be wisely calibrated and provided. Aid needs to take into account the complexity of intra-regional relations, the still murky political geography in parts of the region, the existence of latent conflicts, the prevalence of weak (sometimes *failed*) states, etc. This extremely complex situation links inextricably national economic objectives with other goals, such as peace and security. At the same time, the stability of the region as a whole can be viewed as a collective good, a *public good* for Europe.

It should be said, however, that whereas goals can be easy to define in abstract terms (peace and security, social cohesion, economic growth, etc.), they are much harder to formulate and pursue practically—particularly when they imply hardly reconcilable objectives of governments which do not show a high propensity to cooperate, or when these goals have to be pursued under very adverse circumstances. In the Western Balkans this situation is quite ubiquitous and explains the heavy presence of outsiders (including the provision of economic aid), the existence of protectorates, "hard" and "soft." But foreign presence does not simplify the solution to problems automatically, as the experience of Bosnia-Herzegovina, and not only, amply indicates.

Tackling the problems of South east Europe, of Western Balkans in particular, demands a vision which should frame the policies of both domestic (local governments) and external actors. This vision (and ensued policy) needs to consider: a) The consequences of the years of immense destruction brought about by military conflicts; b) the failures of reform efforts; and c) the still very complicated nature of relations inside the region—all these in conjunction with a developmental challenge. For what is less talked about is the relative backwardness of the area when judged according to European benchmarks. For instance, the income par capita, in many parts of the Balkans, does not exceed 3,000 euro (measured at the purchasing power parity), whereas the EU average is higher than 21,000 euro. In this respect policy-makers and the aid agencies need to take into account the main lessons of development experience and the insights of the "New Theories." Infrastructure is very precarious.

A development-focused policy needs to consider what is realistic to achieve without shunning bold action; it also needs to put the whole endeavour into a longer term timeframe, keeping in mind the intricacies of the situation on the ground. Policy-makers would have to cast their endeavours under three major headings: crisis-management; economic reconstruction; and the change of the regime of functioning of economies (institutional change) without succumbing to policy fundamentalism. In this respect it can be said that dealing with the Western Balkans needs to be judged from two inter-related perspectives. One is the exercise in dual (short- and long-term) crisis-management, which aims, *inter alia*, at arresting (reversing where it is possible) bad dynamics/path-dependencies. The late years in Macedonia are an obvious case of this type of crisis management. The second perspective concerns development, which would have to be a two-pronged strategic endeavour: physical reconstruction (after the years of military ravages); and development proper, that includes institutional change and the political process. In all of this aid has a critical role to play.

The inherent difficulties of dealing with the unsolved and, often, seemingly, intractable challenges posed by Western Balkans, could be compounded by events taking place outside the Region. One such event is the effort to deal with non-conventional threats, which sets new priorities and redirects resources among the major outside players. The USA, for obvious reasons, is likely to reduce its military and material presence in the region, which would ask for an offsetting act on the part of the European Union; the latter would have to increase its involvement accordingly. But this is not a clear option/solution at a time of major economic strain in Western Europe as well, and at a time when "the big game in town" seems to be EU enlargement. On this line of reasoning, one points at another major event, which has a bearing on the concrete attention paid to Western Balkans. It may be that economic pain in the West, combined with a less smooth unfolding of *enlargement*, could keep the region off the immediate radar screen of western chancelleries. This could undermine the EU's attention paid to the region, its overall assistance, at a very sensitive period in time, when there is acute need to support the still very fragile local democracies and help economic reconstruction.

VI. Concluding Remarks

The past decade has been suffused with claims that economic policy, in the advanced countries, is being driven by an emerging new consensus on principles and practice. The ideological fallout was pretty obvious in Anthony Giddens' concocted "The Third Way" sintagma, which connotes neither traditional social-democracy, nor blatant liberalism—in the European sense; this formula was adopted by the "new" Labour Party in the UK as its quasi-philosophical mantra and other social democrats have tried to foray deeply into it. Highly glamorous seminars featuring Clinton, Blair, Schroeder, Persson, Jospin and others were quite *en vogue* in the late 90s. In the United States George W. Bush used "compassionate conservatism" as an ideological means to enhance his presidential quest, which may have helped him in the end. It appeared as social-democrats (in Europe) and democrats (in the USA), on one hand, and centre-right parties (in Europe) and republicans (in the USA) were coming closer, in terms of both principles and practice of economic policy.

The sources of this apparent "new" consensus are, arguably, several. One origin could be traced to the ever longing desire of Man to control his environment (nature) and be more efficient. Thus, in the first quarter of the past century Max Weber's "rationalisation of life" referred to rational accounting, rational law, rational technology, which by extrapolation, can be extended to "rational economics" as a form of *hard science*. Later on (in the seventies), another famous sociologist, Daniel Bell, upheld the primacy of knowledge and theory-related activities in ordering our life, man's technological and economic ascendancy—which would imply that economic wizards can secure a foolproof policy. Even the clash between Keynesianism and monetarism, as the two main competing macro-economic paradigms, could be seen in the vein of searching the ultimate piece of wisdom. Another origin of policy amalgamation comes out of the death of communism. Francis Fukuyama's "End of History" was seen by many as an embodiment of the, presumably, single ideology (liberal democracy) which was meant to rule the world. Last, but not least, globalisation—as an incarnation of unfettered markets and downsizing of government, operating worldwide—also provided an impetus to the vision of the ideal type of economic policy.

At the start of the new century facts are disavowing over simplifications. There are numerous examples which prove that conflicting ideas matter a lot, that reality cannot be encapsulated into a procrustean ideological bed; that economics continues to be softer than some of us try to make people believe. Policywise, it is increasingly clear that trimming the welfare state and the public sector is not enough in order to achieve the expected efficiency gains; this endeavour needs to be accompanied by effective regulations of markets (financial and energy, for example), which, otherwise, can easily be rigged; "the new economy," the "new paradigm" (which claimed to combine high growth rates with very low unemployment), proved to be, simply put, a mirage of the 90s. The developments of the last couple of years in the USA and elsewhere offer ample proofs in this regard—which motivated public authorities to initiate the Oxley-Sarbanes Act. Likewise, as against the prevailing tenets of not many years ago, economic policy, as it is currently undertaken in the USA and Europe, does not preclude running larger budget deficits during a downswing of the cycle; this is the explanation for some basic Keynesian recipes returning to the limelight. It should be said, nonetheless, that, while Keynesian macroeconomics seems to get a higher profile nowadays, the EU member countries are trying to make their markets (labour, product, services, financial) more flexible.

How does globalisation fit into this picture? The pressure of more intense competition forces governments to streamline their public sectors, which does frustrate trade unions and many citizens at large. But rich countries, in the West, remain welfare states, *par excellence*, albeit in an evolving manner. One can detect here a rising/returning Keynesianism in macroeconomic policy-making with a retreat when it comes to social policy; there is an apparent policy contradiction herein. Another consequence of globalisation is the creation of an international policy agenda. By omission and commission, some of the wealthy countries' less inspired policies have given renewed high profile to issues such as: fair vs. free trade, dealing with abject poverty in the world, protecting the environment as a public good for mankind, the code of conduct for international corporations, how to manage contagion effects in the world economy, policy coordination among the leading economies of the world, etc.

As a matter of fact, the traditional ongoing battle between left and right—within the framework of democratic politics—is being shifted, partially, into the international arena. The debate on global governance (which institutions and policies) reflects a growing awareness that there are issues which need to be addressed internationally, in a multilateral context and using collaborative approaches. Arguably, the choice between globalisation and "managed globalisation" is between accepting the effects of completely free markets—with total policy disregard for market failures and their social consequences—, and trying to construct an international policy, which should address/prevent massive coordination failures. The debate on which form of capitalism, and what type of state intervention in the economy, turns, partially, into a debate on which form of "global capitalism."

The second policy route does make sense in a global economy, in which there is acceptance of the need for international public goods. Otherwise, under increasing pressure from foreign markets and other threats (including terrorism, illegal immigration, spreading diseases, etc.), governments would resort to national means of protection—such as trade protectionism and trade clashes, competitive devaluations, etc.

Ideology is not dead, and it does shape social and economic policies—although in subtler forms and following cyclical patterns. It may be less felt nationally to the extent the battlefield of ideas expands increasingly beyond national borders. In any case, globalisation is likely to reflect ever more the battle of ideas, with traditional politics delving increasingly into the international domain. How would policy-makers address the hot issues in the international economy would provide clues regarding its dynamics.

Moving away from doctrinal fundamentalism in policy-making would enhance the room for institutional and policy diversity. Having said that, I do not mean governments reneging on basic rules of sound behaviour in economic policy-making. Instead, I have in mind creative policy-making, which should shun policy fundamentalism and acknowledge particular circumstances. Clearly, "bad governance" in poor countries would have to be fought against unswervingly. The IFIs would have to be more candid about past and present failures in development policy and be faithful to the idea of *policy ownership*, which, it should be said, does not preclude policy conditionality. Likewise, rich countries' governments should practice more what their preach in order to be more credible in their dialogue with the developing world. This would regard policy making at the national level and the production (protection) of public goods for the benefit of mankind (current and future generations).

One should also re-examine the functioning of the international economic system, which should draw on the insights of the "New Theories" and try to deal with the proliferation of bad equilibria, recurrent financial and currency crises, growing economic gaps, the deterioration of the environment and conflicts in the world. Unless the production of international public goods takes place on a proper scale, it would be hard to convince developing countries that the "disciplining" pressure of world markets is positive and in their interest.

Institutional and policy diversity does have a meaning and a future.

REFERENCES

Agenor, P.R. (2000) *The Economic of Adjustment and Growth*, New York, Academic Press.
Arrow, J.K. (1970) *The Limits of Organisation*, New York, Norton.
Bell, D. (1973) *The Coming of Post-industrial Society*, New York, Basic Books.
Bebear, C. and Manière, P. (2003) *Ils Vont Tuer le Capitalisme*, Paris, Plon.
Blanchard, O. (1997) *The Economics of Post-Communism*, London, Clarendon Press.
Dăianu, D. (May, 2002) *How possible is catching up in Europe*, Warsaw, TIGER Working Papers.
David, B. (2000) "Trade, Growth and Disparity among Nations," in *Trade and Poverty*, WTA, Geneva.
Dauderstädt, M. and Witte, L. (2001) *Cohesive Growth in the Enlarged Euroland*, Bonn, Friedrich Ebert Stiftung.
Easterly, W. (2001a) *The Lost Decades: Developing Countries' Stagnation in Spite of Policy Reform 1980–1998*, manuscript.
Easterly, W. (2001b) *The Elusive Quest for Growth*, Cambridge, MIT Press.
Eichengreen, B. (2003). *Capital Flows and Crises*, Cambridge, MIT Press.
Ellis, H.S. (ed.) (1961) *Economic Development for Latin America*, New York, St. Martin Press.
Fischer, S. (2003) "Globalisation and Its Challenges" *American Economic Review*, Proceedings, pp.1–31.

Halpern, L. and Wyplosz, C. (2001) "Economic Transformation and Real Exchange Rates in the 2000s: The Balassa-Samuelson Connection" Chapter 6 (pp. 227–40) in *Economic Survey of Europe 2001*, UN/ECE, Geneva.

Hoff, K. (2000) "Beyond Rosenstein-Rodan: The Modern Theory of Coordination Problems in Development" in *Annual World Bank Conference on Development Economics. Proceedings,* World Bank, Washington DC.

Gao, B. (2001) *Japan's Economic Dilemma*, Cambridge, Cambridge University Press.

Giddens, A. (1998) *The Third Way. The Renewal of Social Democracy,* London, Polity Press.

Gilpin, R. (2001), *Global Political Economy*, Princeton, Princeton University Press.

Greider, W. (2003) *The Soul of Capitalism. Opening Paths to a Moral Economy,* New York, Simon and Schuster.

Guillen, M.F. (2001) *The Limits of Convergence. Globalization and Organizational Change in Argentina, South Korea and Spain,* Princeton, Princeton University Press.

Kolodko, G.W. (2002) *Globalization and Catching-up in Transition Economies,* Rochester and Woodbridge, University of Rochester Press.

Krugman, P. (1994) *Geography and Trade*, Cambridge, MIT Press.

Lal, D. (1999) *Unintended Consequences. The Impact of Factor Endowments, Culture, and Politics on Long-Run Economic Performance,* Cambridge, MIT Press.

Lancaster, K. (1979) *Variety, Equity and Efficiency*, Oxford, Blackwell.

Lucas, R. (1988) "On the Mechanics of Economic Development" *Journal of Monetary Economics*, Vol. 22 (July), pp. 3–42.

Maddison, A. (1995) *Monitoring the World Economy: 1820–1992,* Development Centre Studies, OECD, Paris.

Mancur, Jr., O. (1982) *The Rise and Decline of Nations. Economic Growth, Stagflation and Social Rigidities,* New Haven, Yale University Press.

North, D. (1981) *Structure and Change in Economic History,* New York, Norton, 1981

Ohmae, K. (1995) *The End of the Nation State. The Rise of the Regional Economies,* New York, The Free Press.

Padma, D. (2003) *Financial Crisis, Contagion and Containment,* Princeton, Princeton University Press.

Pettis, M. (2001) *The Volatility Machine. Emerging Economies and The Threat of Financial Collapse,* Oxford, Oxford University Press.

Rodrik, D. (1996) "Understanding Economic Policy Reform" *Journal of Economic Literature*, Vol. 34, pp. 9–41.

Rodrik, D. (2000a) *The New Global Economy and Developing Countries. Making Openness Work,* Washington DC, Overseas Development Council

Rodrik, D. (2000b) *Development Strategies for the Next Century,* Harvard University, manuscript.

Romer, P. (1986) "Increasing Returns and Long Term Growth" *Journal of Political Economy*, Vol. 94, pp. 1002–37.

Rosati, D. (2001) "The Balassa-Samuelson Effect among the CEEC" *Paper presented at the Balassa Commemoration Conference*, Budapest, 18–19.

Rosen, S. (2002) "Markets and Diversity" *American Economic Review*, March, Vol. 92, No.1, pp.1–16.

Rosenstein-Rodan, P. (1943), "Problems of Industrialization of Eastern and South-Eastern Europe" *Economic Journal*, 1943, Vol. 53 (June–September), pp. 202–11.

Soros, G. (2002) *On Globalisation*, New York, Norton.

Stiglitz, J. (1994) *Whither Socialism?*, Cambridge, MIT Press.

Stiglitz, J. (2002) *Globalisation and its Discontents*, New York, Norton.

Summers, L. (2000) "International Financial Crises: Causes, Prevention and Cure" *American Economic Review*, Papers and Proceedings.

Vranceanu, R. (2003) "Opening the Capital Account in Transition Econo-mies: How Much and How Fast?" *Acta Oeconomica*, Vol. 53, No. 3, pp. 245–70.

Weber, M. (1927) *General Economic History*, London, Allen and Unwin.

Williamson, J. (1994) *The Political Economy of Policy Reform*, Washington DC, The Institute of International Economics.

The World Bank (2000) *Progress Toward the Unification of Europe*, Washington D.C., World Bank.

CHAPTER 2

Ethical Lapses of Capitalism: How Serious They Are[1]

> *Trust and similar values, loyalty and truth-telling ... have real, practical, economic value; they increase the efficiency of the system, enable you to produce more goods or more of whatever values you hold in high esteem. But they are not commodities for which trade on the open market is technically possible or even meaningful.*[2]

I. Introduction

Adam Smith is seen by many as the father of economics for his book *The Wealth of Nations* (1776). But he also wrote *The Theory of Moral Sentiments* (1759), which underlines moral underpinnings of a vibrant and socially cohesive society. As the Nobel Prize winner Amartya Sen points out, "not only was Adam Smith a professor of moral philosophy at the University of Glasgow, but the subject of economics was for a long time seen as a branch of ethics."[3] Arguably, if a market-based society is to function properly, its members have to behave decently toward one another, according to socially accepted seals of approval; the latter would explain why individuals care about how they relate to each

---

[1] This chapter builds on a presentation made at the international seminar on "Economy and Ethics" organized by the New Europe College, the Romanian Economic Society and the Konrad Adenauer Foundation, Bucharest, 12–13 December 2003. I thank the participants of this seminar, Rachel Epstein, Laurian Lungu and Michael Keren for their suggestions and remarks on an early draft. The text was published in D. Dăianu and R. Vrânceanu, *Ethical Boundaries of Capitalism*, Aldershot, Ashgate, 2005, pp. 65–84.
[2] Arrow (1974, p. 23).
[3] Sen (1987, p. 2).

other. These seals form a code of morality.[4] Some may be tempted to discard ethical boundaries in social and economic life in the name of ethical relativism; an analogy could be used, in this respect, with Arrow's Impossibility Theorem of constructing social preferences.[5] But, as in case of comparative advantages revealed, social preferences, which rely on ethical motives, operate in society.

One can link Adam Smith's vision to Max Weber's famous work on *Protestant Ethics and Capitalism* in order to strengthen the link between values, institutions and economic performance.[6] A more recent book by a leading development economist, Deepak Lal, highlights the cultural dimension of economic development; in an insightful observation he connects the social cement of a society—which is needed for better economic performance—with the existence of the socializing emotions of *guilt* and *shame*.[7] I would submit that, where shame and guilt are missing, or declining on a large scale, cynicism, unethical behaviour and social irresponsibility get the upper-hand and aggregate economic performance can hardly escape worsening over the long run.[8]

Lately, the issues of ethical behaviour and social responsibility of firms and individuals have come prominently to the forefront of public debate. Some find roots of unethical behaviour in the logic of market competition.[9] At the same time, widespread corruption and unethical behaviour are primarily seen as features of institutional fragility and lack of democratic credentials, which are to be found in the developing world, in particular. Most transition (post-communist) countries have been, by definition, placed in this category. And not a few in the Western world were quick to attribute the financial crises in Southeast Asia, in the late 1990s, to wide-ranging corruption and cronyism and institutional fragility. Nonetheless, the vigorous economic recovery in the Asian economies, of recent years, illustrates a more complex reality.

---

[4] As mentioned by Shearmur and Klein (1997, p. 36), "Morality, its maintenance, and its effective internalization as our conscience all depend upon the monitoring of our conduct by others."

[5] Arrow (1951).

[6] Weber (1958).

[7] Lal (1999).

[8] Ethics assumes a socially accepted (codified) judgment of what is right and wrong in society.

[9] Shleifer (2004).

Likewise the spate of corporate scandals across the Atlantic, in recent years, and similar cases in rich parts of Europe points in the same direction. One should remember that a similar wave of scandals gripped the US in the 1980s.

If institutional fragility in the developing world seems to have relevant explanatory power regarding behavioral patterns, the situation in advanced economies is begging for clearer answers. Is there a cyclical pattern in advanced economies, linked with unavoidable behavioral excesses during periods of economic exuberance, which would subside over time following policy and institutional adjustments? Or, one can establish institutional circumstances and peculiar policies which enhance unethical behavior, and which do not trigger adequate/counter-acting responses automatically. Can social and economic dynamics of capitalism be linked to apparent shifts in some of the values which drive entrepreneurs' behaviour? Is the profit motive similar to greed, or to use Alan Greenspan's famous words, when does it turn into "infectious greed" and "irrational exuberance"? What is the role of norms (formal and informal), or standards of conduct, in constraining socially irresponsible behaviour?

Questions like those mentioned above prompted the writing of this chapter. Against this background ethical lapses in economic behaviour are considered by using the concept of reputation as an *asset* of individuals and firms; the build up of reputation capital would enter the utility function of an individual, or firm. Why bad equilibria persist and the macroeconomic context is also examined through this interpretation of reputation. Likewise, self-regulation and the regulatory functions of the state are judged from this perspective. The chapter broadens the analysis to the international framework.

II. Ethics and Economy

The early 1990s were accompanied by great euphoria following the collapse of communism; this euphoria seemed to engulf Western intellectual and political circles. Fukuyama encapsulated this outburst of optimism in his *The End of History*,[10] which extolled the virtues of

---

[10] Fukuyama (1990).

liberal democracy and talked about the end of ideology. It was like human society was on the brink of entering a golden age, unconstrained by social and political inhibitions. The only concern would have been the pace of technological advance and its economic reverberations. In a sense Fukuyama was right; communism was coming to an end as an economic and political system. But his optimism was less warranted in terms of the vistas for rapid economic development, as these were deemed to open to the rest of the world; similarly, his vision of the demise of conflicting ideas/paradigms was less convincing.

A fallacy, or *naivité*, of those years was an apparent underlying belief that capitalism, as the big victor of a century-long ideological war, was liable to shed its own weaknesses and become a perfect society. Not a few seemed to forget Winston Churchill's famous aphorism. Interestingly enough, Fukuyama himself became much more subdued in a subsequent work.[11] Nowadays, social scientists are more sober in their analysis of social and economic dynamics. As Shearmur and Klein mention: "Market-based societies are living upon moral capital—capital that they cannot themselves replenish. This moral capital is eroded by some of the very factors that seem to make such societies so attractive."[12]

Post-communist transition has offered an immense social laboratory for those immersed in the study of social and economic behaviour. Transformation of former command systems was based in Europe on fast privatization, liberalization and trade opening. This policy thrust was strongly imbued with the *neo-liberal zeitgeist* of the past decade. In this context corruption and deviant behaviour, in general, were put under scrutiny, as post-communist transition has been replete with unethical attitudes.

Two trains of reasoning can be detected with respect to explaining behavioural patterns during transition, which can be extrapolated to developing economies in general. A handy answer would be the very institutional weakness of post-communist societies, a precarious functioning of checks and balances and a corrupted judiciary together with very feeble law enforcement capacity. In an optimistic vein, this reasoning highlights the advance of structural and institutional reforms,

---

[11] Fukuyama (1999).
[12] Shearmur and Klein (1997, p. 29).

which would allow transition societies to diminish malign (unethical) behaviour considerably over time and reduce what Blanchard called "disorganization."[13] Gradually, both micro-inefficiencies and resource misallocation would diminish. This approach seems to rely and favour an organic institutional development—very much in the Hayekian mould.

Joining the European Union can be seen through the lenses of this upbeat logic as the EU would, arguably, provide an extraordinary anchor for systemic transformation. As a matter of fact, the entry of eight transition countries in the EU on May 1, 2004, seems to substantiate this line of reasoning. On the other hand, one could say that these new member countries are in the proximity of the EU and have benefited on more lenient communist legacies. It should be said, however, that these countries still evince substantial institutional fragility; this should provide a stimulus to examine the linkage between regulations (*alias* public policy) and economic performance, on the one hand, and values/norms and economic behaviour, on the other.

A pessimistic answer on explaining behavioural patterns would stress a bad "path dependency" and point at the persistence of widespread corruption, precarious institutions and malfunctioning markets in large parts of the world. Latin America offers a glaring example in this regard. *Mutatis mutandis,* one can say that Latin American countries have been in transition for more than a century and that this undermines ground for robust optimism. Thence a question arises: what explains the persistence of bad social equilibria and poor economic performance over long stretches of time? The plight of Argentina, in the last decade, is the most recent and vivid case of overblown expectations of economic reforms and durability of substantially improved economic performance. Why is it that vicious circles, traps of underdevelopment, are so hard to break away from?[14] The media in and outside these countries constantly reveal instances of corruption that involve top politicians and business people.

---

[13] Blanchard (1997).

[14] Albert Hirschman, Gunar Myrdal, Ragnar Nurkse Paul Rosenstein-Rodan, who are famous names in the panoply of development economists, wrote extensively about the resilience of these traps decades ago.

It appears that the experience of Latin America is a very bad omen for less advanced transition countries—for Balkan countries and former Soviet republics. In South East Europe, for instance, the weak state syndrome and the fragility of institutions, in general, as well as the large criminality in economic life should be a cause of deep concern regarding the ways and means for reversing an unfavourable path dependency. The counter-argument would be that the European Union can provide an extremely powerful anchor and transformation tool for this region as well, as it did for central Europe. But, there is little doubt that the process will be more time consuming and painful in view of specific local conditions, including political and inter-ethnic conflicts.

The rich, advanced countries have not been immune to big scandals in the business world. The turn of the century will, probably, go down in economic history books through a series of big corporate scandals in the USA, in particular, and Europe. The burst of the Internet bubble, the demise of the "new economy" and the "new paradigm," the disgrace which accompanied the fall of Enron, WorldCom, Tyco, etc., the involvement of illustrious Wall Street institutional names in a series of financial scandals with multifarious ramifications, the collapse of LTCM, the ignominious disappearance of Arthur Andersen, the Parmalat case, widely rigged financial and energy markets, etc., tell a lengthy and significant story. It is increasingly clear that the years of intense deregulation favoured not only more aggressive and innovative business behaviour, but they also entailed a wide array of breach of trust, of decent relationships between agents and principals. The recent years have revealed egregious and wide-ranging situations of conflict of interests and irresponsible damage done to shareholders' interests by unchecked (greedy) managers and defective principal-agent arrangements. The last two decades can be judged, in advanced economies, via a combination of excessive deregulation and erosion of moral values, as well as weaknesses in the corporate structures of governance.[15]

The alternative lines of reasoning which were mentioned for developing economies can be used for interpreting behavioural patterns and excesses in advanced economies, too. Thus, an optimistic

---

[15] Among business circles this loss of moral ground has raised serious concerns and triggered a process of soul-searching. See Bebear (2003).

interpretation would look into history and observe recurrent cycles of manias, panics and crashes, albeit these evolved in mitigated forms after the Great Depression.[16] Michael Milken and Ivan Boesky's names as individuals and Drexel Lambert as a corporate entity, in the financial world, remind us of excesses perpetrated two decades ago, which culminated with the crash of the New York Stock Exchange in 1987 (the Black Friday). A pessimistic reading of events would look at what may perpetuate bad equilibria and cause big damage in an increasingly interconnected world economy.[17] It is not accidental that Larry Summers insightfully remarked that "[c]entral to global integration is financial integration … as the events of the late 1920s and early 1930s remind us, central to global disintegration can be international financial breakdowns."[18]He rightly highlights the international dimension of public governance. And Stanley Fischer, a leading macro-economist and former deputy managing director of the IMF says that "the overall challenge to economic globalisation is to make the global system deliver economic growth more consistently and equitably."[19]

Economic and social dynamics reveal a constant play between forces which ask for liberalization and those that deem regulations as useful public goods. Individual and collective agents (entrepreneurs), who pursue their interests under various constraints, operate in specific institutional contexts that influence behavioural patterns. These contexts include formal and informal codes of conduct and explain economic performance over the long haul. Arguably, national economies compete in the global space in terms of institutional contexts, though actual drivers of competition are firms.[20] This is why national policy-makers are concerned about the quality of local business environments. Liberalization may be pursued in order to invigorate sclerotic, rigid structures,[21] and this may lead to positive outcomes. But there is also a dark side of the story, amply illustrated by cases of fraud and wide ranging unethical behaviour. From here arises the importance of

---

[16] Kindleberger (1989).
[17] Eatwell and Taylor (2000). See Stiglitz (2003) as well.
[18] Summers (2000, p. 1).
[19] Fischer (2003, p. 23).
[20] Krugman (1994).
[21] Olson (1982).

striking a right balance between the private and the public sector and the need for an optimal degree of regulation.[22]

The public outrage in the USA and Europe at the cases of misbehaviour in the corporate world and the perceived insufficiency of regulation of certain markets has prodded governments to react. It appears that society does not accept complacency in this regard and is not likely to bet recklessly on the optimistic line of reasoning—which assumes the organic capacity of institutional regeneration. Likewise, it appears that Western societies have judged the social costs of waiting for such regeneration to take place as too large. Hence the policy response of introducing new regulations and new auditing and accounting rules at the start of this decade. Obviously, pragmatic motives have been asking for a policy response. But, it can be argued that "virtue ethics"[23] has also played a role.

III. Understanding Micro and Macro Behaviours

A. THE DISTINCTION BETWEEN ETHICS AND LEGALITY

Unethical behaviour can be met in both advanced and underdeveloped societies; it can be met in both the official economy and the informal sector. The official economy reveals unethical behaviour as the outcome of breaking laws, regulations and codes of conduct. In advanced economies unethical behaviour has more scope for operation in times of liberalization and institutional innovation like financial innovation, which can lead to under-regulation.

There is a need to make a distinction between ethics and legality. Some business operations may be legal, but unethical. Whenever

---

[22] There is need for an optimal combination of self-regulation by industries (which rely on market incentives), state regulation and internal regulations by firms (Argandoña, 2004).

[23] Virtue ethics focuses on the conformity between right thinking and desire (Koehn, 1995, p. 536). In this respect it differs from a deontological ethic which "always runs the risk of developing schizophrenic agents who are compelled to do what duty dictates irrespective of whether they want to perform that act." Virtue ethics can be linked to altruistic behavior. For an analysis of altruism, morality and economics, see the volume edited by Phelps (1975).

conflicts of interest are poorly regulated, or legal frameworks present major loopholes, some individuals leave aside ethical considerations for the sake of making big gains. It is of high notoriety Arthur Levitt's endeavour to introduce more severe regulations in the securities industry in the USA in the early years of the last decade. Though as powerful he was as chairman of the Securities and Exchange Commission, his attempts proved futile when confronted with the formidable lobbying power of vested interests. As some would argue, morality has no place in business. Only the crisis that burst out at the end of the decade compelled many interested parties to revisit this issue, which led to the Sarbanes-Oxley Act to be enacted. But some people are regrouping and fighting bitterly back—claiming that "over-regulation" hurts business. One can see that this is an ongoing battle.

Monopoly power can be blatantly abused and ethically misused. Microsoft got into trouble because of its endeavours to keep a market captive and abuse its power. Even more questionable ethically are operations of the big pharmaceutical companies, which have used R&D related expenditure as an argument for justifying the high prices they charge for their products in poor countries. In this case ethics is clearly divorced from business, although practices may be perfectly legal.

The underground sector is made up of legal and illegal operations. For instance, subsistence agriculture is legal and pretty extensive in many poor countries. Some activities in the informal sector may be illegal from a narrowly defined perspective; I am referring to very small manufacturing and repair activities which do not pay taxes, but do not bring damage to the public at large. Are such activities unethical? In one way they are, for the individuals who undertake them may use public goods in the course of their work. On the other hand, these activities are useful and provide jobs and incomes to people who, otherwise, may be unemployed and would strain the public budget when safety nets operate and individuals are entitled to them. It is also true that, in developing economies, the underground sector reflects also the attempt by individuals (firms) to go around red-tape and survive under very adverse circumstances. These attempts frequently mirror inadequate incentives. Therefore, the picture is pretty clouded in this respect.

The underground sector hosts criminal activities, which, *ipso facto*, involve unethical behaviour. This situation is encountered on a large scale in developing economies, where institutions to fight organized crime are quite weak.

An interesting case is offered by post-communist countries (transition economies), which have experienced a period of institutional interregnum (vacuum) in the aftermath of the collapse of the command systems. This state of affairs has allowed many individuals and firms to operate unethically without fear of penalties. A distinction should be made, in this respect, between questionable practices, which are the result of missing institutions (regulations), and unethical behavior, which may become deeply entrenched and damage economic performance through time. Developing economies, in general, provide ample leeway to ethically "fuzzy" behaviour because of precarious institutional contexts. This state of affairs has prompted De Soto to emphasize that large efficiency gains, and overall development could be achieved in poor countries, by defining and enforcing property rights adequately and by empowering citizens.[24]

B. Over-regulation and Under-regulation

Regulations impact aggregate economic performance. Arguably, the more regulated (and taxed) is an economy the more induced are agents to operate in the underground sector. It can be submitted that there is an optimal *structure* and *level* of regulation of the economy which maximizes societal welfare; the optimal structure and level of regulation depend on social norms, values and principles which validate what people at large appreciate as being positive and negative externalities.

This optimality can be illustrated graphically by dividing the economy into two sectors: the official and unofficial sectors which both consume factors of production—labour and capital.[25] Both over-regulation and under-regulation lead to inferior compositions of the economy in terms of societal welfare. Thus, over-regulation means an expansion of the underground economy against the background of reduced overall efficiency. Likewise, an under-regulated system (as in the case of environmental protection, or securities legislation) can bring about an "official" expansion of socially pernicious activities, which also

---

[24] De Soto (2000).
[25] Dăianu (1997).

reduces societal welfare. The shape of the combination curve indicates that both hyper-regulation (as in a command system) and the lack of regulation (no rules) can lead to a worse economic performance.

When regulations (or taxes) rise, there is a shift of the price line in favor of the unofficial sector in the sense of stimulating its expansion—this happens because the goods produced in the official sector become more expensive. Another effect is an increase of the nominal prices of the goods and services in the underground economy—although they become relatively cheaper—which can only partially be mitigated by its expansion (which puts downward pressure on prices in the unofficial economy).

In a simplified way agents' behaviours can be understood by comparing the benefits and costs of operating in the underground sector. The benefits are: the avoidance of the tax rate and the cost of regulations compliance. The cost of non-compliance includes, *inter alia*, the penalty fee, which can be adjusted by the probability of being caught. A variable whose size is most critical is the cost of non-compliance. A main thesis of this chapter is that when standards of reputation are low, the cost of non-compliance is diminished, which enhances the functioning of the unofficial sector. This issue is revisited when the emphasis will be put on explaining reputation as an asset.

The minimum price acceptable in the unofficial sector can be defined as the official ruling market price from which the tax rate and the cost of regulations compliance are deduced, and the penalty fee adjusted by the probability of being caught is added. Clearly, the price mentioned above is the minimum for not incurring losses. The equilibrium price in the underground sector depends on the intensity of competition, which further depends on the cost of non-compliance. Thus, when the modified cost of non-compliance goes up, the underground economy shrinks and vice-versa; likewise, the equilibrium price, rises. When the cost of non-compliance goes down, the underground economy expands, but eventually the equilibrium price goes down since competition intensifies.

More intense competition in the official economy and a rise of the cost of non-compliance would tend to bring closer the values of the minimum price and the equilibrium price. As it was emphasized, the cost of non-compliance depends essentially on the entrenched rules of the game in the local environment. To be more specific, the size of the probability of being caught depends on rule enforcements, social norms and the local standards of reputation. It can also be assumed that the rules of the game depend on how agents (companies) view their reputation as an asset to be built up.

C. Variety of Institutional Contexts and of Economic Performance

The variety of institutional circumstances, with their correspondence in regulatory frameworks and economic performance, is studied by comparative economics. This field of economics is staging a comeback lately, but under a new guise: instead of examining market based systems as against communist (command) systems (as until 1989), the focus now is on examining the variety of capitalism, various brands of market economy.

Djankov et al. show that specific institutional contexts can be conceptualized through an IPC (institutional possibilities curve);[26] this curve illustrates various combinations of private orderings, independent judges, state regulations and state ownership; an optimal state of affairs would be when social losses are at a minimum. This analysis can explain both the pressure for deregulation in the last couple of decades, against the backdrop of intense technological change and financial innovation, and consequences of excessive deregulation.[27] While EU member countries seem to be over-regulated in certain regards (the Lisbon Agenda tries to address this situation), the US economy appears to have accumulated increasing social losses in the late 1990s because of too much deregulation (or the lack of proper regulations). For, it is fair to say, technological advance and financial innovation created major new opportunities, which were not envisaged by those who had conceived regulatory frameworks. But these new opportunities contained seeds of evil as well. Thus, referring to the cynicism of energy and financial companies during the boom of the last decade an

---

[26] Djankov et al. (2004).

[27] The IPC framework, as an illustration of the so-called "new" New Comparative Economics, is regarded with some skepticism by the proponents of the "old" New Comparative Economics (see Dallago, 2004). In my opinion, the IPC framework, in spite of its limitations, provides an interesting way of examining institutional settings and can be much fruitful for analysis.

International Herald Tribune editorial notes that "[o]ne energy trader gloats about cheating 'poor grandmothers.' Another suggests shutting down a power plant in order to drive up electricity prices ... *Enron* and other major energy companies manipulated California's energy markets in 2000 and 2001 in ways that cost the state billions." The same editorial observes that "...Wall Street analysts acknowledged that the stocks they were peddling were mostly dogs..." (8 June 2004).

The IPC framework suggests that too much regulation, as well as too little regulation, is not good for the economy, or society as a whole. But the optimal combination changes over time, in view of evolving institutions and technology. Individuals' behaviors can be included in this picture. In general, developing economies are less adept at identifying optimal institutional combinations.

Informal sectors tell much about institutional contexts, for such portions of economy are the cover for illegal, criminal activities. By definition, criminal behaviour is unethical. Nonetheless it is notable that some people may enter the underground sector because of an improper structure of incentives—as these are constructed by public policy. In this case, analysis has to use analytical nuances; what is qualified as unethical behaviour (because it is in the informal economy) can easily come into the open, and be positively judged provided the set of incentives changes in the right direction. An example is the huge social security contributions which are practiced in not so few European countries, which induce many entrepreneurs to use black market labour. The bottom line is that a large informal sector is more likely to present unethical behaviour as against the formal economy. Both over-regulation and under-regulation can favour illegal activities and unethical behaviour.

A big question is why socially precarious equilibria are resilient, albeit most of the players would be better off by changing their behaviours. This looks like an obvious coordination problem, which this chapter tries to answer by examining the concept of reputation.

D. Explaining Low Equilibria: Reputation As an Asset

I would submit that *reputation* is the source of all positive social externalities, be they *trust*, *trustworthiness*, *truth-telling*, *loyalty*, etc. By accumulating reputation individuals and communities increase the amount of individual[28] and social capital. Likewise, the quest for better reputation necessarily contains unethical behavior and implies less illegal acts.[29]

One can think about the accumulation of reputation in both static and dynamic terms, as stock and flow. Thus, it should be quite appealing to common sense to view higher reputation (and, consequently, trust and loyalty) as a means to reduce X-inefficiency (at micro-level) and allocative inefficiency, as an addition to the stock of overall capital. Higher stocks of reputation can be captured analytically in two ways: either by increasing the stock of overall capital (capital augmenting) and, therefore, output; or by enhancing efficiency and, concomitantly, output. In the latter case one can easily resort to the concept of transaction costs[30] and conclude that higher reputation as an average trait of a system reduces transaction and information costs. Reputation can be viewed as a means to reduce the trade-off between specialization of work and trust under conditions of anonymity of participants to exchange. This would be the static portion of analysis. On a diagram this can be shown by an outward shift of the production possibilities curve.

In the dynamic case one can think analogously of the role of human capital build-up, and particularly of education, in economic growth.[31] Higher *reputation* has several implications. By making agents more efficient, this likely raises their propensity to accumulate and invest over time. In addition, higher reputation raises overall efficiency (including allocative efficiency) within the national environment and, thereby, it creates higher rates of return, which further may stimulate saving and investment. Krugman argues that nations do not compete.[32] However, when economies are seen as "clusters of activities" which create synergies, they do compete. Summing up, one can dray an inference: higher reputation, seen as asset accumulation, is liable to make both individual agents and a national environment more efficient and competitive; this would enhance R&D, growth prospects— like in endogenous growth model stories. On the one hand, this shifts

---

[28] A company's reputation for ethical behavior is part of its brand-name capital (Brickley *et al.*, 2002).

[29] For various ways of dealing with reputation in formal models, see Klein (1997).

[30] Williamson (1985).

[31] See Becker (1964) and Schultz (1961).

[32] Krugman (1994).

the production possibilities curve of economy outwards; on the other hand, it does raise the growth path of the economy.

E. REPUTATION IN TRANSITION ECONOMIES

Intangible goods (which are positive social externalities) like *trust*, *truth-telling*, *loyalty* were scarce commodities in the command economies. This legacy cannot be overcome instantaneously during transition. The explanation for this state of affairs is essentially twofold: institutional change, and social relations in general, are time-consuming—*natura non facit saltus*; society and the structure of property rights are still too fuzzy in order to shape behaviours clearly and penalize misconduct. One can talk in this respect about a certain ethos, a business culture which reflects the nature of institutions; this business culture does not encourage better economic performance.

Unethical behaviour is a facet of the lack, or neglect, of reputation. In a society where clear rules of behaviour and codes of ethical conduct (as "seals of approval") are the norm, reputation is highly valued; reputation can be built up, or destroyed, and this affects the evolution of individuals in society as well as their expected income streams in economic life. This logic would apply to enterprise life as well. An individual who optimizes for the long run, would be much concerned about his or her reputation and would not undertake actions inimical to it. Why isn't this type of optimization the rule of the social game during transition? There can be several explanations in this respect. One, which was already alluded to, is linked with the fuzzy state of property rights. Another explanation can be connected with uncertainty, which reduces the time horizon used by individuals and organizations. These are, certainly, valid arguments. But what frequently motivates people is the appeal of easy to obtain gains by speculating legal loopholes and by overlooking social consequences of their acts.

Neglect of reputation can be met in politics, too. Usually, a politician should be much concerned about deeds which can harm his or her reputation. Frequently, one sees politicians' behaviour much focused on the short term, which can hardly be rationalized by the pressure of current events. This attitude seems to be related more to an optimization that involves the public position as a purveyor of *rents*. The public function is conceived as a good business, but not for a long time, and a *big discount is applied to reputation*. One could argue that this type of behaviour fits those who enter politics for extra-political (economics) reasons. On the other hand, since this behaviour is quite pervasive, the resultant "competition" leads to increasingly bigger discounts. In this way society as a whole is a loser and the "rule of law" becomes a long distanced image.[33] This social low equilibrium can persist for a long time.

How could this biased behaviour be captured at a micro-level? A possible way is to use a utility function which includes *reputation* as a variable. The optimizing (satisfying) behaviour implies the maximization of a function, namely a utility stream. The utility stream depends on the stock of reputation at the present time *t*, a time horizon used by agents (which cannot exceed the potential active life), and a discount factor applied to future utility flows. Obviously, the assumption is that higher reputation implies higher utility. The dynamic of the stock of *reputation* can be illustrated by its own function. In a normal environment, an agent would be interested in accumulating reputation and maximizing the utility function in the long run.

The analysis can incorporate the degree of *fuzziness* (including property rights) in the system. A relationship can be established *between fuzziness* and the time frame used by economic and political agents. It thus makes sense to assume that the higher is the degree of fuzziness, ceteris paribus, the bigger is the propensity to work with a reduced time horizon.

F. WHY DO LOW EQUILIBRIA PERSIST?

An interesting aspect can be brought into the analysis at this point, which may shed light on and explain why relatively low standards of reputation and high corruption are resilient in many areas of the world. This would also illuminate why people seem to accommodate their habits and condone what some may consider to be unacceptable patterns of behaviours and which should, presumably, change over time. It can be submitted that, when it is seen in relative terms, *reputation* depends on local standards of ethics and morality (corruption),

---

[33] A fallacy of composition is involved here; what seems to be rational for individuals becomes detrimental for society. A negative externality thus emerges.

on local seals of approval. This is a different sort of ethical relativism than the one that basically dismisses ethical considerations. The existence of local yardsticks of ethical behaviour is more realistic when globalisation of economic life, and of universally held standards of business ethics, has less of an impact. Therefore, a revised form of a reputation function, takes into account what is perceived as "normal" by the local environment. The above formulation says that the degree of corruption or the moral (ethical) laxity in the system regarding the observance of normal (not local) standards of reputation affects the perception of one agent's reputation. When corruption is widespread and the interpretation of laws is highly arbitrary, agents become almost indifferent to *reputation* as an asset.[34] Under such circumstances concern about reputation, namely its consolidation becomes insignificant, or even negative. It is a case of sacrificing any trace of reputation for the sake of realizing exceptionally high material gains in the short run. In this case the trade-off between *reputation* and other factors that enter into the utility function do not favour the build up of reputation.

When short-term materials gains get the upper-hand *vis-à-vis* the accumulation of reputation the optimization process gets more complicated. Thus, the optimal stock of reputation can be seen as being dependent on the local rules of the game, and the specific "weight" of the agent. In this case the utility function is revised by making a distinction between reputation as a goal in itself, and the marginal utility

---

[34] One can imagine situations of multiple equilibria—good or bad—related to individuals' behaviors. An example is when people pay their due taxes, or they evade it. There are models which try to portray such situations. Thus, it is assumed that the production of an individual firm (index i) is an increasing function of a public good provided by the state. It is assumed now that the level of public good $g=nt$, where t indicates the degree of fiscality, and n denotes the number of firms that pay taxes. The individual production function can be written as $qi=q+ag$, with $a>0$. In the case of tax evasion, $qi=q$. Different equilibria appear. Let us assume that $a<1<N$. The firm income after tax is $(q+ag-t)$ if all firms pay taxes and (q) if no firm pays taxes. It seems that the decision is clear for the firm; it tries to avoid taxes as long as $t<ag=ant$, or $n<1/a$. If $n=1$ (which means that all firms practice tax evasion) the firm N is also stimulated to get into tax evasion since $n<1/a$ (according to the assumption made). If $n=N$, then the firm is interested in paying taxes, since $n>1$ (see also Sachs, 1994, p. 48). This reasoning can be applied to any kind of criminal or illegal act.

derived from being concerned about reputation; this latter utility denotes potential material gains to be made by using the "rules of the game" and the knowledge of the local environment (including inside information and the use of networks).

Under sufficiently constraining conditions of the local "rules of the game," or by very small incremental gains which induce agents not to care about reputation, a situation can be imagined when higher reputation is not accompanied by higher utility; it is like a point from which the marginal cost of "puritanical" behaviour exceeds its marginal benefit. This means that material gains, however these are acquired, prevail over the accumulation of reputation. In such a context feelings of guilt and shame of bad deeds do not constrain behaviour meaningfully.

The discount rate (applied to future streams of utility) depends also on the degree of uncertainty regarding the evolution of the legal environment. The less clear and more uncertain is an environment compared to an ideal framework, the lower is the discount rate. Why the specific "weight" of actors is mentioned? For there are people, who, through their critical mass (which includes reputation) can influence the rules of the game and the environment. For such individuals, whose dimension goes beyond the frontiers of the local environment, *reputation* acquires different parameters of definition and possible compromises they may get into have a different nature and other implications. Such individuals may develop the ability to stand up morally and not be forced to "howl with wolves."[35] Virtue ethics, as against narrowly defined deontological ethics, play a high profile in their behaviour. There are cases when highly respected individuals, once they take over public positions, can improve the image of the public entity (or the country) they represent. This can be the situation of a minister of finance, or of a governor of a central bank. Obviously, this reasoning can be extrapolated to a whole government. For such circumstances a collective utility function includes as a variable the reputation of key public servants (ministers).[36]

---

[35] Once, a commercial banker confessed to me that the world of business "does not like those who are more Catholic than the Pope." This prodding meant that one needs to be particularly heavyweight in order to be successful as a businessman, while being "excessively puritanical" in behavior.

[36] One factor that might help explain the persistence of bad equilibria is the annihilation (or even the physical elimination) of individuals that attempt to

When new norms are not rooted socially well enough and since a new moral order cannot emerge instantaneously, the role of "moral models" acquires exceptional importance. Leaders of great charisma and moral probity, with vision and determination are essential in making change for the better possible. But such leaders are not easy to find. *Leadership* is an issue that underlines the moral dimension of a society's transformation. Ultimately, however, repaired or solid institutions have to come into being in order to make societies perform better.

IV. Institutional Responses to Ethical Lapses

Institutional responses follow various tracks. One involves public policy as when governments react by adopting new regulations. Another track is a response by organizations which represent producers and consumers, which leads to new regulations and modifications of codes of conduct; this is change from below. The changes under way in accounting and auditing rules reflect both policy tracks. Likewise, modifications in best practices are a venue for improving (constraining) harmful behavior by individuals and firms. The battle for improving governance in public and private sectors around the world is driven by culture, ethical considerations as well. Not least education gets into the picture. The revival of business ethics courses in business schools' curricula and the efforts to enlist major corporations under the banner of promoting corporate social responsibility is part of the same process.

Institutional responses, of whatever sort, are influenced by major social and ideological cycles. As a matter of fact, the events of recent years have triggered a lot of soul-searching in western societies and people talk more profoundly about the next stage in the evolution of capitalism. On the other hand, the very social and economic dynamics of global capitalism force policy-makers to reexamine the regulatory frameworks under which economies operate.

---

build a stock of reputation—either for themselves or for an institution/group they represent. Examples could relate to situations existent in Italy, decades ago, or, nowadays, in countries in South America.

Ethics can be examined in the international economy as well. The dispute over free trade vs. fair trade revolves also around the perception that rich countries preach what they do not practice; their hypocrisy is amply indicated by agricultural subsidies, while poor countries' main exports are made of farm products. The issue of ethical attitudes concerns financial relations as well; the pressure put on emerging economies to open their capital account in the 1990s was the outcome of powerful lobbies exerted by financial industries in the wealthy economies. Therefore, the crises which erupted in a series of South East Asian countries in the late 1990s have an obvious moral dimension as well. The list of global issues with ethical implications includes poverty, fighting diseases, environmental protection, etc.

The past decade has been suffused with claims that economic policy, in the advanced countries, is being driven by an emerging new consensus on principles and practice. The ideological fallout was pretty obvious in Anthony Giddens' expression "The Third Way," which connotes neither traditional social-democracy, nor blatant liberalism—in the European sense;[37] this formula was adopted by the "new" Labour Party in the UK as its quasi-philosophical mantra and other social democrats have tried to foray deeply into it. Highly glamorous seminars featuring Bill Clinton, Tony Blair, Gerhard Schröder, Lionel Jospin and others were quite en vogue in the late 90s. In the United States, George W. Bush used "compassionate conservatism" as an ideological means to enhance his presidential message. It appeared as social-democrats (in Europe) and democrats (in the USA), on the one hand, and center-right parties (in Europe) and republicans (in the USA) were coming closer, in terms of both principles and practice of economic policy.

The sources of this apparent "new" consensus are, arguably, several. One origin could be traced to the ever-longing desire of Man to control his environment (nature) and to be more efficient. Thus, in the first quarter of the past century Max Weber's "rationalization of life" referred to rational accounting, rational law, rational technology, which by extrapolation, can be extended to "rational economics," as a form of *hard science* (as *Newtonian economics*). Later on (in the seventies), another famous sociologist, Daniel Bell, upheld the primacy

---

[37] Giddens (1998).

of knowledge and theory-related activities in ordering our life, man's technological and economic ascendancy—which would imply that economic wizards can secure a fool-proof policy.[38] Quantitative methods may have also entrenched this intellectual propensity. Even the clash between Keynesianism and monetarism, as the two main competing macro-economic paradigms, could be seen in the vein of searching for the ultimate piece of wisdom. Another origin of policy amalgamation comes out of the death of communism. Fukuyama's *The End of History* was seen by many as an embodiment of the, presumably, single ideology (liberal democracy) which was meant to rule the world. Last, but not least, globalisation—as an incarnation of unfettered markets and downsizing of government, operating worldwide—also provided an impetus to the vision of the "ideal" type of economic policy.

At the start of the new century facts are disavowing over-simplifications. There are numerous examples which prove that conflicting ideas are with us, that reality cannot be encapsulated into a Procustian ideological bed; that economics continues to be softer than some of us try to make people believe. Let's be more specific. Policy-wise, it is increasingly clear that trimming the welfare state and the public sector is not enough in order to achieve the expected efficiency gains; this endeavour needs to be accompanied by effective regulations of various markets (financial and energy, in particular), which, otherwise, can easily be rigged; "the new economy," the "new paradigm" (which claimed to combine high growth rates with very low unemployment), proved to be, simply put, a mirage of the 1990s. Recent developments in the US and elsewhere offer ample proofs in this regard; these events motivated public authorities to intervene. Likewise, as against the prevailing tenets of not many years ago, economic policy, as it is currently undertaken in the US and Europe, does not preclude running larger budget deficits during a downswing of the cycle; this is the explanation for some basic Keynesian recipes returning to the limelight.

How does globalisation fit into this picture? The pressure of more intense competition forces governments to streamline their public sectors, which does frustrate trade-unions and many citizens at large. But rich countries in the West remain welfare states, *par excellence,* albeit in an evolving manner. One can detect here a rising/returning

---

[38] Bell (1973).

Keynesianism in macroeconomic policy-making with a retreat when it comes to social policy; there is an apparent policy contradiction herein. Another consequence of globalisation is the creation of an international policy agenda. By omission and commission, some of the wealthy countries' less inspired policies have given renewed high profile to issues such as: fair vs. free trade; dealing with abject poverty in the world; protecting the environment as a public good for mankind; the code of conduct for international corporations, how to manage contagion effects in the world economy; policy coordination among the leading economies of the world; etc. There is an obvious ethical dimension assigned to this international agenda.

As a matter of fact, the traditional ongoing battle between left and right—within the framework of democratic politics—is being shifted, partially, into the international arena. The debate on global governance reflects a growing awareness that there are issues that need to be addressed internationally, in a multilateral context and using collaborative approaches. Arguably, the choice between globalisation and "managed globalisation" is between accepting the effects of completely free markets, with policy disregard for market failures and their social consequences, and trying to construct an international policy, which should address/prevent massive coordination failures. The controversies surrounding globalisation touch upon ethical considerations as well. Concomitantly, the debate over which form of capitalism, and what type of state intervention in the economy, turns, partially, into a debate on which form of "global capitalism."

A second policy route, namely the setting of an international policy agenda, does make sense in a global economy in which there is acceptance of the need for international public goods.[39] Otherwise, under increasing pressure from foreign markets and other threats (including terrorism, illegal immigration, spreading diseases, etc.), governments would resort to national means of protection—such as trade protectionism and trade clashes, competitive devaluations, etc.

---

[39] The ecological concerns would pay attention also to the fact that future generations cannot voice their concerns on how current generations deplete the Earth's resources; this is a major flaw of revealed "rational calculation" as it is provided by completely free markets and an argument in favor of public intervention. See Boulding (1978) for a wide ranging plea in this respect, as well as in addressing the issue of complexity of economic processes.

Ideology is not dead, and it does shape social and economic policies—although in subtler forms and following cyclical patterns. It may be less felt nationally to the extent the battlefield of ideas expands increasingly beyond national borders. In any case, globalisation is likely to reflect ever more the battle of ideas, including the ethical dimension, with traditional politics delving increasingly into the international domain. How would policy-makers address the hot issues in the international economy would provide clues regarding its dynamics, to what extent ethical considerations come to the fore.

V. Conclusion: Whither Capitalism?

It is hard not to share Sen's thought that "it is precisely the narrowing of the broad Smithian view of human beings, in modern economies, that can be seen as one of the major deficiencies of contemporary economic theory. This impoverishment is closely related to the distancing of economics from ethics."[40] Arguably, this distancing has an impact on real life (economies), on how people live, on how they relate to each other. When people lose the moral compass and virtue ethics fades away, they become oblivious to the Socratic question regarding the purpose of one's life. Sooner or later this brings misery and disappointment in individual lives and causes social pain on a massive scale.

Society reacts one way or another. For instance, the years which followed the Great Depression brought about new regulations that aimed at restraining excesses and unethical behaviour stemming from the free-market social organization of society. An example was the Glass-Steagall Act in the US, which split investment banking from commercial banking. Institutional adjustments followed the end of the Second World War as well. And the big failures in financial and energy markets, in the past decade, have ushered in a new period of market regulation, which reshapes public policy accordingly. The Sarbanes-Oxley Act of 2002 in the US is a clear example of such new activism. Firms, too, are reexamining their internal regulation systems in order to cope with unethical behaviour. And new accounting and auditing

---

[40] Sen (1987, p. 28).

rules are being put in place. Such policy responses, at macro and micro levels, are meant to make capitalism function better.[41]

Policy pragmatism is in higher demand than policy fundamentalism nowadays, although hard-nosed "ideologues" are present in the corridors of power. Nevertheless, public policy is forced to reconsider older themes (e.g., the State needs to provide public goods) in order to regain the moral ground, which was partially lost owing to major scandals in the corporate world. The moral ground relates to domestic as well as international politics.

In European transition economies the prospects of joining the EU have operated as a catalyst for reforms and a strong support for dealing with the pains and frustrations of societal change. But not a few citizens are disappointed by the results of reforms, and the widespread corruption and unethical behaviour incense most of the population; some citizens relate these phenomena to market reforms, and this perception does show up unabashedly in the polls. Once the first wave of EU eastern enlargement would be well underway, benefits would accrue to many citizens, but disappointments, too, are likely to become more intense. Such likely outcomes beg a candid discussion on the linkage between values, morality and the dynamics of capitalism and what it takes to make it more fulfilling for most of the population. This is why the public debate on effective regulations and institutions which should strengthen the ability of markets to deliver for the satisfaction of most citizens (consumers) and avoid massive social exclusion has not lost any relevance. The scope of the state in providing public goods should be judged in the same vein, albeit this role should be judged in conjunction with the need for a streamlined and more efficient public sector, which should not crowd out (undermine) the proficiency of the private sector.

The public debate on ethics and economy acquires new overtones when looking at the world under the impact of globalisation and other forces at work. Aside from international terrorism, one can point at the dark side of globalisation: inability to cope with global issues (such as global warming), massive illegal immigration, increasing poverty in many areas of the world, poor functioning of international financial markets, trade disputes, etc. In this context, the issues of governance,

---

[41] Greider (2003) would call it "reinventing capitalism."

both in the public and private spheres, get more salience. And governance cannot be dissociated from the moral values, the mindsets of those who make decisions.

To sum up: history indicates cycles of policies and institutional adjustments following large economic dynamics. It may be, that after a deregulation euphoria which featured so highly on the agenda of governments, especially in the Anglo-Saxon world during the last couple of decades, a new phase is about to set in; this phase would underline the need for effective market regulations and a more enlightened working together between the public and the private sphere. This logic would have to apply to the international economy as well, which needs public goods so badly, which further demand reshaped international institutions—capable of ensuring global governance. The latter, clearly, asks for more international cooperation and a common vision on how to tackle the major challenges confronting mankind. These challenges cannot be dealt with unless economic rationality blends with social and moral values, unless *shame* and *guilt* maintain the cement of societies.

REFERENCES

Argandoña, A. (2004) "On Ethical, Social and Environmental Management Systems" *Journal of Business Ethics*, Vol. 51, No. 1, pp. 41–52. Also available as a chapter of this book.

Arrow, J.K. (1951) *Social Choice and Individual Value*, New York, Wiley.

Arrow, J.K. (1974) *The Limits of Organization*, New York, Norton.

Bebear, C. and Manière, P. (2003) *Ils Vont Tuer le Capitalisme*, Paris, Plon.

Becker, G. (1964) *Human Capital*, New York, Columbia University Press.

Bell, D. (1973) *The Coming of Post-industrial Society*, New York, Basic Books.

Boulding, K. (1978) *Ecodynamics. A New Theory of Societal Evolution*, Beverly Hills, Sage Publications.

Brickley, J.A., Smith, C.F. and Zimmerman, J.L. (2002) "Business Ethics and Organizational Architecture" *Journal of Banking and Finance*, Vol. 26, pp. 1821–35.

Dăianu, D. (1997) "Reputation as an Asset" Paper presented at a Workshop of the European Association of Comparative Economics in Budapest, 1997. See "Institutions, Strain and the Underground Economy" *The William Davidson Institute Working Paper*, 98.

Dallago, B. (2004) "The 'Old' and the 'New' CES: A Synthesis" Paper presented at the VIIIth Bi-annual Conference of the Association of Comparative Economic Studies, Belgrade, 23–25 September, manuscript.

De Soto, H. (2000) *The Mystery of Capital. Why Capitalism Triumphs in The West and Fails Everywhere Else*, New York, Basic Books.

Djankov, S., *et al.* (2004) *The New Comparative Economics*, mimeo.

Eatwell, J. and Taylor, L. (2000) *Global Finance At Risk. The Case For International Regulation*, New York, The New Press.

Fischer, S. (2003) "Globalisation and its Challenges" *American Economic Review*, AEA Papers and Proceedings, Vol. 93, No. 2, pp. 1–30.

Fukuyama, F. (1990) *The End of History*, New York, The Free Press.

Fukuyama, F. (1999) *The Great Disruption*, New York, The Free Press.

Giddens, A. (1998) *The Third Way. The Renewal of Social Democracy*, Oxford, Basil Blackwell.

Greider, C. (2003) *The Soul of Capitalism. Opening Paths to a Moral Economy*, New York, Simon and Schuster.

Kindleberger, C. (1989) *Manias, Panics, and Crashes. A History of Financial Crises*, New York, Basic Books.

Klein B.D. (ed.) (1997) *Reputation. Studies in the Voluntary Elicitation of Good Conduct*, Ann Arbor, University of Michigan.

Koehn, D. (1995) "A Role for Virtue Ethics in the Analysis of Business Practice" *Business Ethics Quarterly*, Vol. 5, No. 3, pp. 533–9.

Krugman, P. (1994) "Competitiveness: A Dangerous Obsession" *Foreign Affairs*, March–April, Vol. 73, No. 2.

Lal, D. (1999) *Unintended Consequences. The Impact of Factor Endowments, Culture, and Politics on Long-Run Economic Performance*, Cambridge, MIT Press.

Phelps, E.S. (1975) *Altruism, Morality and Economic Theory*, New York, Russell Sage Foundation.

Sachs, J. (1994), "Russia's Struggle with Stabilisation. Conceptual Issues and Evidence" Paper prepared for the World Bank's Annual Conference on Development Economics.

Schultz, T. (1961) "Investment in Human Capital" *American Economic Review*, Vol. 51, No. 1, pp.1–17.

Sen, A. (1987) *On Ethics and Economics*, London, Basil Blackwell.

Shearmur, J. and Klein, D.B. (1997) "Good conduct in the Great Society: Adam Smith and the Role of Reputation" in Daniel B. Klein (ed.), *Studies in the Voluntary Elicitation of Good Conduct*, Ann Arbor, University of Michigan Press, pp. 29–46.

Shleifer, A. (2004) "Does Competition Destroy Ethical Behavior?" *American Economic Review*, Vol. 94, No. 2, pp. 414–8.

Stiglitz, J.E. (2003) *The Roaring Nineties*, New York, W.W. Norton.

Summers, L. (2000) "International Financial Crises: Causes, Prevention, and Cures" *American Economic Review*, AEA Papers and Proceedings, Vol. 90, No. 2, pp. 1–16.

Weber, M. (1958) *The Protestant Ethic and The Spirit of Capitalism*, New York, Scribners.

Williamson, O. (1985) *The Economic Institutions of Capitalism*, New York, Free Press.

CHAPTER 3

Why This Financial Crisis Is Occurring—How to Respond to It[1]

While the Committee strongly believes that large, deep, liquid and innovative financial markets will result in substantial efficiency gains and will therefore bring individual benefits to European citizens, it also believes that greater efficiency does not necessarily go hand in hand with enhanced stability.[2]

I. Introduction

Increasing innovation in financial markets, together with rapidly growing cross-border transactions (globalisation), aided by favourable low-interest rate conditions in developed markets, against the background of inadequate regulatory frameworks, have created the premises for a potentially devastating financial crisis (more severe than the ongoing current crisis). It is too early to tell what the consequences of a full blown crisis would be as it is quite difficult to assess its impact on both the financial sector and the real economy; what is certain, however, is that this impact would be very damaging.

---

[1] This chapter is based on a paper written with Laurian Lungu and presented at an ALDE seminar on the international financial crisis, in the European Parliament, 27 February 2008. We thank Sharon Bowles, Wolf Klinz and Patrick Minford for their very helpful comments. We also thank Eric De Keuleneer, Nigel Phipps, Robert Priester, Ray Kinsella, John Purvis, Ieke Van den Burg and other seminar participants for their useful comments. We assume full responsibility for the content of this paper, which was posted on the website of the TIGER Institute of Warsaw.

[2] Alexander Lamfalussy (2008) making a reference to the final report of the Committee of Wise Men on the Regulation of European Securities Markets (15 February 2001), p. 2.

The purpose of this chapter is to have a look at the main causes that have triggered the current crisis and then review some of the suggestions to tackle it as highlighted by various market participants. From the start it looks as if at the roots of today's unfolding crisis has been market participants' behaviour of making reckless lending, often against no collateral, while regulatory and supervisory institutions were failing. But equally important it has been the very intense financial innovation of the past decade, which has allowed a wide dissemination of risks together with a blurring of the line delimiting who bears them. Without this wide dissemination the subprime mortgage crisis could, presumably, have been contained to a large extent, to the US markets. Ironically, what was thought to diminish risks at individual (micro) level has turned out to increase systemic risks; the latter have to be examined in conjunction with the expansion of global markets.

It has to be said, however, that elements of the ongoing crisis make integral part of the long-standing pattern of booms and busts in asset markets. Often, the mechanism through which these financial crises develop is, as mentioned by Michael Bordo, the emergence of new financial instruments.[3] The latter are often designed in such a way as to avoid regulation and necessarily require a test of financial stress in order to be proved successful or not. Initially, the euphoria of the boom, financed through credit, blurs the distinction between sound and less profitable prospects, a situation which could induce an asset price bubble. Information asymmetries compound the initial problem leading to moral hazard[4] and adverse selection.[5] The bust—often triggered by an increase in interest rates—brings an end to the lending cycle. In hindsight, recent crises, such as the LTCM or Enron, could be considered as stress tests for the financial system. Although they were quite severe, their global effects could be contained in the end because, at that time, the financial markets' degree of sophistication did not arguably reach the level and depth as witnessed nowadays. It seems that delays in the effective implementation and enforcement of

---

[3] Bordo (2007).
[4] See Mishkin (1997).
[5] Moral hazard refers to a situation when market participants take excessive risks, if they believe someone will bail them out if things go wrong. Adverse selection occurs when buyers/traders are unable to differentiate between the quality of financial products, i.e., loans for instance.

changes in regulatory systems, as flagged out by these early warning signs,[6] are at least partially, at the root cause for the turmoil we are witnessing nowadays.

Financial crises are powerful events and can have very serious implications. If the effects of the crisis affect the real economy, this could in turn trigger a fall in consumers' wealth and consumption and it might take years until the economy settles back to the economic path at the point preceding the crisis. In effect, this is one of the main questions addressing the existing situation. Given the current state of short-term credit concerns in an economic environment where GDP has still been growing and house price declines have been rather modest, the question posed is what can be expected if the US enters a full-blown recession and average real estate values fall by a large amount. Spill-over effects to other global asset markets would, undoubtedly, magnify the outcome of such a scenario.

The chapter proceeds as follows: the next section deals briefly with the issue of classification of financial crises, as documented in the literature. It also highlights similarities the current financial crisis has with more recent episodes of this kind. Section 3 describes what is particular of the current crisis, while Section 4 looks at how to respond to the crisis. Finally, the last section summarises points of view expressed in the literature and the media about what can be done to avert the occurrence of such a crisis in the future.

II. A Classification of Financial Crises

A. WHAT CAUSES FINANCIAL CRISES?

Financial crises are recurring phenomena which can have a significant impact on the economy. Depending on how one defines a financial crisis, there are various ways in which these can be classified. For instance, Anna J. Schwartz, a reputed US monetary economist, argued

---

[6] By making reference to the LTCM episode, Krugman (1999, p.162) said, years ago: "The hedge fund scare revealed that modern financial markets, by creating many institutions that perform bank-like functions ... have in fact reinvented the possibility of traditional financial panics."

that a financial crisis should involve a run on the monetary base. Otherwise it would be difficult to distinguish between a pseudo-crisis and a real one. In practice, however, things are more difficult to assess once a crisis is unfolding. Financial crises could involve either bank or currency crises or indeed, both of them could take place at the same time.

Historically, credit booms—that fuelled unsustainable rates of economic growth—seemed to have preceded financial crises. Delargy and Goodhart argue that both the late 19th century crises and those in the late 20th were more likely when loose credit conditions in the lending countries were in place.[7] Subsequently, when credit conditions suddenly adversely changed, it generated a boom and bust economic cycle.

The causes for financial crises are multiple and nowadays, a standard classification of currency crises revolves around one of the three generational models.

The *first generation models*, pioneered by Krugman as well as Flood and Garber, deal with crises that are mainly caused by macroeconomic vulnerabilities.[8] In essence, at their origin is the government's need to finance constantly higher deficits, eventually resorting to monetisation. Because these crises necessarily envisage a dynamic path for economic policies, they are therefore predictable. Classic examples are recent crises in Russia (1998) and Argentina (2001). Moreover, these type of crises could include a broader array of factors that trigger them, including monetary policy indiscipline, overvalued exchange rates and contagion from crises in relevant trading partners countries. Because of improved macroeconomic policies at the global level, however, these crises tend to be rarer nowadays.

The *second generation crises models* focused on macroeconomic trade-offs and decisions. They emphasise non-financial conditions that may abruptly turn adverse in such a way that would present the authorities with a range of policy choices. As an example of the second generation crisis is the series of attacks on some European currencies within the European Monetary System in 1992–1993. Obstfeld has shown how crises can be self-fulfilling in such a situation.[9]

---

[7] Delargy and Goodhart (1999).
[8] See Krugman (1979), Flood and Garber (1984).
[9] Obstfeld (1986).

They also exhibit multiple equilibria and occur mainly because market participants expect them to materialise.

The *third generation crises* address the balance sheet problems. A distinctive feature of those is that their causes reside in the financial sector vulnerabilities.[10] At the root of these vulnerabilities are mismatches between assets and liabilities, whether they are held by financial institutions or by the non-financial sector, and irrespective whether they are a matter of concern for the public or private sectors.

The frequency of this later strand of currency crises has become higher recently, as financial markets have become increasingly integrated. Different third-generation models explore various mechanisms through which balance-sheet exposures may lead to a currency and banking crisis. Thus, according to Mark *et al.* there are four types of balance sheet mismatches that can be identified:[11] a) *maturity mismatches*, where the gap between short term liabilities and liquid assets leaves an institution incapable to pledge its contractual commitments if lenders refuse to roll over debt or if creates exposure in the face of interest rate rising; b) *currency mismatches*, where sudden changes in exchange rates lead to a capital loss; c) *capital structure problems*, where excessive leverage leaves a firm or bank exposed to uncertain revenue shocks in adverse market conditions; and d) *solvency problems*, in cases where assets are insufficient to cover liabilities. Solvency risk can arise from various reasons. For instance, Chang and Velasco show that a liquidity exposure leads to the possibility of a Diamond and Dybvig (1983) style bank run.[12] In Caballero and Krishnamurthy firms face a liquidity problem because they finance risky long term projects with foreign loans but have access to limited amounts of internationally accepted collateral.[13]

It is within the third generation models that most recent financial crisis is part of. A characteristic of the latest financial sub-prime crisis is the collapse of short-term commercial paper market, thus impeding the attraction of new financing or rolling over existing short-term liabilities.

---

[10] Kaminsky and Reinhart (1999).
[11] Mark *et al.* (2002).
[12] Chang and Velasco (2001).
[13] Caballero and Krishnamurthy (2001).

There are quite a few episodes of financial crises in the economic history.[14] Probably the earlier classic example of a financial bubble is that of the Dutch tulip mania of 1634–1637.[15] A single bulb of Semper Augustus traded from a few florins in 1634 and rose to 6,390 florins in 1637, before collapsing to a tenth of a florin, at which price it traded for the next century. But there are more other famous examples like the Overend and Guerney (1866), Barings Bank (1890 and 1995) or The Great Depression (1929–1933). Subsequent to these crises, landmark changes in the regulatory and supervisory rules were introduced.

B. Relevant History Lessons and Policy Implications

After Overend and Guerney went bankrupt in 1866, Walter Bagehot advocated the "lender of last resort" role for the Bank of England. Its main objective would be to avert a systemic crisis by providing liquidity to the financial system during crises.

In the aftermath of the 1929 crisis, the so-called New Deal was introduced by the US President, Franklin Roosevelt. This included extensive regulation of financial markets and the banking system through the creation of the Securities and Exchange Commission (SEC) and the Federal Deposit Insurance Corporation (FDIC). It also led to a separation of banking activities through the Glass-Steagall Act.

Subsequent to the Barings crisis in 1995, the Bank of England restructured its Supervision and Surveillance system. It implemented a new model (RATE) for assessing risk[16] while increasing cooperation with other central banks supervisory departments. Its changes were followed suit by other national Supervisory institutions (for instance Germany's, which introduced minimum requirements for the trading activities of credit institutions).

After the Black Monday crush of 1987, regulatory bodies introduced the so-called "circuit-breakers" aimed at limiting programme trading and allowing them to suspend all trades for short periods.

The seriousness of the LTCM crisis in 1998 prompted the US President's Working Group on Financial Markets to issue a report on

---

[14] See Appendix 3 for a succinct description of the most recent financial crises and their economic consequences.

[15] Kindleberger (2000) offers an account of this episode as well as other renowned financial crises in the history.

[16] RATE = Risk Assessment, Tools of Supervision and Evaluation.

the hedge fund implications for systemic risk in financial markets.[17] Its central policy recommendation was that regulators and supervisors should foster an environment in which market discipline constrains excessive leverage and risk-taking.

Investigations by SEC in the Enron scandal (2001) revealed major flaws in the existing regulatory and supervisory system. Among these were rating agencies' conflict of interests, fraudulent management activities and the extensive leverage of the off-balance financial entities.

Obviously, there are many similarities among this crisis and previous episodes. Reinhart and Rogoff, for instance, provide a historical comparison.[18] They were preceded by periods of credit booms facilitated by low interest rate environments. Often the emergence of crises was facilitated by obsolete framework designs of institutions which have a regulatory and supervisory role. But there are also a number of issues, such as the workability of securitised lending and the roles of central banks and regulators, which make this crisis different.[19]

Table 3. The causes and consequences of recent crises

	Causes	**Consequences**
Enron Scandal, 2001	Conflicts of interest; complex structured finance transactions rolled via through off-books financial entities; fraudulent activities.	Systemic effects—on creditors, banks and other energy trading companies.
DotCom Crash, 2000	Limited investment knowledge of individual market participants.	Temporary closure of the financial markets; business investment falling and the US economy slowing.
LTCM crisis, 1998	High leverage factor; sophisticated computer models to assess investment strategies.	Threatening systemic failure in international financial markets.

---

[17] Hedge Funds, Leverage, and the Lessons of Long-Term Capital Management (1999).

[18] Reinhart and Rogoff (2008).

[19] Wolf (2007).

	Causes	*Consequences*
Asian Crisis, 1997	Indiscriminate investments due to cheap credit availability and premature opening of the capital account.	Credit crunch and widespread bankruptcies; slower global growth.
"Black Monday" Crash, 1987	Programme trading strategies and market perception.	The US stockmarket suffered its largest one-day fall.
Latin American Debt Default, 1982	Economic and financial liberalisation; Indiscriminate investments due to cheap credit availability.	Credit crunch and widespread bankruptcies; slower global growth.
S&L Crisis, 1980	Unsound real estate lending	Potential systemic risk
Penn Central Crisis, 1970	Unable to roll over short-term debt.	Threat of the spill-over into the banking system.

III. The Current Crisis—What Has Triggered It and Its Implications

The first signs that signalled the emergence of the current financial crisis first surfaced in June 2007 when two hedge funds run by the investment bank Bear Stearns got into difficulty.[20] The funds borrowed against collateral which was held by the lenders—known as prime brokers. When one of the brokers tried to sell the collateral, its actions succeeded only in driving prices sharply lower. More than eight months into the crisis it seems that it would continue well into 2008 and, possibly, 2009, and its effects could be felt for years to come.

Although the emerging markets do not seem to be affected so far substantially,[21] it might be only a question of time before the crisis would spill over into their markets because of globalisation effects.

---

[20] In March 2008, the precarious financial position of the Bear Stearns investment bank triggered a classic run-on-the-bank. The FED and JP Morgan, another investment bank, stepped in and the latter agreed to buy the 85-year-old Bear Stearns at a 93% discount.

[21] There are of course, a few exceptions. Some of the emerging markets have experienced a depreciation of their currencies following a flight of money for safety.

The current financial crisis is so severe and many-sided that its implications can hardly be underplayed. Policies and market structures (including supervision and regulatory frameworks) have to be re-examined and mended. This crisis prods us to return to tenets of pragmatism and open mindedness in policy making.

A. THE ROOTS OF THE CURRENT CRISIS

The root causes of the current financial market turmoil are to be found at both macro and micro level.[22] An analytical classification would identify structural and cyclical factors.

1 Structural Factors

– A dramatic rise in the role of capital markets (non-banking financial institutions) in the financial intermediation process. The growing complexity of financial markets has become an issue in itself.

– An increasing use of new financial instruments (securitisation) which have spread out risks across national borders, but which have made markets more opaque (reduced transparency). In part this was due to the lack of due diligence.[23] However, the lack of effective trading of many of the new financial products has made rising opacity quite inevitable.

– Rising opacity of financial markets has accentuated systemic risks. There has been a fallacy of composition at play here. The "origination and distribution" of synthetic products was meant to diminish individual (micro) risks by their diversification and spreading. But micro-rationality clashes with macro-rationality when markets lose transparency. As thoughtfully highlighted by Lamfalussy there is here an apparent trade-off between expected higher efficiency of financial intermediation and the stability of the financial system;[24] the latter is becoming more fragile!

– The pressure of globalisation and the rise in cross-border operations. Transactions costs have been reduced constantly over the last years and, as a consequence, large volume of transactions can be

---

[22] See, for instance Buiter (2007).
[23] As excellently pointed out by Sharon Bowles MEP.
[24] Lamfalussy (2000, 2008).

carried out in short amounts of time. Again, these evolutions may in fact, have enhanced a lack of due diligence.

– Inadequate quantitative methods (risk and econometric models) to the extent they are meant to replicate the functioning of actual markets and decision-making relies heavily on them.[25]

– Seemingly intractable conflicts of interest among market participants.

– Inadequate incentive structures (compensation schemes) in the financial industry that have encouraged excessive risk-taking at the expense of prudence.

– An excess of saving in a number of countries—notably China—and the global redistribution of wealth and income towards commodities exporting countries. But, also, one would have to mention, in this regard, the unusual situation of the US economy as the wealthiest and most developed in the world: instead of showing high domestic savings, and related, substantial net capital outflows (which befits wealthy economies) its savings ratio is stunningly low and it relies on foreign capital in order to finance its large current account deficit; the US economy is overdriven by consumption.

– And most importantly, inadequate and obsolete worldwide regulatory frameworks; regulatory and supervisory failures have compounded the magnitude of the debt and credit risk.

– An over-reliance on the self-regulatory virtues of markets.

2 Cyclical Factors

– Excessively low risk-free interest rates at all maturities in major economies (the US, Euro land and Japan).[26] For instance, Taylor shows that a higher federal rate path would have averted much of the housing boom in the US.[27] A higher interest rate would have decreased the supply of funds to the mortgage market. The excess liquidity was reinforced by countries with large exports to the US, such as China or Asian countries, those who had their domestic currencies pegged to the

---

[25] "Also being questioned are the mathematically elegant economic forecasting models that once again have been unable to anticipate a financial crisis..." (Greenspan, 2008, pp.13).

[26] See Wyplosz (2007).

[27] See Taylor (2007).

US dollar or the oil and commodities exporting countries which wanted to limit their appreciation of domestic currency against the US dollar.

– An unreasonable low credit risk spread across all instruments.

– Structural factors create the general conditions favourable for potentially generating a crisis while cyclical factors are those which help triggering it. The history of financial crises shows in fact, that, with regard to cyclical factors, the current turmoil is no different from previous episodes. Thus, it is the gap between high returns on capital and the low cost of capital, with irresponsible lending, which sows the seeds for financial crises. For instance, Ferguson and Schularick argue that this gap has been widened over the last years due to the recent integration of Asian labour force into the world economy.[28] This has increased global returns while the cost of capital was maintained at a low level—as measured by low real interest rates. This situation is no different from the Barings crisis (1890), the Latin America debt default (1980) or the Asian crisis (1997), when low yield investment opportunities in developed economies made capital from these countries to fly to economies where higher return on capital could have been earned. Eventually, indiscriminate lending led to defaults, bankruptcies and, finally, crises.

3 Features of the Current Crisis

One legitimate question to ask is what makes this crisis different. There is a combination of factors that have led to the current situation. Some of them are similar to the ones that caused previous recent financial crises—as mentioned in the earlier section. However, increased innovation in financial products and their growing complexity, together with the failure of regulatory and supervising institutions[29] to keep up with those innovations, appear to have created the conditions for this crisis to emerge. Without being exhaustive, below are several characteristics that distinguish the current crisis from previous ones.

3a The "Shadow Banking System"

What seems to have been happening is the irrevocable transformation of the modern-day banking system, as we knew it. Traditionally,

---

[28] Ferguson and Schularick (2007).
[29] As Sharon Bowles observed to us, "and understaffing of supervisory institutions has weakened further surveillance operations."

the main source of credit was commercial banks which were attracting deposits and then made loans to companies or consumers. Banks, through their combination of assets (loans, secured or unsecured) and liabilities (deposits withdrawable at demand) were in effect borrowing short and lending long. Thus, they were vulnerable to bank loans by deposit holders. Implicitly, the credit risk was retained on their books. Because banks provided a public utility, they were deemed to be systemically important and, to protect them from bank runs, the government devised measures to protect them, the most common being deposit insurance.

However, over the past 10–15 years, this financial market model has changed substantially. On the one hand, banks have increasingly started to sell their credit risk to other investment groups, either via direct loan sales or by repackaging loans into bonds.[30] This process, known as securitisation,[31] allows banks to divide up the resulting residential mortgage-backed securities and place them in instruments called collateralised debt obligations or CDOs. The latter are then sold to a wide range of investors, depending on their appetite for risk. For instance, one set of securities, known as an equity tranche, pays the highest returns but is the first to suffer if the underlying bonds default. Other securities offer a lower yield but a triple-A credit rating, because a lot of defaults would be needed to trigger losses.

More generally, asset securitisation involves the sale of income generating from various financial assets (mortgages, car loans, leases) by a company or bank to a special purpose vehicle (SPV). SPVs are the broad category of vehicles that can qualify as off balance-sheet. They are used for a broad range of items, from term securitisation issuance, conduit securitisation issuance, and other entities. Many of the SPVs, which could be a trust or a company, have financed the purchase of these assets by the issue of short-term commercial paper, secured by those assets.

---

[30] Mortgages were bundled into residential mortgage-backed securities or RMBSs.

[31] The first companies to began the process of securitisation of residential mortgages in the 1970s were US government sponsored entities, Fannie Mae (Federal National Mortgage Association) and Freddie Mac (Federal Home Loan Mortgage Corporation).

Structures such as Conduit Financing Vehicles (CFVs) or Structured Investment Vehicles (SIVs) dis-intermediate banks by enabling a range of long dated debt instruments to be financed by short-term debt. A SIV is a type of SPV, most commonly associated with having CDOs and other longer-termed assets. The main benefit of SIVs is that they exploit an arbitrage, using higher-rate assets funded by short-term, lower rate, liabilities. SIVs are often called "conduits" because they create a channel through which the long-term debt they invest in can be funded by short-term debt. Because SIVs conduct their operations through capital markets—being often offshore entities—they evade the capital adequacy regulations to which banks are subject to.

Because of this, the resulting "shadow banking system"—as it is often called[32]—is exempt, to a large extent, from regulation and supervision as undergone by the banking system. And, as recent experience has shown, activities that involve a high degree of risk could take place undetected, or indeed ignored, until adverse conditions materialise—much in the same vein as in the LTCM or Enron crises. Moreover, recent regulatory reforms have even allowed some banks to reduce the amount of capital that they need to hold against the danger that borrowers default.[33] Moreover, recent regulatory reforms have allowed even banks to reduce the amount of capital that they need to hold against the danger that borrowers default.

In this respect, the recently introduced Basel II capital framework has been aimed at improving Basel I, which was adopted nearly two decades ago. Basel II is intended to provide a more conceptually consistent and transparent framework for evaluating systemic risk in the banking system, particularly through credit cycles. It represents a capital framework consisting of three pillars. Pillar 1 seeks to enhance the way minimum regulatory capital is calculated while Pillar 2 provides a supervisory review and oversight of the institution's overall capital adequacy. The first two pillars are reinforced by the Pillar 3, which deals with transparency requirements. However, this approach is more focused on the microeconomic risk and less on the overall implications of systemic risks. A new approach towards including systemic risk in

---

[32] See Tett and Davis (2007).

[33] This largely happens because of the Basel II regulatory framework, whose Pillar 1 is risk based.

the design of regulatory institutions would be beneficial. This is, arguably, the crucial challenge in reassessing supervisory and regulatory frameworks.

One of the effects of the "shadow banking system" is the lengthening of intermediation. With more market players, it becomes increasingly difficult to assess the nature and magnitude of the risk involved or to locate those who bear the risk. Securitisation of mortgages has spread the financial risks around the economy in such a way that banks were no longer deemed likely to go bankrupt because of holding the bad loans they originated. The repackaging of mortgages in complex collateralised debt obligations has made it difficult to identify who is holding what. As a consequence, this has led to fears of credit risk among banks when dealing in the inter-bank lending market, pushing up the spread between three-month inter-bank rates and the policy rate in the US, the UK as well as in the Euro-area.[34] As a matter of fact, financial innovation of the less benign sort operates as an in-built de-stabilizer for the financial system (creating a *Minsky effect*[35]).

The unexpected losses incurred by assets backed by US sub-prime mortgages have highlighted the potential high costs investors face regarding the type of loans underlying the assets they acquire. As a result, at the moment, the markets in these instruments have become extremely illiquid. Vehicles financed by short-term commercial paper, namely the SPVs, find themselves unable to issue more debt. More and more banks—which created the SPVs in the first place, are forced to take these losses on their balance sheets.

The current crisis resembles an old-fashioned bank run[36]—in what a sudden demand for liquidity can lead to a fire sale of assets that depresses their price, making otherwise solvent institutions insolvent.[37] The difference is that it takes place outside the banking system, namely in the "shadow banking system." But the economic principles of the current crisis are still the same; it is only the market actors that have changed. In the traditional "banking system crisis" the institution was a bank, its long term assets were loans, and its short term liabilities

---

[34] See Appendix 4.
[35] See Minsky (1986).
[36] See Krishna (2007).
[37] See Ennis and Keister (2007) for implications of the central bank's strategy in such a scenario.

were deposits. In the "shadow banking system crisis" the institution could be either a bank or an investment fund whereas the assets could be mortgage-backed securities or their derivatives, and the short-term credit is commercial paper.

3b The High Level of Concentration

According to a report by Autorité des Marchés Financiers (AMF, 2007), concentration has been one of the main characteristics of the structured finance market. In Europe for instance, the structured finance market grew by an impressive 25% in 2005 reaching 450 billion euro in 2006. Over 70% of these deals are structured by 12 banks and the three rating agencies, Fitch, Standard & Poor's and Moody's cover the whole market.[38] The high level of concentration has also been identified as one of the main issues arising from changes in banking fundamentals in the Institute of International Finance Report (2007). Nowadays, there are a few large firms which provide a large part of the volume and liquidity in specific markets. This aspect raises liquidity issues because of the way in which market players are interconnected.

3c The Breadth of the Crisis and the Lack of Trust

Another salient feature of the current crisis is its extensive breadth across a large spectrum of financial market products. Consumer confidence has already been affected beyond the home loan sector. The trend on losses on credit card and auto loans is going up. Moreover, mortgage-related losses have started to be felt outside the banking sector. For instance, widening credit spreads on senior tranches of structured instruments have resulted in marking to market losses on the value of insurance written on these products. This, in turn, triggered market concerns which increasingly have affected higher-rated products and assets other than credit.[39]

The latest concerns relate to the impact of the sub-prime crisis on the Credit Default Swaps (CDS) market. If the current trend of increased insolvency rates in the economy is maintained, the impact on the CDS market, which is worth a staggering 45 trillion US dollars, would be significant. Such a scenario could lead to contagion, an

---

[38] With Standard & Poor's and Moody's covering around 80% of the market.
[39] Fender and Hordahl (2007).

abrupt contraction in credit and a sharp downturn in both the US[40] and, to a lesser extent, the Euro-zone economies. Higher uncertainty regarding the distribution and extent of losses has made investors to take a flight for quality, which, in turn, has led to an increased liquidity demand. Central banks have responded to this by injecting large amounts of liquidity in the money market.

However, the pursuance of such a policy is unlikely to bring an end to the current crisis for two reasons. Firstly, this measure does not address the root of the problem, namely that of the underlying fear that banks' balance sheets are in a precarious position. Until banks, hedge funds, private equity funds and the rest acknowledge their losses, confidence will not be restored in the money markets and trading of structured finance products will continue to be impaired. Unfortunately, losses can be unduly magnified because of strong multiplier effects. At the moment, the existence of counterparty risk is prevailing in the money markets.

Secondly, the liquidity does not reach the market participants which mostly need it—i.e., the "shadow banking system." This happens because liquidity is offered by central banks mainly through their discounted window operations, where only the banks have access. Moreover, these banks seem to be reluctant to access the offered available credit due to the stigma associated with this action. At the moment this effect seems to be more predominant in the US than in the EU. A bank tapping into central bank's credit lines could be perceived as being in trouble by the other banks. The latter could cease of being involved in inter-bank transactions with the ailing bank.

3d Extensive Leverage on a Large Scale
by Some Market Participants

An issue often raised during current debates concerning the causes of today's crisis refers to a certain class of investors and the incidence of their decisions on the financial markets. In recent years, highly leveraged vehicles have been very active in foreign exchange transactions as globalisation spread and opportunities in more traditional markets became scarce due to reduced volatility and low returns. Carry trades, a preferred investment choice for hedge funds, for instance, seem to

---

[40] See Pimco (2008).

be an important driver of cross-border bank lending. This magnifies their exposure to exchange rate fluctuations. One of the reasons why hedge funds decisions could have a strong impact on financial markets—even with systemic consequences, because of the institutions which are counterparts to hedge fund transactions—is that they use a very high leverage, required to ensure a high return on investors' capital. True, so far, systemic risk has not been proven in this scenario but if hedge fund activities grow at the current rate it may well happen. In favourable times this strategy can multiply returns, but, if market prices move against the investment strategy, it also augments risk by the same measure.

Although hedge fund's capital under management is still modest relative to traditional investment vehicles,[41] such as pension and mutual funds, because they are highly leveraged and their operations less transparent, their market impact can be significant.[42] However, hedge fund capital under management has posted a remarkably strong growth in recent years with investor capital increasing by more than three times between 2002 and March 2007, to well over 1.5 trillion US dollars.

As history shows, a small amount of hedging[43] could drive asset prices down significantly. In other words, the amount of asset selling seems not enough to explain large drops in asset prices, which were observed for instance in the 1929 or 1987 crashes. One reason why this could happen is because of the determinants of market liquidity[44] through asymmetries in investors' information sets, which works as follows. Hedging plans[45] create additional supply as asset prices fall. Thus, a relatively minor change in the investors' information set could trigger lower asset prices, which, in turn, due to hedging, lead to an even higher excess supply and a further fall in asset prices. Moreover, contagion is possible and the crisis could spread to foreign markets

---

[41] Hedge fund investor capital has grown from 0.2% of world's GDP in 1990 to more than 3% of world's GDP in 2006 (Becker and Clifton, 2006).

[42] Recently, a number of hedge funds have agreed to voluntary disclosure procedures.

[43] As a percent of total financial markets transactions.

[44] See Gennotte and Leland (1990).

[45] It is worth mentioning that hedging plans and insurance are often compulsory for some market players.

even in the absence of hedging programmes in these markets. The propagating mechanism is through the price signals. Foreign investors observe the drop in asset prices in the hedged market, but because they are unaware of the extent of hedging, revise downwards their expectations, leading to a global fall in asset prices.

Gennotte and Leland's conclusion is that successful policies which would minimise the chance of future crashes occurring involve a wider dissemination of knowledge about hedgers' actions.[46] The authors reckon that increasing market knowledge on the size and trading requirements of hedging programmes could lessen the impact of such trades by a factor greater than 100 and, thus, could radically reduce the likelihood of market crashes.[47]

3e Rating Agencies Deficiencies

As in the Penn Central crisis back in the 1970s, most of the companies selling short-term commercial paper were able to do so because of the prime rating given to those securities by the international rating agencies such as S&Ps, Moody's, Fitch and others. In a number of cases, rating agencies rated investments without the ultimate investors knowing exactly what was behind the bonds.[48] In fact, as in the Enron case, every market player had an incentive to make the deal, regardless of the homebuyers' ability to repay the loan. The buyer hoped to make a fast profit, while the real-estate agent and mortgage broker were taking the fees. The banks in turn, by selling rapidly the loan, alleviated much of the implied risk.

One of the criticisms addressed to the rating agencies is the fact that they have been notoriously slow in spotting the signs of the crisis. This situation resembles once again that of Enron, were credit agencies failed to signal company's huge exposure. Then, the regulatory institutions all over the world designed a voluntary code for the agencies. But this was mainly aimed at sorting out the conflicts of interest whereby agencies were being paid by the companies they rate. Moreover, the

---

[46] Gennotte and Leland (1990).

[47] Although Tobias (2007) finds that in the current crisis there is an unusual high correlation among hedge funds, attributable to low hedge fund volatility. He argues that the current hedge fund environment differs from that existent in 1998, during the LTCM crisis. Also Kambhu *et al.* (2007).

[48] Often, they were not interested to find out this information.

agencies have been criticised for giving upbeat assessments of investments which turned out to be linked to risky home loans in the US.

The failure of rating agencies to warn over the sub-prime crisis has already made both US and EU to take steps to bring in legislation in order to improve and monitor the performance of the agencies and make them legally responsible for their actions.[49] Recently, the US Financial Services subcommittee on capital markets said that it would hold a hearing into the role of credit rating agencies in the structured finance market—including mortgage-backed securities.

IV. How to Respond to This Crisis

Over the last years, there has been an increased interest on the issues concerning financial stability. However, in spite of the warning signals given by preceding crises, changes required to minimise the impact of future crisis have been slow to being implemented. Numerous recommendations have been made by various working groups, supervisory committees, etc. but decisive measures have, so far, been limited. The seriousness of the current crisis has pushed public policy and private initiatives to a new level. The Financial Stability Forum for instance, has released an updated report (FSF, 2007) on highly leveraged institutions in which the focus is on financial stability issues relating to the hedge funds. IMF (2007) published a comprehensive report analysing the causes and consequences of the current financial turmoil together with a list of suggested policy actions. In the UK, the Northern Rock episode is likely to lead to regulatory changes being implemented in order to avoid such events in the future,[50] including credible deposit insurance arrangements and regulating the liquidity position of banks.

One reason why the changes have been slow to implement is the prevailing belief, by some market actors, that markets would sort themselves out in the end. This may well be true, up to a point. After that, however, the risks posed to the real and financial sectors of the

---

[49] So far neither the US nor the EU have actually brought about legislation. The US has Credit Rating Agency Reform Act of 2006—but that was before the crisis. We are thankful for this remark to Wolf Klinz.

[50] See Mervyn King (2007).

world economy might threaten to become greater than the benefits of non-regulation.[51] The practical difficulty is, however, in determining exactly where that point lies.

Structured finance instruments are useful because they offer a higher dispersion of credit risk. But higher dispersion is not automatically a better one; recent events have cast doubts over the functioning of securitised lending, as it is in its current form. One problem is that adding structured instruments to a bank's portfolio has proved that it can lead to unanticipated risk concentrations, which, given the existing state of market knowledge together with the current supervisory and regulatory framework, are difficult to be dealt with.[52] Another problem relates to various aspects pertaining to rating agencies in structured finance operations.[53]

There are a number of proposed strategies for action that would lead to improved financial stability. Strengthening national supervisory and regulatory frameworks; improving transparency, regulatory and public disclosure; and finally, adopting an international approach to exercising effective surveillance, regulation and supervision of financial activity have been suggested quite a while ago.[54] Two of the most important policy challenges ahead are those related to transparency and liquidity.[55] But, arguably, the most arduous task is to combat the scope for higher systemic risks when financial innovation is very intense.

The policy actions which are mentioned below are aimed at dealing mainly with the structural factors identified in the previous section. The roots of cyclical factors are an inherent part of the business cycles and, therefore, more difficult to be dealt with. Nevertheless, sorting out issues relating to the structural factors would greatly enhance the stability of the global financial system.

---

[51] In the aftermath of the Asian crisis, Fisher (1998) suggested that mitigating the crisis would be a better option than non-intervention. Although his remarks actually referred to the IMF role, the principle is the same.

[52] Fender and Mitchell (2005).

[53] BIS (2005).

[54] See for instance Schinasi (2005).

[55] See Dodge (2007).

A. Improving Transparency

– There are certain market players' categories which have minimum disclosure requirements. Given the fact that their trading decisions have significant impact on the overall financial system, it would make sense to strengthen their disclosure requirements. For instance, hedge funds and private equity funds are only a few of the market players that have, at most, rudimentary reporting obligations. As mentioned earlier in the paper, increased transparency of highly leveraged institutions—such as the hedge funds—has the potential to reduce market volatility when market conditions become adverse. It could also lessen the impact of trades by a large factor, thus, lowering radically the likelihood of market crashes. Recently, a number of hedge funds seem to have agreed to make voluntary disclosures of parts of their activities.

– Identifying the "needs" of the "Shadow Banking System." It has become clear with the current sub-prime crises that the regulators' ability to monitor the financial system had been hampered by banks' use of non-transparent off-balance sheet financing. Consequently, addressing this issue would necessarily involve finding the answer for the "needs" to be addressed. Given the large exposure of the financial system to non-bank lenders another option could be to set some kind of "buyer of last resort" to stand behind the markets, much as central banks do for the banking system. With lending becoming so disintermediated, in many sectors this is done by investors and not banks. Then, a run on the markets through the evaporations of liquidity raises the question of who is going to step in and provide that liquidity.

– Finding out who bears the risk. Over the last two decades the pace of product innovation in financial markets has by far outstripped regulators and supervisors capacity to keep up. Therefore, new mechanisms that would address this gap might be necessary. Apart from not being able to set a price for those complex structured products, it is not known who bears the risk. Thus, being able to correctly evaluate the origin of the risk these products possess and who bears it, would be a step forward in aiding to a proper redesign of the regulatory and supervisory frameworks. Recently, the Committee on the Global Financial System (CGFS), which monitors financial market functioning for the central bank governors of the G10 countries, has established a working group to explore the structured finance instruments Fender and Mitchell highlight some of the group's principal findings pertaining to the complexity and riskiness of tranched products.[56] An important result is that, in order to understand the risk properties of these products, the evaluation of the risks should be done according to their contractual structure—as allowed in Basel II. The particularities of transactions make the mission of assessing the riskiness of tranched instruments even more difficult.

– Re-designing the risk assessment specification procedures. Quantitative models employed to model investment decisions and risk assessment in financial markets have, inherently, a built-in conceptual flaw. The main problem is that risk cannot be summarised in a few figures, entailing a more comprehensive description.

– Addressing the costs of failure. The bailout procedures by central banks or the IMF tend to be provided, in general, free of charge. Making the institutions who fail to pay for this would discipline their behaviour. One way to address this could be by imposing some sort of Tobin's tax, the equivalent to a transaction cost aimed at deterring speculation.

B. Resolving Conflicts of Interest among Market Participants

– Credit rating agencies have, inherently, conflicts of interest. They act on behalf of investors but, often, they are being paid by the issuers. Being paid by those they rate, and not by the investors, the common view is that credit rating agencies are under pressure to give their clients a favourable rating. While some credit rating agencies openly acknowledge that they are dependant on investors' fees to stay in business, others argue that this income accounts for a small percentage of their total revenue and deny such conflicts of interest.

– Conflicts of interest between individual and company objectives. There have been several proved cases where individual managers engaged in fraudulent behaviour for their own benefit. As a consequence, the punishment of fraudulent behaviour should be applied at both the institutional as well as individual level. There should be a set of rules

---

[56] Fender and Mitchell (2005).

which could tighten requirements for directors to be vigilant and also provide protection for those who bring improper behaviour to public attention. However, in the end, it is the integrity of directors and executives which would limit the emergence of such crisis in the future. The current credit crisis, LTCM, Enron all involved improper behaviour by individual decision-makers. Absent integrity and in a permissive environment, such individuals will find ways to conceal information or to engage in fraud. Introducing high punishment penalties for such improper behaviour could limit the scale of the problem.

– Perceived conflicts of interest in the current business model. For instance, a set of investors and the issuers have, in general, a clear interest to have a stable financial market and a wide range of high-rate graded assets. On the other hand, the investors who take short-positions and the secondary market participants might have a higher interest to see downgrades so that they could pocket the ensuing financial gains. Financial markets tend to benefit from such speculative activities (though not always). The problem emerges when such actions are blown out of proportions, increasing uncertainty and spreading individual risks in such a way that systemic risk goes up incommensurately.

– Increased coherence between short-term corporate governance objectives and long-term planning strategies. Often, managers' incentives to achieve short-term performance indicators are not consistent with a company's longer term expansion plans. Thus, increased pressure on companies' management to deliver short-term results might not be beneficial in the longer run. Compensation schemes should be revised so that risk-taking is not rewarded at the expense of prudence.

– Increasing knowledge transfer to all market participants. Arguably, the poor knowledge of some of the market participants has a lot to do with the development of the current crisis. The shifting of the risk on to the shoulders of those least able to understand it[57] has been a common feature of the existing crisis. Plans aimed at raising the knowledge base of all market participants, so that they would be aware of the potential risk entailed by their actions should, at least, help create a market awareness that higher risk could, in extreme circumstances, mean virtually negative returns.

---

[57] This has been predominantly a US phenomenon, but the crisis is still unfolding.

C. Improving the Existing Regulatory and Supervisory Frameworks

– Collective regulation. The intrinsic workings of the current financial systems indicate that banking institutions can no longer be separated from the securities markets. If so, it follows that the best option is to create a regulatory framework that would regulate concerned institutions as a whole. The ongoing credit squeeze has proved that risk is apportioned to whoever market participant could bear it, so that regulating institutions individually would fail to close the gaps in the existing regulatory framework. A first step in this direction seems to be taken by the UK, where the Chancellor of the Exchequer has proposed changes to the regulatory regime which would involve all three participating institutions, the so-called tripartite system of HM Treasury, Bank of England and Financial Services Authority.

– Coordinating Supervision and Regulation Activities. Currently there are an increasing numbers of financial institutions which operate across many different national jurisdictions. Supervision and regulation are often organised at the national level, although in several instances national models share a large number of similarities.[58] However, coordination attempts among national jurisdictions are difficult to achieve due to the ongoing creation of new institutions and new instruments. The development of an efficient EU-wide supervision and regulation of financial institutions and markets should allow a reduction in the current number of arrangements to be concluded. In an article in the *Financial Times*, Tommaso Padoa-Schioppa argues for a supervisory structure for multinational financial institutions at the EU level.[59] Moreover, international coordination of supervisory and regulatory

---

[58] Coordination among central banks in the EU seems to have already been working in a close and efficient manner and the challenge lies in the cooperation of supervisory authorities. Supervisory convergence has improved through the Lamfalussy process and the Level 3 Committees. However, coordination attempts among national jurisdictions are yet difficult to achieve. Supervisory cooperation and convergence in the EU is lagging behind as the possibilities of the current framework are not fully realised. We are thankful for this comment to Wolf Klinz. Furhermore, the EU and the G7 operate with different mandates. Some convergence of objectives and means of action has to be achieved in this respect.

[59] Padoa-Schioppa (2007).

policy has to become of commanding interest. The integration of the global financial system means that counterparty and systemic risks ceased to be a national or regional concern.

– Markets for Structured Finance Products. The sub-prime crises effects were compounded because there was no liquid market for the complex structured finance products issued by the banks. These products have tended to be frequently "mark-to-model," with models whose intricate mathematical and computational features have been quite often beyond the grasp of institution's risk managers. Other alternative pricing methods, such as those used by credit agencies, proved to be flawed due to conflicting interests between the designers and the issuers of the instrument.[60] One alternative to sort this out, as suggested by Buiter and Sibert,[61] is through the creation of a market-maker of last resort. This institution would "create" market prices for illiquid assets by purchases and sales of private sector securities and through the acceptance of a comprehensive range of private sector securities as collateral in repos. This could be done through the central bank but another institution could be as easily set up which would have the necessary reputation and credibility to perform those operations. Practical considerations, however, would make this suggestion difficult to implement.

– Steps to integrate banks' balance sheets. Some lessons from Japan's 1989 property bubble bear striking similarities with the sub-prime crisis. As highlighted in an article in *The Economist*,[62] one reason both crises were not detected earlier was because most of the warning signs were not at parent banks but down the intermediation chain, namely in affiliates, subsidiaries or other off-balance sheet vehicles. Pre-crisis condition shared similarities in that in both cases financial engineering made available easy credit which sparked a property-related bubble, commercial in Japan and residential in the US. Integrated

---

[60] Arguably, the rating quality during the subprime crisis has been questionable due to methodological aspects. Some argue that the conflict of interest seems to be a minor issue because of reputational aspects. Moreover, the credit rating agencies were only modeling credit default risk, not market liquidity risk.

[61] See Buiter and Sibert (2007).

[62] *The Economist*, "Lessons from Japan's financial crisis should worry, and embarrass, America," 13 December 2007.

balance sheets reflecting the whole picture of banks' lending would have aided in the identifications of the problems much sooner and would have allowed a timely intervention by the regulatory and supervisory institutions. Thus, measures to report integrated bank balance sheets could be taken to diminish the intensity of future crisis.[63]

– Deposit insurance versus Moral Hazard. As shown by Keely deposit insurance worked well prior to the 1980s.[64] However, increased competition within the banking and financial service industry has led to a moral hazard problem, in fact rewarding banks who took an excessive risk taking. Thus, these commercial banks were provided in fact with a "put" in which the central bank was expected to bail them out in case they went into trouble. Banks could, in effect, borrow at the risk free rate through the issuance of insured deposits and then invest the proceeds in risky assets. This problem appeared to have been compounded in the early 1980s when, increased competition in financial services industry caused banks charter values to decline.[65] Thus, bank charter values, which previously were a high entry barrier in the industry, appear to have lost some ground in the face of demand for higher returns triggered by increased competition in the banking industry. One set of proposals is to give to some national authority enough powers to intervene in banking crises. Such models draws heavily on elements of the US, Canadian and Belgian where emergency roles are given to new institutions, such as Federal Deposit Insurance Corporation in the US, for instance. While this special insolvency regime for banks would allow a badly bank run to fail with diminished effects in triggering a systemic crisis caused by a loss of public confidence, this also compounds the moral hazard problem, and, as recent events in the US have shown, is of limited use when crisis spreads in other markets.

– Raising the capital requirements of the structured finance investment vehicles. This would reduce the liquidity risk—a major factor of concern in the current crisis. Again, these aspects are already covered under Basel II. But the challenge would be to enforce these rules and avoid loopholes to be exploited. Moreover, under Basel II banks were

---

[63] Basel II provides, indeed, a framework for this.
[64] Keely (1990).
[65] *Ibid.*

left with the impression that they have too much equity, thus encouraging excessive risk taking from their part.

– Enforcement of conformity and compliance systems. This is yet to be seen how would be resolved under the Basel II framework. It is true that, at the time when the crisis started, Basel II was half in half out. However, following recent developments, it becomes clearer that Basel II would need to be revised. The current crisis is different from the previous ones in what its spreading occurs in spite of the existing framework of accountancy and Basel II regulations. Therefore, it tends to suggest that these are inadequate to deal with the severity of the crisis. One drawback of the Basel II framework, for instance, is that it fails to incorporate systemic risks into the design of regulatory institutions and risk management (apparently, it relies too much on the efficient capital markets hypothesis[66]). These aspects would need to be addressed.

– Risk management procedures and mechanisms in banks have to improve considerably.

– Use of counter-cyclical control mechanisms or instruments. Some authors argue that bank capital requirements should not only be contra-cyclical but also related to the rate of change of bank lending and asset prices in the relevant sectors.[67] This is because risk models employed today undermine the assumptions that should make them work. They systematically underestimate risk in "good" times and overestimate risk in "bad" times.

– The timing of introducing new changes in the regulatory and supervisory systems is particularly important. Rushing radical changes overnight in these systems might actually exacerbate the crisis by worsening the credit crunch. Caution is therefore needed in the design and implementation phases of changing the regulatory and supervisory systems. At the same time, however, complacency and too slow change are not warranted. The flaws and creaks in the current supervisory and regulatory frameworks are quite visible and demand firm action.

– Cooperation between public and private institutions. This needs to be enhanced and re-designed to account for recent developments in the financial market innovations.

---

[66] This hypothesis is linked with the rational expectations theory.

[67] See for instance Charles Goodhart and Avinash Persaud, "A proposal for how to avoid the next crash," *Financial Times*, 31 January 2008.

V. Summing Up

As the current crisis unfolds and the time passes by, it becomes clearer that we are being confronted with an event whose implications are bound to be long lasting. It is hard to understand why those in charge with regulating markets have been so oblivious to warnings which had been sent by highly knowledgeable individuals years ago. Almost a decade ago Alexander Lamfalussy cautioned against the use of derivatives that enhance instability and increase systemic risks against the backdrop of global markets. And Warren Buffett called synthetic products "financial weapons of mass destruction" in 2003. For them and others "casino type trading" was more than a threat to the financial system.

Addressing the roots of the problem that have triggered this crisis should be of paramount importance. In the past, such crises tended to be more localised and were dealt with more easily. The difference this time has been in the rapid spread of intense financial innovation (the "origination and distribution" which has been undertaken by leading banks), which has occurred during the last couple of decades; this allowed dissemination of risks on a large scale at the expense of transparency. As a consequence, the emergence of the shadow banking system, largely unregulated and lacking appropriate supervision has brought about more opacity in financial markets and has accentuated systemic risk. The excessive trust in the "self-healing" power of markets has not yielded the result some expected.

It follows from here that one line of action should, necessarily, be the regulation of the shadow banking system. Likewise, the intrinsic workings of the current financial system indicate that banking institutions can no longer be separated from the securities markets. Thus, one feasible option would be the creation of a regulatory framework that would regulate concerned institutions as a whole.

Securitisation of mortgages has spread the financial risks around the economy in such a way that banks' exposure to their bad loans has become, nominally, minimal. But, the repackaging of mortgages in complex collateralised debt obligations has made it difficult to identify who is holding what. Ironically, financial innovation that was designed to diminish risk at the individual or micro level has ended up in exacerbating it at the macro level, thus increasing systemic risk. Moreover, this innovation has favoured speculative trading.

Two of the most important policy challenges ahead are those related to transparency and liquidity. But, arguably, the most arduous task is to combat the scope for higher systemic risks when financial innovation is very intense. In these cases traditional ways of risk assessment become obsolete. The complexity of today's financial market instruments render risk assessment models unreliable. Thus, quantitative models employed to model investment decisions and risk assessment in financial markets have, inherently, a built-in conceptual flaw. One of the problems is that risk cannot be encapsulated in a few figures, asking for a more comprehensive description. There is a scope for a redesign of the risk assessment specification procedures.

Another line of action should address the costs of failure. The bailout procedures by central banks or the IMF tend to be provided, in general, free of charge. Making the institutions which fail to pay for this would discipline their behaviour. One way to tackle this could be by the introduction of various measures aimed at deterring speculation.

An issue closely related to this is managers' performance compensation packages. Managers' incentives to achieve short-term performance indicators are not consistent with a company's longer term expansion plans. Thus, increased pressure on companies' management to deliver short-term results might not be beneficial in the longer run. Compensation schemes should be revised so that risk-taking be not rewarded at the expense of prudence.

Although the Basel II regulatory framework has been devised to prevent crises occurring, the current one has highlighted existing flaws in its design. Regulatory measures aimed at dealing with liquidity and system risk ought to be revised. Moreover, the use of counter-cyclical control mechanisms or instruments should be seriously considered. Capital requirements should not only be contra-cyclical but also related to the rate of change of bank lending and asset prices in the relevant sectors.

Last but not least increasing coordination among national supervision and regulatory bodies should be enhanced. Global financial markets require a global approach in dealing with such issues. This cooperation is simply required in order to limit the potential devastating effects such crisis could have in the future on both the financial system and the real economy. Inside the EU this coordination is a must and Padoa-Schioppa's proposals should be given a more sympathetic hearing.[68]

References

Allen M., *et al.* (2002) "A Balance Sheet Approach to Financial Crisis" IMF Working Paper WP/02/210.

Autorité des marchés financiers (2007) "Is Rating An Efficient Response to the Challenges of the Structured Finance Market?" *Risk And Trend Mapping*, No. 2, March.

Bank of International Settlements (2009) "The role of ratings in structured finance: issues and implications," Report submitted by a Working Group established by the Committee on the Global Financial System, January 2005.

Becker, C. and Clifton, K. (2007) "Hedge fund activity and carry trades" *BIS Quarterly Review*.

Bordo M. (2007) "The Crisis of 2007: The Same Old Story, Only the Players Have Changed" Remarks prepared for the Federal Reserve Bank of Chicago and International Monetary Fund Conference, Globalization and Systemic Risk, Chicago, Illinois, 28 September 2007.

Buiter, H.W. (2007) "Lessons From the 2007 Financial Crisis CEPR" *Policy Insight*, No.18, December.

Buiter, H.W. and Sibert, A. (2007) "Central Bank as the Market Maker of last Resort: From lender of last resort to market maker of last resort" Available at: *http://www.voxeu.org/index.php?q=node/459*

Caballero, R.J. and Krishnamurthy, A. (2001) "Smoothing Sudden Stops" NBER Working Paper No. W8427, August.

Chang, R. and Velasco, A. (2001) "A model of financial crises in emerging markets, *The Quarterly Journal of Economics*, May.

Dodge D. (2007) Remarks by the Governor of the Bank of Canada to the Institute of International Finance, Washington, D.C., October.

Dăianu, D. (2008) "Better Regulation is a Must for Financial Markets," *The European Voice*, 31 January, p. 12.

Delargy, J.R. and Goodhart C. (1999) "Financial Crises: Plus ca change, plus c'est la meme chose" LSE Financial Market Group Special Paper No.108.

Diamond, D.W. and Dybvig, P.H. (1983) "Bank runs, deposit insurance, and liquidity" *Journal of Political Economy*, Vol. 91, pp. 401–19.

Fender, I. and Hordahl, P. (2007) "Overview: Credit Retrenchment Triggers Liquidity Squeeze" *BIS Quarterly Review*, September.

---

[68] Dăianu (2008).

Fender, I. and Mitchell, J. (2005) "Structured finance: complexity, risk and the use of ratings" *BIS Quarterly Review*, June.

Ferguson, N. and Schularick, M. (2007) "Chimerica and the Global Asset Market Boom" *International Finance*, Vol. 10, No. 3, pp. 215–39.

Financial Stability Forum (FSF) (2007) Update of the FSF Report on Highly Leveraged Institutions, May.

Fischer, S. (1998) "The Asian Crisis: A View from the IMF," Address by First Deputy Managing Director of the International Monetary Fund at the Midwinter Conference of the Bankers' Association for Foreign Trade, Washington, D.C., January 22.

Flood, R., and Garber P. (1984) "Collapsing Exchange Rate Regimes: Some Linear Examples" *Journal of International Economics*, Vol. 17, pp. 1–13.

Gârleanu, N., Pedersen and Lasse, H. (2007) "Liquidity and Risk Management" *American Economic Review*, Vol. 97, Issue 2, pp. 193–8.

Gennotte, G. and Hayne, L. (1990) "Market Liquidity, Hedging and Crashes" *American Economic Review*, Vol. 80, pp. 999–1021.

Greespan, A. (2008) "We will never have a perfect model of risk" *Financial Times*, 17 March, p. 13.

Ennis, H.M. and Keister, T. (2007) Commitment and Equilibrium Bank Runs, Federal Reserve Bank of New York Staff Reports, No. 274, May.

IMF (2007). "Financial Market Turbulence Causes, Consequences and Policies," Global Financial Stability Report, October.

Institute of International Finance (2007) Principles of Liquidity Risk Management, March.

Kambhu, J., Schuermann, T., and Stiroh, J.K. (2007) "Hedge Funds, Financial Intermediation, and Systemic Risk" Federal Reserve Bank of New York Staff Reports, No. 291, July.

Keely, M. (1990) "Deposit Insurance, Risk, and Market Power in Banking" *American Economic Review*, December, pp. 1183–200.

Kindleberger, P.C. (2000) *Manias, Panics, and Crashes: A History of Financial Crises*, New York, John Wiley & Sons.

King, M. (2007) "Opening Statement to the Monetary Policy Committee" December 26.

Kornert, J. (2003) "The Barings crises of 1890 and 1995: causes, courses, consequences and the danger of domino effects" *Journal of International Financial Markets, Institutions and Money*, Vol. 13, pp. 187–209.

Krishna G. (2007) "Credit turmoil has hallmarks of bank run" *Financial Times*, 2 September.

Krugman, P. (1979) "A Model of Balance of Payments Crises" Journal of Money, Credit and Banking, Vol. 11, pp. 311–25.

Krugman, P. (1999) *The Return of Depression Economics*, New York, Norton.

Lamfalussy, A. (2008), "Looking Beyond the Current Credit Crisis" Remarks made at the meeting of the Economic and Affairs Committee of the European Parliament with national parliaments, 23 January.

Minsky, H.P., (1986) *Stablizing an Unstable Economy*, New Haven, Yale University Press.

Mishkin, F. (1997) "The Causes and Propagation of Financial Instability: Lessons for Policy Makers in Maintaining Financial Stability in a Global Economy" Federal Reserve Bank of Kansas City, Jackson Hole Symposium, pp. 55–96.

Pimco (2008) "Pyramids Crumbling" *Investment Outlook*, January. Available at: *http://www.pimco.com*.

Reinhart, M.C. and Rogoff K.S. (2008) "Is the 2007 U.S. Sub-Prime Financial Crisis So Different? An International Historical Comparison" Paper presented at New Perspectives on Financial Globalization (AEA), January.

Schinasi, G. (2005) "Preserving Financial Stability" *IMF, Economic Issues*, No. 36.

Padoa-Schioppa, T. (2007) "Europe Needs A Single Financial Rule Book," *Financial Times*, 10 December.

Taylor, J. (2007) *Housing and Monetary Policy*, September.

Tett, G. and Davies, P.J. (2007) "Out of the shadows: How banking's secret system broke down" *Financial Times*, 16 December.

Tobias, A. (2007) "Measuring Risk in the Hedge Fund Sector" *Current Issues in Economics and Finance—Federal Reserve Bank of New York*, Vol. 13, No. 3, March–April.

Wolf, M. (2007) "Why the credit squeeze is a turning point for the world" *Financial Times*, 11 December.

Wyplosz, C. (2007) "No more easy cash: banks must take their losses" *Financial Times*, 20 December.

CHAPTER 4

What This Financial Crisis Tells Us[1]

The significance of the current financial crisis is huge, and its policy implications are manifold—and one of those is that we need to learn from previous crises. I heard one leading central banker say that the depth and magnitude of this crisis could hardly have been predicted. His is not an isolated voice. But such remarks should be a surprise, for it is the job of a central banker to focus on the health of the financial system, and not just the stability of prices.

There were various crises over the past decade and there are people who learned from them. Some financiers and economists—such as Warren Buffett,[2] Edward Gramlich, Paul Krugman,[3] Alexander Lamfalussy,[4] Nouriel Roubini and Paul Volcker—warned another crisis was in the making, underlining the menace posed to financial stability by new types of financial innovation. Studies of the Bank of International Settlements and the Bank of England had examined roots of the

---

[1] This chapter is based on four articles which were published by *European Voice*: "The Calculation Debate revisited" (13 June 2008), "What this crisis teaches us" (9 May 2008), "Purging the toxins" (27 September 2008) and "Limits of Openness," (4 December 2008).

[2] In a BBC interview, in March 2003, Warren Buffett named derivatives "financial weapons of mass destruction."

[3] Krugman (1999, p. 162) writes: "...modern financial markets, by creating many institutions that perform bank-like functions but do not benefit from bank-type safety nets, have in effect reinvented the possibility of traditional financial panics."

[4] Lamfalussy (2000, pp. 88–89): "...even if we were to reach a state of generalized competition on a worldwide scale financial markets ought not be left to their own devices. Those who attribute the virtues of global stability to a fully competitive and liberalised financial system may be right. But how can we know? ...I believe that we should not try to find out in practice how smoothly and swiftly self-correcting our system would be in the absence of the active care of the public authorities."

current crisis before it erupted. I would add here reports of the European Parliament, from years ago, that pointed the finger at issues that have been widely debated during the last couple of years.

I. The Calculation Debate Revisited

The failings of rating agencies and financial institutions in evaluating synthetic financial products and the rising opacity of financial markets have reminded me a famous debate in economic thought.

The calculation debate took place among several leading economists during the interwar period, in the last century. One camp fielded, among others, Ludwig von Mises[5] and Friedrich von Hayek,[6] who stressed that free markets and clearly defined property rights (private property) are essential for proper calculation of costs and benefits and economic development; these were very dear tenets of the Austrian school of economic thought. Hayek highlighted also the ubiquity of information/ knowledge in society and, in this context, the role of entrepreneurship (like Joseph Schumpeter did) in promoting technical change. The other debating camp used the intellectual guns of Oskar Lange.[7] The latter, while being against private capital, acknowledged the importance of markets in economic development and tried to build on them a mechanism of "market socialism" (which relied on social property). But Lange's model had its own major flaws. One originates in the inadequate pricing of capital, which undermines its accumulation as a source of economic growth over the long run. Moreover, entrepreneurship could not blossom in conditions of market socialism, where capital and risk-taking are not properly rewarded.

What came closest, in modern history, to an implementation of market socialism was the texture of socially owned firms in the former Yugoslavia, which has brought some prosperity to its citizens as against what occurred in the typical command economy in the former soviet system. Goulash communism in Hungary was also an attempt to introduce market reforms in a socialist economy. Much worse than "market socialism"

---

[5] von Mises (1935).

[6] Hayek (1972).

[7] Lange (1972).

was the command (communist) system. While having the power to mobilize resources for major projects, it suffered from fundamental original sins: lack of proper valuation of factors of production and stifling of innovation (apart from the suppression of political liberties). The collapse of the command (communist) system, as well as the market economic reforms in China and, later on, in Vietnam, have proven, in a spectacular way, which camp of economic thought won the debate.

To put more emphasis on this victory and make the hook-up with the current financial crisis, I would recall something of great significance. There was a group of soviet economists—Leonid Kantorovich[8] and V.V. Novojilov among them—who thought that quantitative models can replicate markets and offer scarcity valuations to capital, labour and land. They tried hard to work out general equilibrium (input-output) models and came up with so called "shadow prices" as substitutes for free market prices. Interestingly, Kantorovich got a Nobel Prize for his work. But his models were far away from being able to help the command system—for nothing can substitute real markets and clearly defined property rights as foundations for an efficient economy. In addition, entrepreneurship cannot be simulated, or stimulated by decree; it has to happen in reality, as a result of incentives and economic freedom. That there is need for a public sector (that supplies public goods) in a modern economy and that markets have their own failings which need to be addressed is another serious matter for discussion and public policy response.

Above I have linked the calculation debate to the current financial crisis. A financial system which has been increasingly based on capital markets (securitization)—as it has evolved in the last couple of decades—has brought the key issues of transparency and proper valuation to the fore. Ironically, these are exactly some of the main negative traits which have brought the command system down. As a matter of fact, models which were used by leading investments banks (brokers) and rating agencies in assessing risks, and the ratings that were assigned to new (synthetic) financial products, have proven to be highly erroneous. Likewise, a certain type of securitization, which has distanced lenders from the consequences of their actions more than dangerously, has obfuscated risks (the counterparty risks) and enhanced

---

[8] Kantorovich (1965).

the opacity of markets. The non-existence of effective markets for derivatives (OTC) has compounded the diminishing transparency of markets and added to inadequate valuation. The credit crunch could not be avoided due to an overwhelming lack of transparency and trust. The bottom line is that missing genuine markets (for various derivatives) and highly questionable valuation of securities pushed toward a freezing of credit markets.

The causes of the current financial crisis should prod many to remember the lessons of the famous calculation debate: we need genuine markets, transparency and proper valuation of factors of production and products (services). Simulation and models cannot be but a very imperfect and insufficient substitute of actual markets. And the transparency and smooth functioning of markets need to be propped up by adequate regulations and supervision. For, markets, by themselves, cannot protect themselves against their inherent weaknesses and the public good needs, sometimes, the work of a visible hand.

II. Is Only Greed to Be Blamed?

As the markets come to terms with what is happening and as thoughts focus on how to save and re-build the financial system, there is one statement among Paulson's remarks on 19 September 2008 that deserves particularly close attention: "We must now take further, decisive action to fundamentally and comprehensively address the root cause of our financial system's stresses." Do we understand the root causes that have transmitted the diseases that now ail every branch of the financial system inside and outside the US? What is the transmission mechanism that has been at work so intensely?

The media is now full of condemnations of greed; for many this is the quintessential source of this financial crisis. But is it only greed that should be blamed for this mess? What about the flaws of the originate-and-distribute model, which decouples loans from assets, has spread risk and facilitated the emergence of systemic risk? What about skewed pay schemes in the financial industry that has stimulated reckless risk-taking at the expense of prudence (not to mention the ethical dimension these schemes carry)? What about the nonchalance with which rating agencies have assigned investment-grade values to derivatives of more than questionable value (such as "collateralised debt obligations" and "credit default swaps")? What about the conflicts of interest that plague the financial system? What about banks engaging in casino-type transactions on a massive scale? And, not least, what about the lightness of or the absence of any regulation of the "shadow" banking sector, made up hedge funds, private equity funds and the like that are extremely leveraged and engage in speculative operations?

These questions highlight a thesis: the root cause of this crisis is an inadequately and under-regulated financial system. These are in part the effects of the Phil Gramm-Leach-Bliley Act passed in the US Congress in 1999, which was, basically, a repeal of the Glass-Steagall Act of 1934.[9] That act triggered a further wave of deregulation in the financial industry that, inter alia, brought to the market a plethora of fancy products whose risks were poorly understood. Mortgages are not toxic *per se*; badly constructed securities based on them are toxic. The packaging and repackaging of financial products are toxic, making their valuations increasingly unclear and reducing their tradability. Reward schemes that shape the decisions of managers and agents in markets and that make their behaviour irresponsible, when judged from a systemic perspective—that is toxic. Misleading quantitative models are toxic. Not to address these and other problems would be totally wrong. The tripwire for this financial crisis may have been in the housing industry, but housing is not the structural cause of the crisis.

What this crisis should make plain to everyone is that not all financial innovation is benign. It is therefore baffling to hear the argument that fresh regulation is bad because it would stifle financial innovation. Fresh regulation is necessary because there has been a lack of proper regulation and supervision. The enormous mistakes that have been made by allowing finance to develop its own, highly risky *raisons d'être* must be undone.

But are we capable of learning that lesson? Why is it that we fail to learn from previous crises? At a recent Eurofi conference in Nice, Nout Weelink, the governor of the Dutch central bank, cited greed as a key factor driving people's propensity to forget and repeat behavioural patterns conducive to euphoria, excesses, over-indebtedness and finally, panic and crisis. A famous book on financial crises by the

---

[9] Which put Chinese walls between commercial and investment banking.

Massachusetts Institute of Technology professor Charles Kindleberger traces the same sequence of mindsets and behavioural patterns.

I accept this explanation, but not without qualification. A market economy involves cyclical movements and ups and downs. The entrepreneurial spirit lifts the economy, but, together with the herd instinct, it can also bring it down, by overshooting. This is indisputable, and a reflection on how free markets function. But just as modern economies need public policies, so they need regulations. As traffic needs rules and lights in order to protect people's lives, so market economies need regulations to limit collateral damage and enhance the production of public goods and restrict negative externalities. A lax monetary policy can lead to higher inflation and, ultimately, to a recession, but cannot, by itself, cause the meltdown of a financial system. This is the crux of the matter: the features of the financial system that have brought the threat of collapse are structural features of the "new" financial system, including a breakdown of due diligence.

Regulators and supervisors are supposed to think about the good of economy and of society, rather than to pursue specific interests. And they are supposed to learn. They may espouse ideological beliefs, for none of us is devoid of intellectual kinship. But, even so, they are supposed to learn and think in terms of what is good for society. They are supposed to have a good grasp of systemic risks.

Vested interests can have a long arm and try to influence regulations and supervision (the mortgage industry pressed Congress hard to roll back state rules aimed at stemming the rise of predatory tactics used to lure homeowners into high-cost mortgages). But vested interests must be strongly resisted, and with all means. Regulators and supervisors should know that financial markets are volatile and prone to instability, and that the efficient-markets hypothesis—that prices reflect all known information—is a fantasy.

In the real world, we need regulators and supervisors who have a good understanding of how financial markets function in practice and who do not succumb to market fundamentalism. They should never underestimate systemic risks; they should always be alert to financial stability. Strains and crises cannot be entirely avoided—but we can limit the damage they cause. For that to happen, we need to learn from mistakes and establish better, more effective and comprehensive regulatory and supervisory setups.

III. What This Crisis Teaches Us

Some use the complexity of financial markets as a *leitmotiv* when explaining this crisis. But this is pretty much a self-serving argument, hard to accept without qualification. Not all financial innovation is sound. Not all products and services are accepted by markets, and regulations are needed to protect consumers and investors. Some financial products are better than others; some are flawed by design, among them those that underpinned the international quasi-Ponzi scheme that has enabled companies to report abnormally high profits that do not reflect revenues generated by their businesses. It therefore makes sense to judge the nature of various financial products, and to regulate the financial industry as a whole.

One of the questions posed by this crisis is about policies. As a rule, the pro-cyclical use of monetary and budget policies should be avoided. One can argue that price stability should play second fiddle when financial stability is at stake, but one has to keep in mind the effects of injecting liquidity into the system when inflation is on the rise. This crisis reminds us again about the risks of financial liberalisation when institutions are not congruent or when markets are not functioning smoothly.

Market structures should be re-examined. We have undoubtedly seen a massive failure of regulatory and supervisory frameworks. Risk management, at both micro and macro levels, has failed miserably in countries that claim to epitomise good practices in banking and finance. Those who keep saying that things are better in Europe than in the US have to think twice about the national fragmentation of regulatory and supervisory structures in the EU, a fragmentation that clashes glaringly with the logic of single markets. The Lamfalussy process, which has been developing regulation of the financial service industry in the EU since 2001, needs much improvement if it is to cope with mounting challenges. Some argue that since the crisis started in the regulated sector of the financial system, its non-regulated area should be left alone. But this argument is ridiculous: banks have made use of loopholes and poor regulations to develop the non-regulated sector, creating a shadow banking sector.

The current crisis is a stern indictment of the incentive structures in the financial industry, which have stimulated reckless risk-taking at the expense of necessary prudence. Some banking turned into a "casino"-type activity, through the creation and selling of new types of securities. This asymmetric compensation scheme has to be corrected and the culture of investment banking has to change for the benefit of the economy as a whole. But inappropriate compensation schemes operate in other industries, too. There are numerous CEOs who receive incredibly high salaries and bonuses despite the shaky performance of their companies. There is a huge ethical issue here, one that needs to be addressed by politicians and policy-makers: How can we ask citizens to bear the brunt of painful adjustments when some of those who have been deeply involved in creating this mess are shunning responsibility or are not accountable?

The structuring of fiscal policies also has to change. It is, for example, quite odd to see Americans saving so little and their deficits being financed by emerging economies. Moving further along this line of reasoning one reaches the issue of policy coordination against the backdrop of financial globalisation: is coordination appropriate? Do we have proper structures of global governance? Unless we manage globalisation adequately, rising nationalism (principally in the form of protectionism) and populism in policy-making could reverse the evolution toward more open markets. The quest for energy security and affordable food could easily make things worse.

This financial crisis, in conjunction with the "food crisis," brings to prominence another issue: Is there an optimal degree of openness for an economy? The debates about international financial institutions, prematurely asking emerging economies to open their capital account, about energy dependency and about food dependency make glaring the question of the optimal openness of a market. In addition, open markets should not to be confused with deregulated markets; deregulated markets could easily backfire and cripple the functioning of a free society, one in which social cohesion and social justice are meaningful. Open markets, in order to operate as such, have to be accompanied by wise public intervention, which should consider both market and government failures. The bottom line is: full openness is not necessarily advantageous economically and socially.

Arguably, the view that the market should be seen as the solution for all decision-making, a view that has much influenced policy-making in the last couple of decades, has been fatally wounded by this crisis. It is high time to be pragmatic, open-minded and commonsensical. Open trade, markets and competition are good. But we need effective regulations and sensible public policies if the majority of our citizens are to benefit from free markets.

IV. Limits of Openness

In the midst of the deepest financial crisis after the Great Depression, the instability of the world's financial system is all too evident. But that is not a momentary instability: there have been several crises in industrialised countries in the past couple of decades, numerous financial and currency crises in emerging markets, trade liberalisation has left many poor countries in the dust, the myth of the "new economy" has dissipated, corporate scandals have shown that cronyism and bad governance are more complex and widespread than thought, wealth is more unequally distributed than it was and social fragmentation and exclusion have risen in rich and poor countries alike.

And yet this disorder has co-existed with a "consensus" on the principles and practice of economics, translated into policies that have unbridled markets, privatised the economy and downsized the public sector to the maximum. This "rational economics" is perhaps of a piece with what Max Weber referred to the "rationalisation of life," our tendency to ascribe primacy to knowledge and theory and the search for the ultimate piece of wisdom. The death of communism helped give birth to a single cosmology, dubbed "neo-liberal" in an economic context. That cosmology was also boosted by an international regime based on overwhelming US superiority.

This crisis should deal a *coup de grâce* to the belief that economics is a hard science. It has certainly revealed the serious weaknesses of market fundamentalism. There have, of course, been significant market-driven transformations—but they too appear a little different under close inspection. Liberalisation and privatisation transformed post-communist societies—but their unique geography, cultural and political consciousness combined with considerable support from the US and Western Europe made these countries exceptional. Market-oriented reforms have spurred China and India forward—but their reforms have been pragmatic, with close attention paid to social issues and rural development problems, while financial and trade markets have not been liberalised recklessly.

Globalisation (and liberalisation) does not, though, need to be an ideological mantra; it could be an open-ended concept that purports to define the "opening up" of societies, under the impetus of technological change and the manifold quest for economic progress. Such an interpretation would encourage pragmatic and flexible policies, and would rid globalisation of its perceived Western-centred origin.

Such an unconstrained interpretation of globalisation would have major repercussions for national public policies and international politics. Thus, national public policies could become fairly pragmatic, varied and geared towards the traditional goals of economic growth, price stability and social justice. Some might say that too much variety in institutional and policy design would damage a level playing-field and prevent markets from functioning effectively. There is truth in this argument, but it underplays the importance of working out policies that keep in mind the extreme diversity of conditions in the world economy and the fact that market forces do not automatically bring convergence.

We may already be seeing the start of a significant change in financial policy-making. One of Keynes' intellectual legacies—namely, that highly volatile capital flows are inimical to trade and prosperity— has demonstrated its relevance in this crisis. For decades now a mantra has been heard worldwide: that not much can be done in national policy-making because global markets would punish a government. This crisis encourages fundamental questions (such as: is the complexion of global markets God-given?) and questions that raise the prospect of policy changes (are not global markets, aside from their technological drivers, also the product of human beings' decisions to set rules for finance, trade and investment?). The claim that nothing can be done about financial flows, when they bring about misery, is unconvincing. There are plenty of specific regulations that can be imposed and restraints that can be exercised.

Similarly, free trade is likely to be re-examined as states' concerns grow about its impact on security. One concern—shared by leading and developing economies alike—is the cost of adjustment to competitive pressures. Another set of concerns relate to "hard security." How much "trading with the rival" is likely before restrictions are imposed?

Will the US, or major EU member states, accept big chunks of their most sensitive manufacturing and IT sectors being acquired by China's and Russia's companies and sovereign-wealth funds? Food security and climate change will concentrate minds on preventing over-reliance on overseas suppliers. We may think globally, but risks may force us to limit ourselves to "safer" patterns of trade and production.

In other words, we may well see a partial domestication of market forces in national governments' quest to cope with systemic risks and social strain. This would involve a greater state presence in the economy (state capitalism) and broader regulations; elements of "war economy"-style conduct in public policy will also be quite visible, even in liberal democracies. Perceived needs will trump ideological propensities.

Such concerns could stimulate the formation of alliances among groups of countries that share common interests. The EU is one such a bloc. A transatlantic trade area could also emerge. We could see a replica of it in Asia. Rivalry and experience—no monetary union emerged after the Asian crisis of 1997 despite speculation—suggest this might not happen; however, if the yuan turns into a reserve currency, the rationale for creating an Asian monetary area would grow.

Several sub-global clusters might, then, emerge to mitigate the potentially devastating effects of a completely open world system. They would operate in a multi-polar world of major global state powers—and the presence of poles that are alternatives to US power could itself create barriers to unrestrained free world trade, investment and finance.

How might the EU evolve in such a context? The logic of single markets might remain dominant, but policy-making would be quite nuanced at national level. In the absence of a common foreign and security policy and faced with greater security risks, national governments would be more active in the economy. The EU would therefore continue to have a fairly complicated policy-making structure.

So, who would formulate and enforce a suitable international regime for the twenty-first century? The US will not have the capacity do so any longer. In its current shape, the EU could not take over such a role. And an overhaul of the international architecture of financial institutions hinges on what the main international actors wish to do and on how they relate to each other. If the US, the EU, and the emerging global powers can strike a deal on reform, other significant players would eventually come along. Their challenge would be to make openness work for the world as a whole. That implies shedding a blind belief in the self-healing and self-regulatory virtues of markets. That may be happening.

REFERENCES

Hayek, F. von (1972) "The Use of Knowledge in Society" in *Individualism and Economic Order*, Chicago, Henry Regnery Co., 1972.

Kantorovich, L.V. (1965) *The Best Use of Economic Resources*, London, Pergamon.

Krugman, P. (1999) *The Return of Depression Economics*, New York, Norton.

Lange, Oskar (1972) "On the economic theory of socialism" in Nove, A. and Nuti, M. (ed.), *Socialist Economics*, London, Penguin, pp. 92–110.

Lamfalussy, A. (2000) *Financial Crises in Emerging Economies*, New Haven, Yale University Press.

Mises, L. von (1935) "Economic calculation in the socialist commonwealth" in Hayek, F. von (1935) *Collectivist Economic Planning*, London, Routledge, pp. 88–130.

CHAPTER 5

A Strained European Model—Is Eastern Enlargement to Blame?[1]

I. Introduction

Euro-pessimism is not of recent vintage. Rather, it has resurfaced from time to time after the Second World War, even during periods of relatively rapid economic growth and low unemployment. I recall here the famous book by the late French essayist J.J. Servan Schreiber, *Le Defi Americain* (The American challenge) that triggered a wide-ranging debate on the ability of European firms to compete with American multinational companies.

One counter-argument may be that this competition has constantly prodded top European politicians to push ahead with the European Union (EU) economic and political project. But there have also been bouts of Euro-optimism over the decades that induced fears across the Atlantic. As recently as the 1990s, some American pundits viewed the "Continental Model" as a viable alternative to the "Anglo-Saxon model."[2] This fear was encapsulated in the term "Fortress Europe."

In the end, however, the world economy was viewed in triangular terms: the USA, EU, and Japan (the non-Western exception) and nothing more.[3] One might think that there is nothing new here, for cycles are an unavoidable pattern in economic life.[4] But this reading of

---

[1] This analysis was presented at a Policy Network Seminar in Bucharest on 7 September 2006; the text was posted on the website of Policy Network (*http://www.policy-network.net*).

[2] Albert (1993).

[3] Thurow (1993).

[4] I refer to possible cycles in overall productivity dynamics, which can change hierarchies in terms of income per capita. These cycles can be linked with business cycles and longer term or secular cycles.

modern history, and the prognosis it leads to, is deceptively simplistic and intellectually defective.

There have been deep currents at work in European societies and in the world over the last two decades that beg for another approach and fresh policy thinking. These currents motivated Anthony Giddens to look beyond conventional theoretical and policy responses.[5] Bavarez, Sapir, Sinn, Rifkin, Bofinger and Fitoussi, among others, have joined this debate with their insightful contributions.[6]

The debate on the European Social Model (ESM) is highly relevant for several reasons. Most of the EU-15 member countries are under economic and social strain, and policy-makers are being challenged to devise appropriate answers to society's ills. Consequently, this debate is designed to make policy more effective in addressing social problems. In addition, the entire purpose of the Union is meant to give a particular social and economic meaning to European societies, which purportedly goes beyond the quest for international competitiveness.

This chapter examines various factors which have strained the ESM and which arguably make this period of Euro-pessimism quite peculiar. It looks at the race for competitiveness in today's world and the rise of economies in Asia. It also analyses the inner dynamics of European societies (demographics, the crisis of the welfare state, a sort of decadence) and tries to forecast what lies ahead, including relevant policy options. The underlying thesis here is that eastern enlargement is not solely to blame for the pain currently being experienced by EU member states, though it may have accentuated these problems.

II. The ESM and the Roots of Its Strain

Despite some persuasive arguments to the contrary, the existence of a single "European Social Model" is open to dispute. On the one hand, one can identify certain traits in European capitalism, which distinguishes it from what is generally called the "Anglo-Saxon" model, or

---

[5] See Giddens (1998, 2006).
[6] See Bavarez (2003, 2006), Sapir (2003, 2005), Sinn (2004), Rifkin (2004), Bofinger (2005) and Fitoussi (2005).

from the model encountered in advanced economies of Asia. On the other hand, the welfare state, in various forms, is a ubiquitous feature of advanced capitalism worldwide. Some convergence among the capitalist patterns of functioning has occurred in the last couple of decades under the rubric of globalisation.

Inside Europe there is significant social and economic variety, which has led to a differentiation between the Scandinavian model (with its emphasis on social redistribution[7]), the British model (which is closer to the American model), and the Mediterranean model (which is characterised by a sense of "disorder"). This categorisation is complicated by the bulging budget deficits in Germany and France. Likewise, some analysts point to the new EU member states from Central and Eastern Europe, which, seemingly, practice a more liberal form of capitalism. So where do we stand regarding the "European Social Model"?

In order to answer this question, one should not underestimate the influence of the EU construction as a process of depth and scope. The EU project can be considered from two perspectives. One is the construction itself, which aims to spread common standards throughout the Union and impose common rules of policy-making and institutional arrangements. The "Social Charter" is relevant here, as an attempt to increase the social uniformity of the Union.

That the EU project is mired in the throes of the policy dilemmas and trade-offs of enlargement and deepening is another story. The fact remains that the Union assumes a high common denominator in various social and economic aspects. The second perspective refers to the EU's meaning outside its boundaries. The EU, in spite of differences among its member states, is viewed by the rest of the world as a model that has brought prosperity and peace to its citizens.

Why is the ESM under strain? One major challenge is EU's own growing complexity. This challenge is illustrated by frequent failures of coordination among EU member states with regard to policy-making in various fields. The very institutional arrangement is the subject of heated debate when it comes to effective economic policy-making. An example is the coherence of macroeconomic policy in a single currency area where fiscal policies remain in the national realm.

---

[7] Illustrated by the share of taxes in GDP (above 45%).

One line of reasoning, though not uncontested, is that this asymmetry imparts a deflationary bias to macroeconomic policy, and that this bias brings about an unfortunate equilibrium (with high unemployment and low growth). The Constitutional Treaty itself has fallen prey to the limited ability to manage a rapidly growing complexity.[8] Poor leadership in a number of EU countries is more salient under such circumstances.

The EU is strained by an apparent contradiction between its well-entrenched social model and the need to make its markets more flexible so that economic growth is enhanced and unemployment reduced. Arguably, this contradiction is rooted in its inner dynamics and would not be so acutely felt in the absence of the tremendous pressures exerted by globalisation and by competition from low wage economies, including neighbouring eastern European countries.

The inner dynamics of the EU relate to a gradual institutional decay. This process demonstrates that social and institutional structures do not maintain their vitality in perpetuity, and that they can succumb to vested interests.[9] With considerable justification, some speak of a democratic deficit in the EU that is apparent at both national and supranational (EU) level.

There are areas in society where stalemates are ominous, including blockages in reforming educational and pension systems, or in enhancing public and private research and development (R&D). Another inner dynamic relates to an ageing demographic that is crippling the social security system. Last but not least, the functioning of labour markets places "insiders" and "outsiders" in opposition; and is symptomatic of the erosion of social cohesion. Difficulties in maintaining social cohesion are compounded by difficulties in integrating a rising number of immigrants.

Globalisation and the rise of Asian economies place today's world competition in a new context. The latter has to be understood against the background of the new information and communication technologies (ICTs) that are creating a new age of uncertainty.[10] ICTs foster a

---

[8] Students of organisational change could tell a lot in this regard and use the EU as a case study.

[9] See Olson (1982) and North (1981).

[10] Reich (2000).

labour-saving type of growth in many industries and services in industrial countries. This can lead to high economic growth combined with high unemployment and the erosion of social cohesion.

III. The Race for Competitiveness

President Bush's most recent State of the Union address touched on challenges to competitiveness, expressing concern that the United States risks falling behind in science and technology. For citizens in the EU, this "wake-up call" came as a surprise. From a European perspective, the United States appears to be well ahead in fostering technological innovation.

A 2005 report from the Conference Board shows that for the period 1995–2005 annual growth in national output for every hour worked in the EU-15 averaged 1.4%, compared with 2.4% in the United States. Likewise, data compiled by the European Commission (EC) in Brussels also suggest the EU lags behind the United States in key areas. Research and development (R&D), for instance, represented only 1.93% of the EU's GDP in 2003, as opposed to 2.58% in the United States and 3.15% in Japan. True, there is considerable diversity in performance across the EU, with the Nordic countries overtaking the United States in the amount invested in R&D.[11] However, the stark truth is that the heavyweights of the EU do not spend nearly as much in this area as the EC considers appropriate—namely, three per cent of GDP.[12]

The ambitious EC blueprint known as the Lisbon Agenda was formulated with an eye to the performance of US companies and the excellent results of American blending of academic research with high-

---

[11] Some data would suggest some catching-up lately: "More efficient Europe helps hold down rates" *International Herald Tribune*, 16 October 2006, p. 16. Other data would indicate, however, the reverse: in 2005 R&D corporate spending rose by 8.2% in the US as compared to 5.8% in the EU ("US widens gap with Europe on R&D" *Financial Times*, 30 October 2006, p. 1).

[12] A recent Booz Allen Hamilton study finds no solid link between R&D expenditure and economic performance ("R&D spending frenzy may be a waste of time" *Financial Times*, 13 November, p. 1). The study is, in my view, conceptually questionable.

tech and industrial pursuits. For instance, the EC proposed setting up a European Institute of Technology, modelled on MIT. The idea was criticised for being "top-down," and diverting resources from supporting high level research through a European Research Council. Indeed, controversies have often arisen over specific measures aimed at implementing the Agenda, and much remains in the hands of European national governments.

However, it is clear that the United States represents a kind of benchmark for policymakers, and also that the EU, on average, has been sluggish in achieving its goals in terms of competitiveness. This last point needs qualification, however, for there are European companies that have achieved stellar performance in world competition. And the EU, as a whole, and Germany in particular, continue to out-perform competitors in manufacturing. But how long will this continue and what are the social implications of labour-saving technology and inadequate upgrading of people's skills?

The success of the EU's Nordic fringe has been due, not only to major R&D undertaken both by governments and private companies, but is also a result of flexible product and labour markets, and a clever overhaul of welfare networks—the so called "flex-security" model.

The newer EU member countries seem to fare comparatively well in terms of productivity growth.[13] The 2005 report of the Conference Board shows annual growth increases of over six per cent annually in these economies. Accession states which have capitalised on their potential to catch-up. Arguably, however, simply catching up is insufficient (see Section four of this paper). Over the longer run, demographics and a predicted sharp rise in wages (according to the Balassa-Samuelson Effect) will diminish the growth differential sharply unless appropriate policies are in place.

If we compare the EU and the United States, then the latter's concerns about competitiveness appear to be without grounds. However, there is another factor to be considered: the newly industrialised economies of East Asia. China, India and other emerging East Asian

---

[13] The divisive and acrimonious domestic politics in some of these countries in the last couple of years would suggest that things are not as good as they look according to economic growth rates.

economies are increasingly a source of competitive pressures in the global economy. These economies are absorbing advanced technologies at a rapid pace and excel in innovation—India's remarkable engineering institutes, like those in Bangalore, can match the best in the Western world. Scientists from Asian nations are becoming an increasingly noticeable presence in top scientific journals, illustrating the region's potential to shape the research agenda of the future.

When Asia is introduced into the picture, we can see that the United States and the EU both face challenges of maintaining competitiveness, although the nature of these challenges is somewhat different. For the United States, they appear to be mainly related to global strategic interests, which are further affected by the emergence of new global powers. For the EU, they involve worsening demographics and crises of the welfare state, together with insufficient resources devoted to R&D and the difficulties in managing its growing complexity. There is a common denominator, however: both the United States and the EU will increasingly face stiff competition from Asian economies.

A couple of decades ago, global competition was defined in a triangular formation: US–EU–Japan.[14] The picture today is not as simple. The evolving global economy brings with it new major competitors and a change of competitive hierarchies. Unless governments and companies exercise clear foresight and adjust to trends by investing more in R&D and education, painful corrections are likely to be in store.

Those who believe that only positive-sum games prevail in the world economy need to be questioned. The dramatic changes under way open up the possibility for co-operative relationships, but also for emerging tensions. Consider, for instance, the growing need for energy and basic commodities in Asia, with China and India as the prime consumers, the unresolved geopolitical crises in various parts of the world (in the Middle East in particular), nuclear proliferation, and the visible and hidden aspects of the struggle against terrorism.

---

[14] The composition of the Trilateral Commission is quite telling in this regard.

IV. Who Fears Globalisation?

The less benign aspects of global free trade are ascribed to its affects on countries that either cannot make good use of their comparative advantages, or face stiff protectionism from wealthy economies—for example in the case of agricultural products. In general, such economies are in the developing world, and are afflicted by poor governance and the inability to absorb new technologies.

Recent years, however, have witnessed increasing disquiet in advanced countries as to the impact of global trade on their economies. In the USA, leading politicians have voiced their concerns over what they perceive to be runaway jobs, due to outsourcing and off-shoring. This feeling is even more acute in Western Europe, where top national policy makers have not demurred from making public their worries about industrial relocation. And they have not refrained from blaming new EU member countries for, allegedly, practising unfair competition via lower taxes.

Fiscal competition would, it is argued, further entice jobs to the less affluent economies of Eastern Europe. How is it that advanced economies, which have traditionally been staunch supporters of free trade, are having second thoughts and resurrecting a new brand of economic nationalism under the guise of patriotism?

There are both theoretical and more practical reasons for this apparent partial turnaround in the public rhetoric in rich economies. In economics, the arguments which stress the virtues of free trade form the basis for rationalising commercial exchanges between countries. Nonetheless, these arguments lose some of their appeal when the distribution of gains is largely asymmetric and dynamic competitive advantages dominate.

Brander and Spencer as well as Krugman and Helpman wrote seminal pieces on what they call "strategic trade."[15] One can posit that the rise of Asian economies in the last two decades, and most impressively of China, is to be judged through the lens of strategic trade poli-

---

[15] See Brander and Spencer (1983), Krugman and Helpman (1985).

cy, and was embedded in a development industrial policy by intelligent use of market forces.[16]

Nowadays, the new ICTs bring about great opportunities for those developing economies which benefit from well educated populations. Again, Asian economies fare quite well in this respect. India's growth over the last decade is the outcome of market-oriented reforms utilising the vast pool of English-speaking engineers and computer software specialists. However, this rapid economic progress has only reached particular parts of India, with much of the population still mired in abject poverty.

What matters in the global economic game, and what drives industrial relocation, is the existence of substantial wage differentials between countries and regions. These differentials induce globally-oriented companies to shift operations to areas which combine cheap labour with adequate technologies. The intensity of this process depends on how great the wage differentials are the quality of other production factors and the emergence of industrial clusters. Leading mainstream trade economists, such as Jagdish Bhagwati, would argue that advanced economies have little to fear since they are increasingly specialising in higher value-added products and services, and that all countries will end up better off.

This train of thought has been contested by the Nobel Prize winner Paul Samuelson from MIT. He argues that "sometimes a productivity gain in one country can benefit that country alone, while permanently hurting the other country by reducing the gains from trade that are possible between the two countries."[17] He also states that "post-2000 outsourcing is just what ought to have been predictable as far back as 1950," in the sense that other economies in the world have assimilated advanced technologies and are catching-up with the US economy.

Samuelson's argument finds solid underpinning in empirical research done by Richard Freeman from Harvard. Professor Freeman estimates that the entry of China, India and countries from the former Soviet bloc into the world economy resulted in a doubling of the

---

[16] Rodrik is, probably, the most articulate and sophisticated development economist in this field (1996, 1998).

[17] See Samuelson (2004, p. 142).

number of workers to almost three billion. Consequently, the ratio of capital to labour fell to 60 per cent of what it would otherwise have been. Moreover, the newcomers have good technical skills and much lower wages than their western counterparts, exerting a strong downward pressure on wages in western economies.[18]

That some German workers have accepted cuts in their wages is testament to this pressure. Lawrence Summers makes a similar argument that "middle-class workers and their employers—whether they live in the American Midwest, the Ruhr valley, Latin America, or Eastern Europe—are left out" in a competitive global environment that rewards the combination of low wages and diffusible technologies, and the ability to access global product and financial markets.[19]

Against the backdrop of the new ICTs and considerable wage differentials between economies in the world, significant shifts in the global distribution of industrial and services activities looks unavoidable. At the same time, public budgets are increasingly under strain due to ageing populations.[20] These factors produce the fear of outsourcing and off-shoring. One can easily understand this fear in western European countries, where wages are significantly higher than earnings of well-educated workers in eastern and central Europe.

The Lisbon Agenda responds to this fear, albeit framed in global (and not continental) terms. The large EU member states most fear Asian countries and the US economy and regard the Lisbon Agenda as a policy response aimed at lifting competitiveness.[21] The European Commission's update of the Agenda has scaled down the highly ambitious ultimate goal, but the policy thrust is unaltered.

The fear of outsourcing and off-shoring is analogous with the anguish surrounding the transformation depression of the last decade in post-communist economies. There was a dramatic reduction in output because resource reallocation—at the new market clearing prices—could not happen rapidly enough. Similar pains can be detected nowadays among some groups of workers in rich economies, who cannot compete in the new global economy.

---

[18] Brittan (2006, p. 13).
[19] Summers, (2006, p. 13).
[20] Gros (2005).
[21] Maincent and Navarro (2006).

The theoretical explanation presented above can be complemented by examining the reality of protectionist measures in various countries, which makes the picture more complex. The bottom line is that countries which have skilled people, which invest in education and have forward looking public policies, are more likely to enjoy the fruits of the global dissemination of technology.

V. High Growth Rates Are Not Enough: The Case of Central Europe

The political situation in Hungary, Slovakia, the Czech Republic and Poland over the last few years has raised eyebrows among observers of European politics. How is it that after EU accession, domestic forces have produced fragile and stalemated governments? Coalitions in these countries have brought together strange bedfellows with opposing political philosophies, puzzling those who expected a consolidation of democratic politics.

It is worth remembering that these economies are part of the dynamic area of Europe, with annual economic growth rates far higher than those registered in the old core of the EU (five to six per cent as opposed to one to two per cent). Moreover, their economies appear to be embedded in higher value-added European industrial networks, as against other transition economies. These networks, therefore, should lead to greater optimism regarding the chances of these countries to sustain rapid economic growth over the longer term.

Conventional wisdom, blending politics and economics, states that wherever economic growth is relatively high, there is a greater likelihood of social stability and sound politics. To be more specific in the case of Central Europe, a logical inference would be that owing to significant economic growth in this decade, a large part of the population would be enjoying tangible economic benefits and, therefore, support the ruling coalitions. Moreover, EU accession was presumed to consolidate the solid underpinning of these young liberal democracies and further enhance democratic politics.

There is yet another factor to consider. As opposed to the citizens of most of the EU-15 (discounting Spain and Portugal due to the decades of authoritarian rule under Franco and Salazar), most of the post-communist countries' citizens have personal experience of the communist command economy. Therefore, a fair assumption might be that they are immune to the erosion of basic constituent parts of orderly democratic life, and be better able to detect false democrats and cheap populism, be it on the right or the left.

I will now elaborate on these explanatory variables. When it comes to economic growth, post-communist *Mitteleuropa* glaringly shows that high growth rates are not sufficient for securing tranquillity in social and political life. Among economists there is an ongoing debate on the fundamentals of economic growth and on the relationship between democracy and prosperity. Some would argue that what matters most of all is economic growth, even if that may inevitably mean substantial inequalities between social partners.

Another line of reasoning suggests that sustainable economic growth should not impair social cohesion when accompanied by provision of public goods. The debate emphasises the importance of good practices in both the public and the private sector and effectively combating corruption. Arguably, wherever numerous citizens in central and Eastern Europe have lost out in the economic race, or have been marginalised from the benefits of economic growth, their frustration is likely to be captured by extremist parties. As a result, parties closer to the centre risk losing political ground.

Another explanation for the political flux in central and eastern Europe is the disappearance of the EU anchor. This anchor allowed politicians, irrespective of their political persuasion, to rally citizens behind the banner of EU accession, symbolising a "return to Europe." Not a few of these citizens had assumed that the "return to Europe" would bring them immediate considerable social and economic benefits. These people have observed no such dramatic change since May 2004. On the contrary, some additional pains have been brought about by the rigors of complying with EU regulations. A confrontation with reality was thus unavoidable.

This confrontation concerns the resurrection of "economic nationalism" in major EU member countries as well. In order to join the EU, Eastern European countries have diligently observed the intellectual and operational matrix of the Union such as the opening of markets including those for financial services and public utilities. As a matter of fact, in these sectors, Eastern Europeans have been more liberal than their Western counterparts. It is easy then to comprehend the frustration in some political circles in Central Europe when EU heavyweights preach what they do not practice. This is also an explanation, among others, for the revival of economic nationalism in the East, a tendency that can be amplified by other issues. One example of this is Poland's concern over Germany and Russia, both of which are working together in the sensitive field of energy procurement.

Collective memory does not seem to be an effective tool for promoting the EU due to its selectivity. There seems to be an asymmetry at play here: people enjoy political liberties and the opportunity to voice their satisfaction or frustration, but at the same time, they seem to have forgotten the period when those liberties were non-existent. Likewise, the generations of young people who do not have a personal experience with communism lack this insight.

A fourth explanatory argument can be made: the working of actual democracy is quite distant from textbook democracy. Actual democracy essentially means the functioning, for better or worse, of checks and balances and refers to the morality and the sense of accountability of political rulers. The actual state of democracy has had an impact on the mythology created after the fall of communism with numerous myths and clichés fading away in the "New Europe."

Eastern European societies are much less prosperous than their western counterparts. At the same time they are facing similar structural challenges: ageing, the crisis of the welfare system, socio-economic polarisation, identity-related confusion and the rising pressure of immigration. High economic growth is not a panacea where governments are incapable of dealing with the social challenges that accompany modernisation against the background of globalisation.

Furthermore, high economic growth may not be durable if wages keep rising rapidly because of catch-up dynamics inside the Union. There are no easy solutions in this regard. Nonetheless, what is certain is that national politicians will be severely tested in the years to come. What they do would influence domestic politics and their countries' economies greatly. What is happening in central Europe is a lesson and a harbinger to other post-communist countries as well.

VI. The Future of the ESM

How the European Social Model will evolve in the future hinges on the interplay of many different factors. One factor is the challenge of managing the increasing complexity in the Union. Students of organisational change know how difficult it is to make ever larger and more complex organisations function efficiently. For the sake of economic and social functionality, the EU has to find more appropriate institutional and policy constructs. The Constitutional Treaty is part of this endeavour. For this to happen, better leadership and actual statesmanship have to come to the fore.

Unfortunately, these political commodities have been shown to be scarce in Europe at present. It may be that rising variable geometry is inescapable in the EU, but this does not simplify the challenge of managing the increasing complexity. Serious issues would remain such as: tax competition, creating genuine single markets, reform of the Common Agricultural Policy, energy, and reform of the European Commission and its links with other EU governing bodies.

The clash of paradigms and ideas would also shape developments. For instance, the big failures in financial and energy markets have ushered in a new period of market regulation, which reshapes public policy accordingly. The Sarbanes-Oxley Act in the USA, which has also had reverberations in Europe, is a clear example of this dynamic. Public policy is forced to reconsider older convictions, for example that the state has to provide essential public goods, in order to regain moral ground.

Policy pragmatism is in much higher demand, in spite of the hard-nosed "ideologues" continuing to walk the corridors of power. There are a growing number of signs that market fundamentalists are on the retreat and that pragmatic considerations, of social and environmental issues should find an easier way into mainstream policy-making. However, the pressures of globalisation make it difficult for western governments within the EU to strike the right balance between social concerns (dealing with the "underdogs" or "les exclus") and environmental issues, on the one hand, and reforming and streamlining the welfare state, on the other hand. This is because failures of coordination exist not only within the EU, but in the world economy as well.

Missing or ineffective institutions for global governance should also be mentioned in this context.

Education must be tackled much more effectively by national governments. People have to rediscover the merits of engineering, mathematics and the physical sciences. This would help create a competitive edge based on technological advance and higher value-added products and services. The economic battles of the future, in an expanding global economy—wherein China and India will play an ever bigger role—, cannot be won by armies made up exclusively of lawyers and MBA graduates.

Can a new social contract be entered into by social partners? If wage earners would accept a slower rise in their incomes (or even a freeze or a cut), would capital accept lower profits or dividends for the sake of more public and private productive investment? It is public knowledge that recent years have witnessed an astonishing rise in the incomes of CEOs at a time of modest or even stagnant wages at the lower end.

Income polarisation has increased in almost all western societies and the middle class has frequently lost out. Can we ask wage earners to accept cuts in their incomes when CEOs gain ever more? If this dynamic is judged by considering the myriad of corporate scandals, one has to question the morality and social responsibility of numerous corporate leaders.[22] This is why ethics and morality are part of the equation when trying to address social problems.

Ethical and moral considerations suggest that we need to "go back to our roots," in order to regain moral values of honesty and trustworthiness, honour and respect, loyalty, hard work, education, family, community, altruism, compassion, and the love of one's country.[23] In order to strengthen the social cement of society, guilt and shame need to be recovered as socialising emotions.[24]

---

[22] See Bebear, (2003).

[23] "Trust and similar values, loyalty, truth-telling ... have real, practical, economic value; they increase the efficiency of the system, enable you to produce more goods or more of whatever you hold in high esteem. But they are not commodities for which trade on the open market is technically possible or even meaningful" (Arrow, 1974, p. 23).

[24] Lal for insightful observations on the cultural dimension of development, differences between Europe and Asia (1999).

Cynicism, the lust for power and money, hypocrisy and a disregard for fellow citizens have been spreading. They point to a decadence that has to be fought against tenaciously. It is dismaying to see high-profile politicians reveal themselves as villains, who use the intricate democratic procedures to enrich themselves and their cronies, and maintain a hold on power. This behaviour is undermining democracy and crippling the effectiveness of public policy. One could argue that virtue and vice have accompanied human history from the very beginning, and that actual democracies are not textbook, ideal creatures. Nevertheless, I would argue that in times of duress, lofty ideals and moral values can make the difference and turn the boat in the right direction.

The role of religion is to be highlighted when examining the importance of moral values. The Church as an institution is also facing its own challenges, including a credibility gap. At the same time, interreligious dialogue is essential in a Europe that has to show that the "clash of civilisations" can be averted on its own turf.

The moral ground plays a role in international politics as well. Issues such as environment protection (dealing with global warming), containing and combating diseases in the developing world, securing drinkable water, fighting poverty, and resuming the Doha trade round for example, constitute an urgent agenda for action which would also help to alleviate the threat from international terrorism. When highlighting the moral ground, the EU has to undergo its own soul-searching. It has to practise more what it preaches in its dealings with emerging economies, and with developing countries in general. It is worth keeping in mind how and why the Doha trade round failed.

The European Social Model remains deeply relevant on all moral issues mentioned above. Its progress would make a significant contribution to how the world evolves economically, socially and politically in the years and decades to come. Were it to occur, this progress, would not, in my view, be spectacular.

There are many more uncertainties, and the world has changed considerably as compared with a few decades ago, when the EU project included less than a dozen European countries. The economic rise of Asia is quite momentous historically and produces tectonic shifts in the balance of power in the world. It also changes the flow of pressures worldwide, sometimes dramatically. A period of muddling through awaits the European Union.

REFERENCES

Albert, M. (1993) *Capitalism vs. Capitalism*, New York, Four Walls Eight Windows.

Arrow, J.K. (1974) *The Limits of Organization*, New York, Norton.

Baverez, N. (2003) *La France Qui Tombe* (France that goes down), Paris, Perrin.

Baverez, N. (2006) *Que Faire?* (What to do?), Paris, Perrin.

Bebear, C. (2003) *Ils vont tuer le capitalisme* (They are going to kill capitalism), Paris, Plon.

Bofinger, P. (2005) *Wir Sind Besser als Wir Glauben* (We are better than we think), Munich, Pearson.

Brander, J.A. and Spencer B.J. (1983) "International R&D rivalry and industrial strategy" *Review of Economic Studies*, 50.

Brittan, S. (2006) "Globalisation depresses western wages" *Financial Times*, 20 October.

Fitoussi, J.P. (2005) *La Politique de L'Impuissance* (Politics of impotence), Paris, Arlea.

Helpman E. and Krugman, P. (1985) *Market Structure and Foreign Trade. Increasing Returns, Imperfect Competition and the International Economy*, Cambridge, MIT Press.

Giddens, A. (1998) *The Third Way*, New York, Blackwell.

Giddens, A. (2006) *Europe in the Global Age*, London, Polity.

Gros, D. (2005) "Prospects for the Lisbon Strategy. How to increase the competitiveness of the European economy" CEPS Working Document No. 224, July.

Lal, D. (1999) *Unintended Consequences: The Impact of Factor Endowments, Culture and Politics on Long-Run Economic Performance*, Cambridge, MIT Press.

Maincent, E. and Navarro, L. (2006) "A Policy for Industrial Champions. From picking winners to fostering excellence and the growth of firms" *DG Enterprise and Industry*, Brussels, April 2006.

Olson, M., Jr. (1982) *The Rise and decline of Nations. Economic Growth, Stagflation and Social Rigidities*, New Haven, Yale University Press.

North, D. (1981) *Structure and Change in Economic History*, New York, Norton.

Reich, R. (2000) *The Future of Success*, New York, Vintage Books.

Rifkin, J. (2004) *The European Dream*, New York, Penguin Group.

Rodrik, D. (1996) "Understanding economic policy reform" *Journal of Economic Literature*, Vol. 34.

Rodrik, D. (1998) *The Global Economy and Developing Countries: Making Openness Work*, Washington D.C., Overseas Development Council.

Samuelson, P. (2004) "Where Ricardo and Mill rebut and confirm arguments of mainstream economists supporting globalisation" *Journal of Economic Perspectives*, Vol. 18, No. 3, pp. 135–47.

Sinn, H.W. (2004) *Ist Deutschland noch zu retten* (Can Germany be saved), Berlin, Ullstein.

Sapir, A. (2003) "An Agenda for a Growing Europe. Making the EU Economic System Deliver" Report of an Independent High Level Study Group, EC, Brussels.

Sapir, A. (2005) "Globalisation and the reform of the European social models" Background document for the presentation at ECOFIN informal meeting in Manchester, September, Bruegel.

Servan Schreiber, JJ (1968) *Le Defi Americain* (The American challenge), Paris, Gallimard.

Summers, L. (2006) "The Global middle cries out for reassurance" *Financial Times*, 30 October.

Thurow, L. (1993) *Head to Head*, Cambridge, MIT Press.

CHAPTER 6

The Monetary Union: The Decade Ahead. The Case of Non-Member States[1]

I. Introduction

Since its emergence in 1999, the euro zone area[2] (as a proxy for the EU) has established itself as a major global economic power. From the financial and monetary point of view it has been a remarkable success. The credibility of the European Central Bank (ECB) has been established rather quickly, owing, inter alia, to the positive long-track record of some of the member countries central banks, such as the Bundesbank. In addition, the eurozone has proved to operate as a shelter during the current world financial crisis. But some of its weaknesses have also been better revealed during this crisis.

It goes without saying that the main indicator of this success is the low inflation rates in the single currency area during the past decade. The euro's share in total identified official holdings of foreign currency exchange increased from 18% to over 26% between 1999 and 2007[3] and the medium to long term trends tend to suggest that it will grow further.

---

[1] This chapter was written together with Laurian Lungu and was posted on the website of the William Davidson Institute as Working Paper 947, January 2009.

[2] For the purpose of this chapter, the Euro zone countries are: Austria (AT), Belgium (BE), Cyprus (CY), Finland (FI), France (FR), Germany (DE), Greece (EL), Ireland (IE), Italy (IT), Luxembourg (LU), Malta (MT), the Netherlands (NL), Portugal (PT), Slovenia (SL), Slovakia (SK) and Spain (ES). Although Slovakia will join the Eurozone in January 2009, it has been included in the euro countries group. The Non Member States, NMSs, are defined as Bulgaria (BG), Czech Republic (CZ), Estonia (EE), Hungary (HU), Latvia (LV), Lithuania (LT), Poland (PL) and Romania (RO).

[3] Although much of this has occurred largely due to the fall in the US dollar.

However, on other fronts, in particular the real economy, the adoption of the euro has failed do deliver expected results. Economic growth and employment have been considerably inferior to the US economy. And this, in spite of the fact that the 1999–2007 period has been, largely, one of macroeconomic stability, with low inflation and interest rates. Also, the euro has not worked that well in bringing prices of the same products and services together across the euro zone.

These weaknesses are best exposed nowadays, at a time of an unprecedented global financial crisis. The intensification of financial turmoil together with the impairment of the functioning of credit markets would restrain economic activity in the near future. Both households, with good credit histories, and businesses, confront themselves with diminished access to credit. The more prolonged the current financial crisis becomes, the deeper it would affect the real economy, impacting on output and unemployment. From the euro zone economy's point of view two issues stand out. First, does the MU have the adequate mechanisms in place to deal with crisis like this? Second, how fast would the MU economy recover, following these shocks? Are its markets (i.e., goods and services, money and labour) resilient enough to have a quick recovery? Complex decision mechanisms required getting an MU-wide consensus, the absence of some sort of a Central Fiscal Authority, which would have made possible a more effective coordination with monetary policy, and rigid labour markets would likely impair both the timing response to the crisis as well as the recovery process.

Most of the issues related to the functioning of the euro zone are found in the optimal currency area theory. Some of the euro zone economic challenges have been highlighted since its inception; others have emerged with the subsequent expansion of the euro zone. More recently Slovenia joined the single currency in 2007, Malta and Cyprus in January 2008, and Slovakia entered the EMU in January 2009. However, for the remaining NMSs there is an increasing uncertainty regarding the timeline of joining the euro zone. Most of the NMSs are a long way from fulfilling the Maastricht criteria, and the current global macroeconomic environment of increasing inflation and reduction in GDP growth creates additional uncertainty.

Expanding the euro zone further presents additional challenges. Currently, the euro zone has a population of 320 million and the remaining 8 NMSs would add another 100 million. This would exacerbate some of the existing problems, such as health care and aging costs, for instance, and raise issues on the required levels of public debts and fiscal deficits.

From an economic point of view, the challenges the NMSs face are threefold. The first set pertain to internal macroeconomic conditions: achieving sustainable inflation, reduced exchange rate volatility, prudent fiscal policy. The second set addresses the current global macroeconomic conditions and the effects of the financial crisis. Third, a set of conditions relate to the institutional underpinnings of innovation and competitiveness—education being a paramount ingredient herein. Obviously, the three sets of challenges are interlinked and this is what makes it more difficult for the NMSs to fulfil the Maastricht criteria. It has been argued that the Maastricht criteria were devised for a different group of countries facing different problems in the 1990s and that some of these should be relaxed for the new countries joining the EMU.

The prevailing view, both in the academia and in official circles has advocated strict compliance with the Maastricht Treaty's convergence criteria, ruling out any relaxation of those. The concerns are more related to the long-term stability of the euro area, in this respect the macroeconomic stability of the new entrants is paramount. Moreover, it may not be in the interest of some NMSs to join EMU in the near future. Their economies need the flexibility of exchange rate to address their structural problems. With their monetary policy run by the ECB, the economic convergence with the rest of the euro zone countries would be harder to achieve. But there is another argument, too, which would highlight the benefits of a faster track of accession, which would look at dynamic costs and benefits for the countries involved and for the euro zone as a whole.

II. The First Decade of Monetary Union

The effect of EMU on financial markets in the euro zone has been quite impressive. One important factor has been the elimination of exchange rate uncertainty and transaction costs, which in turn has led to increased efficiency of financial markets in the euro zone. However, as the current financial crisis has highlighted, credit markets within the euro zone continue to remain relatively fragmented because of regulatory and tax differences. Cross border competition among banks has also been quite limited.

The divergence of real economic growth across the euro zone countries continues to be a major drawback. Moreover, low growth performance of the euro zone, as a whole, was another minus. Countries which opted to stay out of the EMU improved, on average, their growth performance compared to euro zone countries.

There is some evidence of cyclical convergence within the euro area, but, overall, convergence still remains largely incomplete. This, in spite of the fact that, over the last two decades, the business cycles across the globe, especially among the wealthier nations, tended to become more synchronized.

Price dispersion continues to be high. Prices should, in theory, be equalised within the EMU but this is not the case. Low levels of intra-European migration, and the absence of a system for cross-national fiscal transfer, place the burden of adjustment squarely on wage flexibility. The inadequate level of economic integration leaves the national economies within the euro area exposed to asymmetrical shocks, since they do not benefit of on independent monetary policy.

During the first decade of the euro, inflation in the MU has been, on average, lower when compared to previous years. Clearly, the ECB mandate to price stability was paramount but a global low inflation environment also played a large role in easing the ECB's work to keep inflation below its agreed target.

III. Old and New Challenges for the Monetary Union

The challenges for the functioning of the MU are rooted in the economics of currency areas. The theoretical foundations for these are derived from the optimum currency area (OCA) theory[4] which shows that the adoption of a single currency pays off when the monetary area is highly integrated economically and has the capacity to adjust quickly to asymmetrical shocks.

Traditionally there are five core OCA properties namely: wage and price flexibility, trade integration, cyclical convergence, factor mobility and fiscal federalism, which are used to assess a success of an OCA area. On these accounts, the euro area still seems to have some way to go in order to achieve high efficiency.

---

[4] See for instance Mundell (1961) or McKinnon (1963).

Wage and price flexibility — Wage setting continues to be done, predominantly, at the national level, and quite often at the sectorial level. This mechanism reinforces the relative inflexibility of the individual countries labour markets. Within the euro area real wages have tended to be downwardly rigid with a relatively high level of indexation. Moreover, although nominal interest rates have largely converged, there is a wide discrepancy among real interest rates of the euro zone members.[5] In many euro zone countries there is a high and persistent rise in the price of services—often largely influenced by changes in local administered prices.

Trade integration — The common currency appears to have boosted trade flows between member states. The effect, however, is rather small[6] and, although it could well increase in the future, the economic benefits of trade integration are likely to be hard to disentangle from other endogenous effects generated from the currency area.

Cyclical convergence — This is a process that started long ago, with the Internal Market programme. Although business cycles synchronisation appear to have increased within the euro zone countries, much of it has to do with the recent fall in the amplitude of global business fluctuations, which benefited from low interest rates, high economic growth and low inflation. However, structural differences still remain at the euro zone country member level. Spain and Ireland are recent examples where rapid economic growth rates, driven by their construction sectors, could slowdown markedly.

Factor mobility — The mobility of the two main production factors, capital and labour, is crucial for the economic success of the euro zone. While the European capital markets are substantially more open and integrated than they were a decade ago, to some extent this is part of a global trend. Within the euro zone, FDI has gathered pace, however there are still barriers in place, such as incomplete liberalisation of the rules for mergers and acquisitions, which hamper a more complete integration of those. On the other hand, European labour mobility remains fairly limited, despite persistent differences in regional unemployment. Only around 2% of the total EU workforce appears to have increased working mobility.

---

[5] For instance, in 2006 Spain had the lowest real interest rate in the euro zone, around 0.4% while Germany the highest, around 2.4%.

[6] Between 5–10%, according to Baldwin (2006).

Fiscal federalism — Given the existence of an independent EU monetary authority, the ECB, the argument for an EU Fiscal Authority appears to be compelling. This would create more room for manoeuvre for the fiscal mechanisms of purchasing power transfers in the face of idiosyncratic shocks. It would also place less pressure on the ECB when dealing with regional divergences. The EU budget is little more than 1% of the EU GDP, providing limited scope for stabilising cross-state transfers. Moreover, a large part of that budget is allocated towards spending on Common Agricultural Policy and Structural Funds, which are weakly related to cyclical fluctuations in the individual member states.

Given these shortcomings in the functioning of the EMU, it is not surprising that many EU officials have voiced their concerns of how best to address those issues. At the Euro's 10-year anniversary, in June 2008, the President of the ECB, Jean-Claude Trichet, acknowledged that over the next decade the euro zone will be confronted with three major challenges:

> This anniversary is no time for complacency. But for continuous efforts, because the challenges lying ahead for Monetary Union will be numerous and demanding. As one of the major central banks in the industrialised world, we, like the others, have three challenges to cope with in our monetary policy-making: rapid technological progress, globalisation in all its dimensions, including the transformation of global finance, and population ageing.[7]

Some of the old challenges, such as the full and complete implementation of the Stability and Growth Pact—which is seen as a paramount component of EMU in the absence of a European federal budget— the pursuit of structural reforms aimed at raising Europe's long-term growth potential, and reduced fluctuations in national competitiveness indicators within the euro area members still remain.

There are two views on the OCA. The first one advocates the so-called "specialisation hypothesis." This argument, based on trade theory, argues that single currency areas lead to greater geographical specialisation through higher economies of scale and lower transaction

---

[7] Jean-Claude Trichet, "Address at the ceremony to mark the 10th anniversary of the European Central Bank and the European System of Central Banks" Frankfurt am Main, 2 June 2008.

costs to trade. The resulting increased regional specialisation in turn, generates an increasing vulnerability to asymmetric shocks. The second view[8] has been build around the "endogenous currency area" argument and asserts that that monetary integration reduces trading costs beyond those related to nominal exchange rate volatility. Moreover, a currency area could, by itself, induce the required changes to allow member countries to integrate enough to make the currency area viable. If so, the currency union could produce political commitments which contribute to its optimality. There is some empirical support for each of the two theories and the next ten years would test which one of these views is more valid.

A. Old Challenges

1 The Speed of Real Convergence

Probably this has been the most disappointing effect of the euro zone so far. Member countries in the euro zone have been growing at different rates. Moreover, real GDP growth among euro zone countries has been, on average, inferior to that recorded in the NMSs (which is not surprising in view of their catching up potential). As it can be seen in Figure 1, there have been wide disparities among average GDP growth rates in the euro zone.

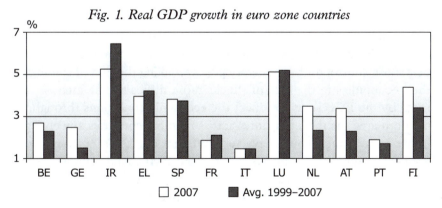

Fig. 1. Real GDP growth in euro zone countries

Source: Author's calculations based on AMECO data.

---

[8] See for instance Corsetti and Pesenti (2004) or Frankel and Rose (1996).

Between 1999 and 2007, average GDP growth in France, Italy and Germany, the countries which together account for three quarters of the euro zone GDP, was the weakest among euro zone countries. Ireland has been by far the fastest growing economy, averaging 6.5% over the same period.

In contrast, as expected, economic growth in NMSs has been fastest (see Fig. 2). Except Hungary, during the 1999–2007 period all NMSs recorded growth in excess of 6%.

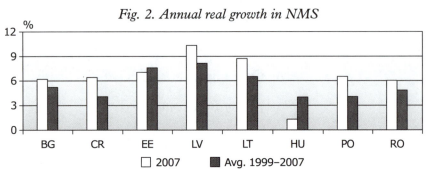

Fig. 2. Annual real growth in NMS

Source: Author's calculations based on AMECO data.

As growth differential between euro zone countries and NMSs would continue to persist in the medium term, one important issue is the individual timing of the NMSs adoption of the euro.

2 One Size Fits All Monetary Policy

In normal circumstances a country uses both monetary and fiscal policy to react to economic shocks. Within the EMU however, its members loose control of the monetary policy, making the task of stabilizing their economies in the face of shocks more difficult. The interest rate is set by the ECB so as to reflect the economic conditions throughout the euro area. As the latter differ across member countries any changes in the interest rates could have very different effects on economic and financial conditions in various parts of the EMU. And, unless there is a reasonable convergence of the monetary policy transmission mechanism across the euro zone members, this could give rise to serious strains and inefficiencies.

The experience of Ireland and Spain within the euro zone has been illustrative in this respect. Since adopting the euro the countries have been growing much faster than the euro zone average, and would have needed higher nominal interest rate to stem off rising domestic inflation. On the other hand, the current global supply shock which raises inflation throughout the euro zone, would require higher interest rates. However, the consequences of this monetary action would differ from country to country in terms of timing and its impact on real variables, as there are differences in the monetary transmission across EMU countries. Since convergence within EMU has not been achieved yet, inevitably, the effects of the output-inflation trade-off in individual countries would be magnified. Thus, as even in good times (i.e. periods of macroeconomic stability), the cost of maintaining price stability will be unevenly spread across the monetary union, in bad times these costs will necessarily be higher.

The Case of Ireland

Prior to joining the MU, Ireland's average growth over the previous 10 years was over 6%, the highest growth rate in Europe. A reason for that strong performance was Ireland's attractive business investment, namely an English-speaking work force and relatively low labor costs and real estate prices.

After joining the MU, the Irish economy continued to boom, but, because the largest euro zone economies needed lower interest rates, monetary policy, set by the ECB, tried to accommodate the latter. This, in spite of the fact that the Irish economy would have benefited from higher interest rates. As a consequence, higher demand in Ireland pushed up domestic prices and wages, eroding Irish competitiveness.

Between 1999 and 2007 Ireland grew at an annual average rate of 6.5%, still the highest among the MU countries. But inflation was also the highest at an average of 3.4%. And this in spite of the fact that this period was characterised by low global inflation and low interest rates. High economic growth rates have been possible due to an exceptionally elastic labour supply, largely because of migration effects, in stark contrast to rigid labour markets in most of the euro zone countries.

The Case of Portugal

Starting with the second half of the 1990s, the commitment by Portugal to join the euro resulted in a sharp drop in local interest rates. On the other hand, expectations of faster economic growth led to a decrease in private saving and an increase in investment. The outcome was high output growth, a fall in unemployment, higher wages, and a rapidly increasing current account defficits.

Today Portugal finds itself in a trap of high unemployment and low economic growth. Investment failed to pay off and productivity growth has been advancing at a dismal pace. High wages have been a major reason for that. Labour markets are rigid, average duration of unemployment is very long and the main cause for that is the high degree of employment protection. The continuing increase in labour unit costs reduced Portugal's competitiveness affecting primarily its non-tradable sector profitability. Unit labour costs also increased in relative terms, which maintained a sizable current account deficit.

Part of the solutions to Portugal's problems lies in issues related to real and nominal wage rigidities (see Blanchard, 2006). Both mechanisms would necessarily impose an adjustment cost on unemployment. Fiscal policy could also play a part, but its role is rather limited in Portugal's case.

The Case of Italy

Since entering into the euro zone, in 1999, Italian economic annual average growth was a dismal 1.5%. Primarily, this poor economic performance is due to the rapid rise in domestic wages which, in turn, pushed up unit labour costs (ULC). For instance, between 2000 and 2006, Italian ULC rose by 20% compared to those of France and by 10% when compared to those of Germany.

The loss in competitiveness is due to both inefficiencies at the micro level and a deficient fiscal policy (see Sibert 2007). Italy has the most regulated market products in the euro-zone, with high prevalence of price controls, administrative burdens and barriers to ownership. Moreover Italy has one of the most rigid labour markets in the euro area; hiring and firing workers are both especially difficult and costly processes.

Between 2003 and 2006 Italy's budget deficit has been consistently above 3% of GDP. As a percentage of GDP, government debt is, at 104% in 2007, the highest among euro zone countries. With future pressures on public debt, such as the cost of population ageing, mounting, it is likely that, at some point, Italian debt would be priced at a premium over other euro zone countries. This would dampen further the country's economic prospects.

Other euro zone countries, such as Portugal, Spain or Greece find themselves in a similar position. This divergence in competitiveness among euro zone countries is largely caused by differences in both national micro-level and fiscal policies.

3 Fiscal Policy and Strained Welfare Systems

The euro area is the only region in the world which has a centralised monetary policy but favours a rather independent approach to fiscal policy. The foundation for the latter is laid out in the Stability and Growth Pact (SGP), which is politically and legally binding and acts as a coordinating instrument across the EU. In order to maintain fiscal discipline within the EU, the deficit to GDP and debt to GDP ratios should not exceed 3% and 60% respectively over the economic cycle. As noted in a multitude of papers, from a longer-term perspective, these constraints puts into question the sustainability of public finances.

The largest threat is, undoubtedly, the *ageing of population*. Between 2010–2050, the EC projects a 16% fall in the EU working age population (48 million people) with the number of elderly people rising sharply by 58 million, or 77%. Thus, the old-age dependency ratio is set to double to slightly over 50% by 2050. The population ageing would require a substantial increase in public spending, mostly on pensions, health care and long-term care.

EU's projections of age-related expenditures in its "no-policy change" scenario[9] envisage an average debt-to-GDP ratio for the EU

---

[9] See Commission (2006).

in 2050 of over 180%. Individual country debt-to-GDP ratios could be much higher with Greece at 450% and Portugal at 520%.

Long-term sustainability finances are important for the EU as a whole because the negative effects caused by the un-sustainability in public finances from any individual EU country could spill over to other member states. Moreover, risk premiums for EU countries with a more precarious state of public finances could rise relative to other EU members, making harder for the former to refinance their debt.[10]

Adopting a long term view for the EU's fiscal policy, in which these issues will have to be addressed, is mandatory. Multi-annual budgetary frameworks are useful because they limit the scope for opportunistic government interventions in fiscal policy but adopting a longer-term vision for the EU public finances would require changes in the way fiscal policy is conducted.

Ideally, from the point of view of coordinating monetary and fiscal policy, a monetary union should have a central fiscal authority. As responsibilities of the two institutions are different, it would be important to have a single fiscal authority counterpart to the MU's monetary authority. In practice, however, this is likely to be difficult to achieve. Resistance of national governments, which would like to have some discretion over their fiscal policy and control their national budgets, would, most probably, continue to be very high.

Although the SGP provides a general framework for the euro zone governments to conduct fiscal policy, in situations with extreme economic conditions, such as the one the world faces nowadays, there is scope for overriding the restrictions imposed by SGP. Economic policies are implemented more effectively when there is coordination between monetary and fiscal policies. As Ben Bernanke has declared recently,[11] "the intensification of the financial crisis in recent weeks made clear that a more powerful and comprehensive approach involving the fiscal authorities was needed to solve these problems." Fiscal authorities of the euro zone member countries have started to

---

[10] So far, risk premiums for Belgium, Greece or Portugal, countries which have had the highest debt-to-GDP ratios within the EU, have not risen. It may be because the markets thought that this trend could be reversed, which actually has started to happen.

[11] Speech by Ben S. Bernanke, Chairman of the Board of Governors of the US Federal Reserve System, at the National Association for Business Economics 50th Annual Meeting, Washington D.C., 7 October 2008.

be involved but their coordination efforts and asymmetrical responses would likely cause delays with respect to the timing of implementing their decisions. And, in times of crisis, the speed of reaction is crucial.

The reform of the SGP in 2005 has allowed medium-term budgetary objectives to be differentiated across countries, according to individual member countries economic conditions. However, when a global shock, such as the current credit crunch, hits so severely, from a fiscal point of view this would impose an additional cost to government's current and future financial commitments. This could leave the finances of some governments in a precarious state, which could weaken the euro zone's credibility, and thus have an impact on the euro exchange rate.

4 Diminished Adjustment Capacity in the Global Economy

The globalisation of financial markets together with the continuous acceleration of financial deepening in world markets have led to increased interconnection of the world's financial markets. The ongoing financial crisis revealed, once again, how difficult is to contain the propagation of shocks, especially financial shocks. In today's world, large money flows take advantage of investment opportunities across world's economies, facilitating an efficient allocation of resources. On the other hand, however, the sudden outflow of foreign funds could leave domestic financial markets depressed, which, in turn, could have a negative impact on the real side of the economy, with output contracting, sometimes threatening the very existence of the entire sectors, and unemployment going up. Subsequently, the recovery of the economy could take a long time.

In today's global economy, individual economies have a less limited adjustment capacity, compared to, two-three decades ago, let's say. They are much more flexible, indeed, but their desired economic objectives could be often difficult to meet. This is because the control over economic conditions is to a large extent, at least in the short term, outside the individual country's institutions powers. Take, for instance, monetary policy. The response from most of the Asian central banks over the last years has been to purchase massively US T-bills in order to take advantage of the low interest rates in the US and keep their domestic exchange rates against the US dollar at favourable terms, required for maintaining their export growth to the US economy. The efficacy of a unilateral action from the part of the US Federal Reserve is much more reduced compared to an alternative of a coordinated response from a large number of representative central banks.[12]

5 The International Role of the Euro

In its anniversary report, EMU@10, the EC acknowledged the fact that "the euro area must [...] build an international strategy commensurate with the international status of its currency." While, undoubtedly, building an international strategy that focuses on changes at the institutional level in international organisations, for instance, would help, the economic dimension itself, plays a major role in strengthening the euro's international exposure.

A currency has three major roles, namely as a unit of account, medium of exchange and store of value. The international role of the euro focuses on enhancing the last two of these as the unit of account role is, implicitly, already fulfilled by giving the euro a meaningful interpretation of prices.

Clearly, the euro will further develop as a medium of exchange as the euro zone gets engaged more actively and openly in the international trade of goods, services and capital. But displacement of the US dollar, which is currently the leading global exchange currency, is likely to take time to materialise.

As a store of value a common indicator is taken to be the euro share in central banks total foreign exchange reserves. As the central banks diversify away their US dollar foreign exchange reserve holdings, the euro share is bound to increase. However, for this process to continue more preconditions have to be met. More generally, according to Dehesa, the best way to measure the role of the euro internationally is "through its relative presence in three international different markets: the international liability management market, the international asset management market and the foreign exchange market."[13]

---

[12] On Wednesday, 8 October 2008, major central banks across the world engaged in the biggest coordinated emergency interest rate cut in the history. The interest rates were cut without reference to their respective governments. Coordinated governments action plans were made at G7 and G20 meetings a few days later.

[13] Dehesa (2008).

Credibility of the issuer plays an important role. And this comes with time, as the ECB will establish a longer track record. Stability of the euro will be another characteristic which will enhance euro's international role.[14]

As an international currency, the euro will need to be supported by financial instruments denominated in euro which can be easily traded in a liquid financial system. Here, however, the US bonds and T-bills market still offers investors a wider diversity. Moreover, the largest part of energy trade is still denominated in US dollars. A number of countries which are global suppliers of oil and gas for instance, have their domestic currencies pegged to the US dollar.

B. New Challenges and Re-emerging Threats

Apart from the challenges presented above, nowadays there are renewed pressures, some derived from the changing structure of the global economy and some from accelerating processes such as climate change or energy supply concerns. It would be interesting to see whether the impact of the spreading economic crisis on energy and commodity prices would annihilate much of the inflation expectations which were so much an obsession to central banks until not long ago.

1 Labour Productivity

In the absence of an individual exchange rate for any euro zone member country, one possible measure of competitiveness within the monetary are is given by domestic unit labour costs. Figure 3 below shows the percentage deviation, relative to EU-27, of the real unit labour costs of individual member countries in 2007.

According to the data, Poland and Romania appear to have been the most competitive countries in EU.[15] Slovakia, the soon-to-be euro

---

[14] Although, as a ratio to GDP, the euro appears to have surpassed the US dollar as currency holdings circulating outside the euro area. In 2006, the ratio of UD dollar banknotes in circulation to euro banknotes in circulation reached 0.9.

[15] It is true that, in Romania for instance, wages have been growing fast over the last years. But the increase in wages has been a phenomenon observed throughout NMSs, so in relative terms the increase has been much less. Moreover, the aggregate wage level in Romania is among the lowest in NMSs.

zone member follows suit. Unsurprisingly, Spain which has had this advantage for the last decade, still benefits on a lower unit labour cost than the EU average. Among the core group of EU countries, Germany and Austria have been doing remarkably well. In part this is due to structural measures, in particularly taken by Germany, to rebalance their economies. The agreement on wage policy German government had with trade unions has paid off.

On the other side of the spectrum, among the NMSs, countries which have their domestic currency pegged to the euro, i.e., the Baltic countries and Bulgaria, fare the worst. Their currency board monetary regime prevents them to adjust and a strong euro puts an upside pressure on their domestic labour costs.

Fig. 3. Real ULC relative to EU-27 (2007=100), % deviation

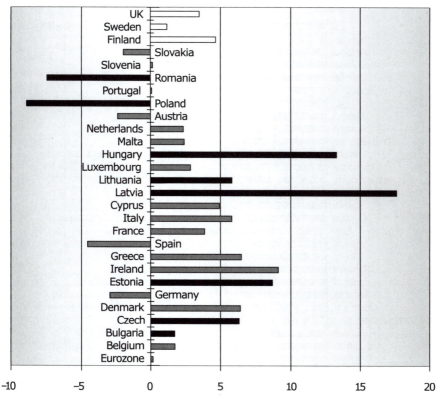

Source: Author's calculations based on AMECO data. Black lines are NMSs, grey lines are euro zone members.

Overall, the euro zone appears to be slightly less competitive than average EU-27, but this happens mainly due to the large positive contributions of Poland and Romania.

2 Energy and Climate Change

The European energy policy plays an increasingly important role in the overall EU's policy framework. The energy package drafted by the EC envisages the fulfillment of a number of targets by the year 2020. Taking the year 1990 as a benchmark, the aim, at the EU-level, is to reduce by 20 percent the EU's greenhouse gas emissions, use a 20 percent share of renewable energies in the energy mix, and improve energy efficiency by 20 percent. These policies highlight the need to se-

Fig. 4. Real ULC relative to EU-27 (2007=100), % deviation

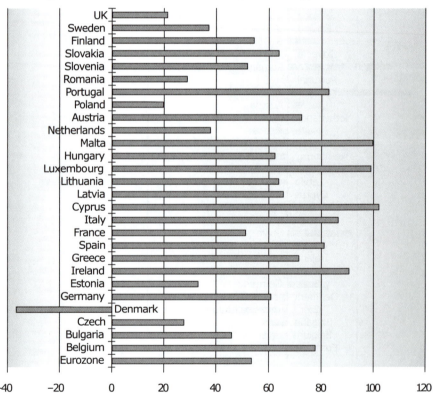

Source: Eurostat

cure supply, fight climate change and build a competitive energy sector within the EU as a whole.

However, the initial costs associated with these changes are going to be large and they will affect various EU members to different degrees, and implicitly the euro zone members as well. This happens because of the existent different energy supply and economic structures countries within the EU. The relative price of energy shock would impact quite severely on the economies which have low valued added and consume energy disproportionately (most NMSs range among them); this curse will show up in adverse dynamics of ULCs.

The EU energy dependency ratio, expressed as net energy imports divided by gross energy consumption, is set to rise from the current 53% to some 65% by 2030. These changes alone are bound to bring about changes in the energy supply mechanisms and could transform profoundly the economic structure of individual countries.

For instance, industries which rely too much on oil and gas will become uncompetitive as the price of these goes up and the price of alternative energy supplies comes down.[16] Moreover, the costs associated with these changes are both monetary and non-monetary. This makes it more difficult to come up with scenarios that quantify their impact on the individual EU countries.

3 The Financial Integration

Although countries in the euro area appear to have continued the process of integration in European financial markets, there are still segments of these markets which are not sufficiently integrated. Financial integration is an important issue in the context of a monetary area. Both economic theory and empirical findings tend to suggest that integration and development of financial markets contribute to economic growth and allow capital to be allocated more efficiently—provided financial innovation is of the right nature.[17]

---

[16] Also, in transport, energy use has grown rapidly over the last decade. A key characteristic that distinguishes energy use in transport is the almost total dependence on oil as a fuel. The social and economic effects of the measures aimed at maximising energy efficiency and renewable energy substitution in this sector are difficult to quantify yet.

[17] This is easily to illustrate by examining the episodes of financial crises of recent decades. As the report on securitization produced by the Committee of

A study by the ECB (2004) performed over five key euro area markets namely, money, government bond, corporate bond, banking/ credit and equity markets, shows that these have achieved different levels of integration. Money market appears to be the most integrated of the five but even so, differences persist between various sectors of the money market itself.

As euro zone financial institutions have extended their activities across national borders, the financial systems of different countries have increasingly become intertwined. This, in turn, increases the risks of international contagion. As the current financial crisis has shown, the emergence of a crisis in a specific country and a specific sector can rapidly propagate to other countries and financial sectors. In this context, the establishment of an adequate regulation and supervision system becomes important for the functioning of financial markets.

The European Parliament has been very active in the setting up of the Lamfalussy framework in order to improve financial market supervision and regulation. However, there are notorious difficulties in coordinating more national authorities. Such a euro zone authority, if there was to be created, would face great challenges. The large number of the institutions to be coordinated[18] in an event of a cross border crisis would raise issues of timing, efficiency and information streamlining.

As the ongoing financial crisis has shown, the financial stability has become a major issue in itself. The financial sector has an important role to macroeconomic stability for a number of widely acknowledged reasons. First, a financial crisis can cause major economic disruptions and sizable fiscal costs. Second, the resilience of the banking sector is paramount for pursuing a flexible interest rate policy, as well as a predictable and effective monetary transmission. Third, an efficient financial intermediation is essential for enhancing growth. Fourth, risk management is very important, as it limits unhedged borrowing and discourages flows driven by moral hazard.

The current financial crisis has exposed a number of flaws, two of which stand out. The first relates to the control of monetary aggregates

---

Wise Men, which was headed by Alexander Lamfalussy, underlines, there is a trade-off between financial innovation (especially if it is not well regulated) and financial stability (2001).

[18] The number of national authorities involved would have to be multiplied by the number of countries.

when credit expansion is very intense and financial innovation loosens the relationship between the monetary base, M0, and broad money, M2. Over the last three decades, the relationship between M0, over which a central bank has control, and M2, over which a central bank does not have control, has weakened considerably. This has made the task of implementing monetary policy by a central bank slightly more difficult. In hindsight, the increase in M2 in a low global inflation environment has been made possible with increased leverage by the financial institutions—helped by the development of complex financial product and the creation of a parallel architecture to the banking system—as it used to exist two decades ago. This leads to the second flaw exposed by the ongoing financial crisis, namely, that related to the regulation and supervision of the so-called shadow banking system.

Undoubtedly, the need to act is compulsory. The seriousness and global implications of the crisis underscore the need for creating institutions for global governance. In practice, however, this could be difficult to achieve. Even if such institutions were to be created, their effectiveness would still need to be tested in times of crisis. Each crisis is slightly different and the means to address it could be different. Local disequilibria could trigger global disequilibria—as the US-originated subprime crisis has shown. With this it comes higher volatility. For instance, in 2008 alone, stock markets in Eastern Europe have fallen by 60–70% from their peak levels in a matter of several months.[19] In turn, this leads to volatility of the exchange rates and uncertainty about investment decisions.

This crisis has outlined the need for preventing a regulatory arbitrage in the global economy. Arguably, an institution which would perform such a task would be faced with a rather complicate supervision process. Coordination with national supervisory institutions would be essential and this could increase the likelihood of a delayed response in the event of a sudden crisis. Nevertheless, some form of co-coordinated action plan among MU member countries, should be in place *a priori*, with contingency plans drawn up.

---

[19] As of 11 October 2008, all global stock markets recorded dramatic falls since their peaks only a year ago. Dow Jones, for instance, fell by 39%, while S&P 500 fell by 42% compared to their peak levels.

4 Regulation and Supervision in the MU

The ongoing international financial crisis should compel everybody to reexamine financial regulatory frameworks. Some are tempted to see the crisis as a recurrent accident, albeit more severe, along an economic cycle and following worldwide very cheap credit for several years in a row. But a careful reading would go at structural roots of the crisis. Globalisation of financial markets and very intense financial innovation, with precarious and, sometimes, missing regulations, and a plethora of conflicts of interest, have created the milieu for the current crisis. There is a growing debate among top policy makers on how to address the causes of this crisis.

One type of arguments refers to cooperation among supervisory agencies. Thus, the former Italian minister Tommaso Padoa-Schioppa makes a cogent argument when he advocates the setting up of a single European rulebook and an integrated supervision of EU-wide groups. In our view, these proposals deserve a more sympathetic hearing from ECOFIN minister members and EU governments. As a matter of fact, the logic of the single market and increasing cross-border operations ask for increased cooperation among supervisory authorities in the EU. But, arguably, it is not sufficient to focus on strengthening the supervision of banking institutions. For, apart from an irresponsible relaxation of lending criteria in the US sub-prime mortgage and other markets, the origin of the current financial crisis is to be sought in implications brought about by massive cross-border capital flows and the increasing use of financial instruments/derivatives (the securitization of various obligations) which are not transparent and traded effectively.

Financial markets have become, in certain areas, increasingly opaque and, identifying those who bear the risk together with evaluating it, represent formidable tasks. The size of the so-called "shadow banking sector," which is lightly regulated, has been constantly increasing over the last 10–15 years. This evolution brings to memory the Gurley-Shaw Report of decades ago, which highlighted the imprecision in distinguishing between credit and money, and, consequently, major hurdles for effective monetary policy. Banks themselves have been caught in this game by their origination and distribution operations, flawed risk management practices.

Not a few leading banks have engaged in highly questionable packaging and selling of debt tied to high risk mortgages. And several Wall Street major banks have come under the scrutiny of prosecutors lately. A Glass-Steagall type recreation of Chinese walls for the sake of restoring trust and transparency would, quite likely, be impossible nowadays, albeit not unimaginable. But there is an obvious need to regulate financial markets more widely and better. The deepening of the financial turmoil refutes glaringly those who said that the financial industry is capable of self-regulation. It is quite unfortunate that more thorough lessons from the LTCM episode, the dotcom bubble, the Enron and Parmalat affairs, etc. have not been learned by national regulators more thoroughly. There is, arguably, a need to revise the regulatory frameworks for the operation of investment vehicles. There is also a need to regulate the very use of financial instruments (of CDOs and CDSs, for instance), so that the transparency of markets be restored and investors be adequately informed. As banks are required to hold minimum reserves a similar rule could apply to other financial institutions. Likewise, the magnitude of the leveraging should be subjected to constraints and efforts to mitigate the effects of procyclicality should be taken into account And a final note: better regulation does not mean a reversal of financial openness; the opposite is true. Financial openness, in order to be sustainable (and not produce irreparable damage), demands proper (enforceable) regulations and effective oversight.

5 Global Governance

The issue of global governance is a pretty wide one; however, from this chapter's point of view three of them would be addressed namely, the regulatory arbitrage in the global economy, local disequilibria and the need for institutions for global governance. In fact, they are all interlinked, one reinforcing the other.

In an article in *Financial Times*,[20] the head of Switzerland's central bank argued for greater harmonization among emergency help provided by world's central banks in order to prevent large global banks to go outside their home country in order to shop around for the best

---

[20] "Banks urged to co-ordinate more in emergencies" *Financial Times*, 19 August 2008.

deal. A closer integration of financial markets facilitates this sort of behaviour.

Another issue which the ECB has been confronted with lately has been an abuse by banks on its financial market liquidity operations.[21] The banks appear to have taken advantage of the ECB's broad-based collateral system and used riskier collateral than envisaged to secure financing form the ECB. This sort of aspects complicates further the supervision aspect and, what is more important, sometimes it fails to sort out the issue for which the mechanism/instrument has been devised in the first place.

In a world of increasing integration of financial services, local disequilibria could propagate rapidly across two dimensions, namely geographical borders and other products. For instance, although the current financial crisis has originated in the US subprime market, subsequently it spread to almost all developed economies and it has done so across a broad range of other products such as car loans, insurance and so on. Apart from the extensive flaws in the US subprime mortgage securitization, there have been wider information and incentive problems originating in the banking system. Moreover, the emergence of the totally unregulated "shadow banking system" and its high levels of leverage compounded the initial problem.

In the view of recent events, the need for global institutions of global governance seems to be well founded. Devising the architecture and the functioning mechanisms of such institutions would probably take time because of the complexities involved in such a process. Response times in period of crisis is paramount this would be a trade-off with the level of complexity, as both national and EU institutions would have to be coordinated

IV. Challenges for the New Member States

The eight New Member States (NMSs) aiming to join the euro are bound to face more challenges in their process of entering the monetary union compared to their predecessors. This is because fulfilling

---

[21] "ECB to tackle possible abuses of liquidity aids" *Financial Times*, August 25 2008.

the required conditions for nominal convergence is bound to take longer today, as uncertainty in global markets deepens and adverse shocks do not abate. Moreover, the EC and the ECB have grown more lukewarm towards the expansion of the EMU and insist that convergence conditions should be met. We shall see whether the very serious impact of the financial crisis on NMSs would alter this stance.

A number of countries which entered into the EU in 2004, such as Poland or Hungary for instance, have been revising their euro adoption date. Others, like Lithuania, were refused the application to join since they did not fulfil the criteria convincingly. Table 4 below displays the intention date—either explicit or inferred—of euro adoption by the NMSs.

Table 4. Planned year of the euro adoption of the NMSs

Country	EU Entry Year	ERM II Entry Year	Planned Year of Euro Adoption
Bulgaria	2007	n/a	n/a
Czech Republic	2004	2008*	2011*
Estonia	2004	2004	2010**
Hungary	2004	2011*	2014*
Latvia	2004	2005	2008**
Lithuania	2004	2004	2010*
Poland	2004	2009*	2012*
Romania	2007	2012	2014

* Forecasts—official date not set yet. ** Under revision

About two thirds of NMSs trade is with the euro area. Also, the degree of integration of the NMSs equity markets has increased more recently, in countries such as Czech Republic, Hungary, or Poland, local bond prices exhibit fairly high co-movement *vis-à-vis* Germany. However, although in many areas NMSs integration with the EMU has gone a long way, the incomplete structural adjustment of their domestic economies would require more time for convergence.

A. PRECONDITIONS FOR JOINING THE MU

The entry preconditions in the euro zone are embedded in the Maastricht Treaty. They require countries to achieve a high degree of sustainable nominal convergence before they can participate in EMU. The fulfilment of the Maastricht criteria is assessed by the EU Council on the basis of the reports prepared by the EC and the ECB at least once every two years or at the request of a member state wishing to adopt the euro.

The Maastricht criteria require the following:

Price stability — The average annual rate of inflation must not exceed by more than 1.5 percentage points the average rates of inflation of the three best performing EU countries. Inflation performance should also prove to be "sustainable".

Long-term interest rates — The average nominal long-term interest rates over the latest twelve months should not exceed by more than 2 percentage points the average of the three best performing EU member countries in price stability terms.

Exchange rate stability — Countries are required to keep their exchange rates within the "normal" fluctuation margins of the European Monetary System (ERM-II) without severe disruptions for at least two years.

Fiscal sustainability — The fiscal deficits should not exceed 3% of GDP, and gross government debt should not exceed 60% of GDP. However, the assessment of fiscal sustainability under the excessive deficit procedure outlined in the Maastricht Treaty is designed to evaluate whether the budget deficit ratio "has declined substantially and continuously and reached a level that comes close to the reference value" or that "the excess over the reference value is only exceptional and temporary and the ratio remains close to the reference value." Similarly, the government debt ratio is allowed to be "sufficiently diminishing and approaching the reference value at a satisfactory pace."

Eventually, countries which joined the EU would have to enter into the EMU. Among the EU countries only the UK and Denmark have negotiated EMU opt-out clauses. They also have the discretion to choose the dates for going into the ERM-II mechanism. But, The Maastricht Treaty leaves the timing of EMU entry open and, in practice there are no legal limits on how long the NMSs can remain outside the EMU.

B. WHAT HARDENS THE MAASTRICHT CRITERIA [22]

To a large extent, challenges in meeting the Maastricht criteria by the NMSs stem from the necessary convergence processes in both prices and incomes to euro-area levels. Furthermore, the ensuing capital inflows and financial deepening could bring about significant developments in inflation and exchange rates. Given the fact that initial conditions are different in each NMSs country, the convergence process is likely to take different paths. In the NMSs, income levels are inferior to those in euro zone, so the speed at which these would converge is an important consideration.

Usually income convergence should occur simultaneously with the convergence in price levels. In practice there are two mechanisms through which this could happen. Either the country involved in the catching up process needs to experience higher inflation relative to the euro zone or its nominal exchange rate must appreciate relative to the euro. Both mechanisms involve the appreciation of the real effective exchange rate.[23] With NMSs expecting to grow at a higher rate, inflation would be growing faster relative to the euro zone,[24] so that there is a large risk that inflation would go up after joining the EMU—unless sufficient convergence has been achieved.

Price growth could be different in the tradable and non-tradable sectors—the Balassa-Samuelson Effect—since in some NMSs productivity in the tradable goods sector tends to grow faster than in the tradable goods sector. The Balassa-Samuelson Effect would be manifesting itself by putting pressure on prices or the exchange rate.[25]

---

[22] A skeptical view on these criteria as applied to the NMSs holds, among others, Wyplosz (2007).

[23] This results from the definition of real exchange rate (or competitiveness), which equals the nominal exchange rate times the ratio of the two price levels.

[24] This is known as the Balassa-Samuelson Effect and arises due to higher differences in productivity growth sectors *vis-à-vis* their corresponding wages. Productivity growth has tended to grow faster in the traded goods sector than in the nontraded goods sector, such as services. Rapid productivity growth in the traded goods sector pushes up wages in all sectors so that the prices of nontraded goods relative to those of traded goods will rise. Because productivity growth is faster in the catching-up accession countries relative to the EU countries, this implies, *ceteris paribus*, that inflation rises more rapidly in the catching up economies.

[25] Empirical evidence on the Balassa-Samuelson Effect estimated it between 0.2% and 2% per annum.

C. Inflation Challenge

As mentioned above, even in a stable global macroeconomic environment, inflation in the NMSs would be higher than that of the euro zone. However, current economic conditions create additional challenges for meeting the inflation criterion because the NMSs would have no choice but to import inflation. It is true that other euro zone countries would also import inflation but for NMSs, which must meet the Maastricht criteria, this is an additional hurdle to be overcome.

The global financial crisis, triggered by the US subprime market events in the summer of 2007, is bound to have effects in the medium term. One of the central banks responses[26] to the crisis has been to inject liquidity in the money markets. This liquidity would not go away easily and with economic growth in developed countries expected to falter, there would be an inevitable rise in inflation. Current economic policies in the US tend to support measures for increasing demand, a recipe for another inflation bout, though one can argue that monetary easing is not unwarranted during periods of bad equilibria and while inflation pressures seems to have largely subsided.[27]

Moreover, the weakness of the US economy triggered a fall in the US dollar during the first half of 2008, which in turn amplified the increase in global commodity, energy, and food prices—most of which are expressed in US dollars. The outcome has been an increase in inflation throughout the world and a rise in inflationary expectations. This process has been reversed after the full eruption of the financial crisis and the entry into a recession of most of the euro area—which has weakened the euro against the USD considerably.

Given that these developments are outside control of the NMSs, they have no choice but to import inflation—at least in the medium term. This creates additional uncertainty in the timing and sustainability of the inflation criterion.

Unsurprisingly, the inflation in NMSs has been higher than that of the euro zone. In 2007, however, in 6 out of the 8 NMSs inflation

---

[26] The Federal Reserve, Bank of England and the ECB have injected large amounts of liquidity in the money markets and created facilities which are still in place in order to offer access to more funds to the distressed banks.

[27] As a matter of fact the FED is acting in a quite Keynesian fashion in order to forestall a deepening of the recession.

was higher than the average inflation recorded in the 1999–2007 period (see Fig. 5). This rises the question on the sustainability of low inflation in the NMSs.

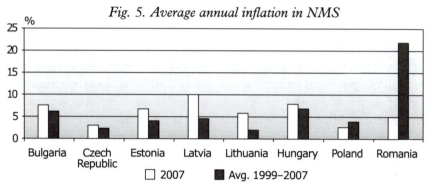

Fig. 5. Average annual inflation in NMS

Source: Author's calculations based on AMECO data.

In contrast, inflation in the euro zone countries tended to be more subdued. New euro zone members, such as Slovenia and soon-to-be member Slovakia, experienced by far the highest average inflation among euro zone economies. Fastest growing countries, such as Spain or Ireland also had higher inflation rates.

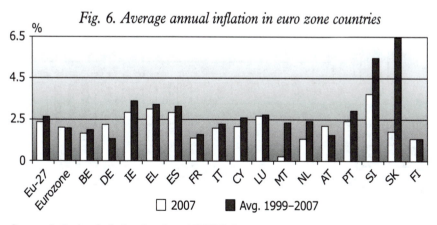

Fig. 6. Average annual inflation in euro zone countries

Source: Author's calculations based on AMECO data.

D. GROWTH AND EXTERNAL DEFICITS

A low real rate of interest and expectations of faster convergence by
the NMSs justify higher private spending, in the form of either consumption or investment. This would require running current account
deficits. As domestic savings rates are too low to finance the current
level of investment and consumption, external borrowing is the only
way to speed up the convergence process. However, with large capital inflows potential vulnerabilities emerge. All NMSs experience rapid
credit expansions, and in some countries there were concerns about
overheating. Higher incomes create the opportunity to borrow more
and banks have been scrambling to offer loans in their pursuit of market share. Domestic borrowers have been contracting loans in foreign
currency—mostly euros—increasing the currency risk on their balance
sheets. Obviously, currency mismatch makes the private sector vulnerable to the exchange rate depreciation, and raises the systemic risk
through credit risk.

Within the EU, the largest current account deficits are run, with
the exception of Greece, by NMSs (see Fig. 7). Again, the NMSs which
have a currency board have the largest current account deficits domestic
adjustment cannot occur in the face of strengthening of the euro.

Fig. 7. Average annual inflation in Eurozone countries

Source: *Author's calculations based on AMECO data. Black lines correspond to NMSs.*

Large current account deficits imply an external disequilibri-
um and, therefore, would necessitate an adjustment in the exchange
rate. As long as transitory changes take place, the settlement of the

exchange rate on a stable path—as required by the ERM-II—would be harder.

E. Exchange Rate Arrangements, Currency Boards or Floating Rates

The exchange rate arrangement plays a crucial role in a country's progress towards its EU accession. Participation into the ERM-II requires a relative stability of domestic currencies *vis-à-vis* the euro for a period of two years. Out of the 8 NMSs, half, the Baltic countries and Bulgaria, have a currency board arrangement. At first, this might be perceived as an advantage since it could smooth out their participation into the ERM-II. Moreover, currency boards also help bringing down inflationary expectations at a time when these are high. The major problem, however, with a currency board arrangement is that countries loose control over their monetary policy. And, during a time of rapid structural change, this could affect competitiveness and hamper the speed of their adjustment.

At the time of writing, the NMSs with currency board agreements were having the highest inflation within the EU, being the only four countries which had double digit inflation (see Fig. 8 below).

Fig. 8. Annual inflation in NMS, July 2008

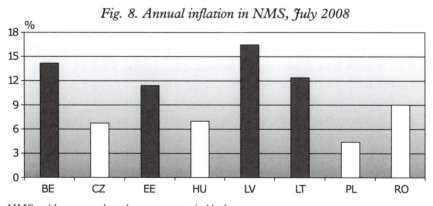

NMSs with currency board arrangements in black.

Part of the reason for this high inflation rates in NMSs with currency board agreement was due to higher wages. Due to the out-migration, the ensuing labour shortage has pushed up wages, which in turn, raised companies costs and thus inflation. A fixed exchange rate has worsen the problem by preventing an appreciation of the domestic exchange rate, which would have taken some pressure off inflation.

In contrast, NMSs countries with flexible exchange rates fared much better—in spite of similar prevailing labour shortage conditions. Romania's July 2008 inflation edged a little over 9%, but inflation in the Czech Republic, Hungary and Poland were between 4–7%, a little higher that euro zone inflation. The return of many Polish workers from abroad over the last months may have played its part in keeping inflation low in Poland.

Currency board arrangements may be a temporary solution when inflation is high and there is a need for rapidly establishing credibility for the disinflation process. But, maintaining them for long period of times, when the economy undergoes a structural adjustment, could prove to be costly. And these costs could be more painfully in the future, if the country enters into the MU at an exchange rate parity which is not adequate with the macroeconomic fundamentals. From this point of view, the floating exchange rates of the NMSs seem to be a far better alternative on their road to euro adoption.

The advantages of different regime options are debatable in both academic and official circles. However, several considerations are worth taking into account by the NMSs authorities when deciding which monetary regime is more suitable for their economies. First, it is important to ensure that the monetary regime will be consistent with the country's inflation objectives. This objective is part of the Maastricht criteria and achieving a low and sustainable level of inflation is possible only when structural economic adjustment has reached its final stages. The two mechanisms available to achieve the required real currency appreciation are to allow either the domestic currency to appreciate in nominal terms or domestic prices to rise. Second, the financial deepening of the economies would raise additional issues regarding the transmission mechanism of the monetary policy. Transition economies have experienced shifts in money demand and, from this point of view, pursuing an IT regime might be perceived as being more challenging. However, this has to be put in balance with the benefits of the central bank having full control over monetary policy. Having a currency pegged to the euro—as Bulgaria and the Baltic states—seriously impair their central bank's response to current events, for instance. In the presence of potentially strong and variable capital inflows, which most of the NMSs economies experience currently, the monetary authority has limited room for manoeuvre. Moreover, large swings in real exchange rate affect output and expectations.

And, as today's ongoing financial crisis reveals, it may be that, for the small countries which have currency boards, their best choice would be to adopt the euro as early as possible. The alternative would be a prolonged recession since adjustment in the nominal exchange rate is not possible.

Allowing monetary policy to operate more flexibly seems to present a greater advantage in current circumstances. Moreover, an IT regime gives the central bank some discretion if unexpected economic circumstances materialise. And, it also allows a better coordination with fiscal authorities in designing and pursuing the appropriate economic policies. This said, however, a free floating of the exchange rate (which is implied by a hard IT regime) poses its own strong perils—especially under the extreme volatility conditions which have been brought about by the current financial crisis.

F. STRAINS TO BUDGETARY POLICY

Within the EMU, the creation of the SGP may have made structural adjustment more difficult. While in a boom, meeting the SGP rules is easier, achieving fiscal balance through tax increases and budget cuts when the economy is weak could prove difficult. The onset of poor economic conditions in 2000 proved this point. The economic downturn reduced government revenues while accelerating unemployment increased government expenditures. These two trends combined to drive budget deficits above the 3% ceiling in several EMU countries. And this could well happen again if the current financial crisis persists.

The NMSs would have to deal with these fiscal strains as well. And, on top of this, they will have to address issues such as co-financing EU projects on environment and infrastructure or large education, health care and pension costs. In the NMSs, public debt—which gives a perspective over the sustainability of fiscal policy in the long run—expressed as a percentage of GDP, is relatively low. Exceptions are Poland and Hungary with the latter already going over the Maastricht criteria limit.

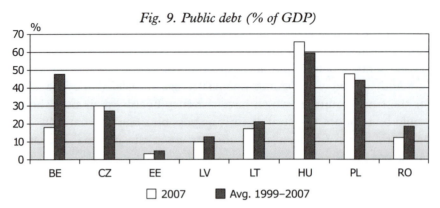

Fig. 9. Public debt (% of GDP)

Source: Authors calculations based on AMECO data.

In contrast, public debt in the euro area is much higher, on average (see Fig. 10). Italy, Belgium and Greece have the highest ratios, around 100% of GDP.

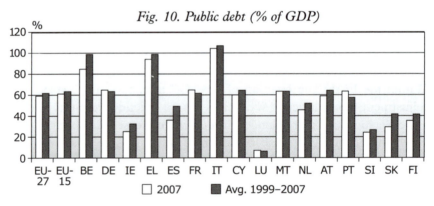

Fig. 10. Public debt (% of GDP)

Source: Authors calculations based on AMECO data.

Fiscal policy, in particular, would need to be carefully devised in the NMSs within a long term framework. Although, in general the level of public debt in NMSs is relatively low, it could quickly grow if left unchecked. The old-age dependency ratio is set to rise drastically over the next 4 decades (see Fig. 11). Aging would put pressure on both government revenues—by lowering them—and expenditures—which would grow.

Fig. 11. Old-age dependency ratios

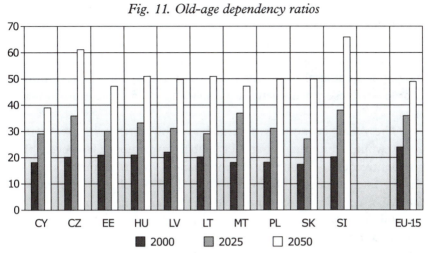

Old-age dependency ratios (% of aged over 65 as % of the working-age population—aged 15–64).

G. DIVERGENCE OF ECONOMIC DEVELOPMENTS

Currently, a large number of countries within the euro zone exhibit divergent economic developments. These divergences are bound to become more prominent with the expansion of the euro zone. Some of these divergences are structural but many of them have a political origin. As long as convergence with the euro zone area is not fully achieved, a set of policies in the NMSs countries such as spending, taxation or social policies would be more efficient implemented at the national level.

H. THE ASIAN ECONOMIES CHALLENGE

Higher competitivity from the Asian economies, notably China and India, would continue to provide a challenge for the NMSs economies. Traditionally, companies in euro zone tended to move further eastwards in Europe, taking advantage of lower labour costs. But, with labour costs growing many of them have been investing in Asia, preponderantly in China. Most of the Asian countries are in a financial position in which they could easily increase consumption. In China, for instance, the share of domestic consumption in GDP is remarkably low. This is partly due to the Chinese high propensity to save, as the lack of a Chinese social security system forces the households to save for their own age. A low level of household wealth and higher demographics could also provide more room for increased consumption. Moreover, these phenomena are applicable to more countries across Asia.

The Asian economies potential to grow further in the years to come would continue to attract global investment. However, their competitiveness is prone to abrupt changes due to shifts in their exchange rates against both the euro and the US dollar. So far, most of the Asian economies have pursued an exchange rate policy based on maintaining a favourable parity against, especially, the US dollar. This has allowed them to increase their export volumes to the US and—to a large extent, Europe. But the recent emergence of domestic higher inflation in Asian countries would put an increasing pressure on their exchange rate policies which is likely to change their attitude towards imports of goods and services.

I. How Does the Financial Crisis Strain the MU?

More than one year after it started, the global financial crisis appears to place an increasing strain on the workings of the European financial system.[28] The functioning of the existing EU arrangements for maintaining financial stability could well be hampered if the crisis continues to deepen. There are three main questions which are worthwhile answering in the current global context. The first is whether the existing Eurosystem operational framework is indeed suitable to deal with the effects—current and expected—of the financial crisis within the euro area. The second relates to the level of support—if any—the ECB should provide to the non-euro zone member states. And finally, what are the major threats to the euro-financial system which the ongoing crisis has been exposing so far.

---

[28] The European financial system can be seen in a strict and a broader sense. The latter would include the EU member states that do not belong to the eurozone.

The answer to the first question is rather unclear. So far, the European financial system appears to have survived a crisis of public confidence, in spite of a number of bankruptcies and large losses incurred by various European banks. But, as the bottom of the crisis appears to be some way ahead, the adequacy of the ECB's instruments remains still to be tested. The ECB has at its disposal three categories of instruments namely, open market operations, minimum reserve requirements and standing facilities. The two commonly used open market operations employed by the ECB during the current crisis have been its refinancing operations—through which liquidity is temporarily lent to counterparties against eligible collateral—and fixed term deposits—used to absorb temporary liquidity from the financial system. The increased instability of money demand[29] within the euro area's financial system has made the ECB to adjust more actively than usual the timing and maturity of its open market operations but there has been no change in the other two instruments.[30] However, if the liquidity problems in the euro zone financial system continue to worsen, the ECB may find itself in a difficult position *vis-à-vis* its capacity to supply the necessary liquidity to the markets. In turn, this would have a negative impact on interest rates—distorting the monetary transmission mechanism signal—impairing access to credit by both households and corporate sector. This has already started to happen in the US and some European countries. It is a serious issue since the euro zone banks' share of loans and deposits in total financial assets and liabilities is rather large.

Dealing with such threats to financial stability would necessarily involve a coordination effort among various financial institutions. The IMF has already announced it would aid financially a number of European countries such as Hungary, Island or Ukraine, to shore up public's confidence in their financial systems. Even so, the scope for the IMF's intervention seems rather limited. In total, it currently has some 260 billion US dollars which could tap into and lend but this amount

---

[29] In fact, the instability of euro zone money demand has been well documented since the inception of the MU. But, in times of stress, the volatility of money demand grows even higher, making the conduct of monetary policy more difficult.

[30] See "The Eurosystem's Open Market Operations During the Recent Period of Financial Market Volatility" May 2008, *Monthly Bulletin*, ECB.

looks dismal in relation to the sums already provided by other central banks to the markets so far.

Coordination would also need to be established within the euro zone countries. The credibility of the euro, as an international currency, would depend of the EU's ability to find a common response to a collapse that transcends its members' borders. For instance, debates about raising guarantees for private savings across the EU showed how large the disagreement still is among member countries. Many European governments have taken unilateral action.

Apart from coordination initiatives, other measures aimed at managing cross border crisis would have to be swiftly implemented. Among these are proposals on reducing barriers to cross border asset transferability by subsidiaries of a banking group—on which the EC was expected to report in March 2009—clarifying the circumstances in which a bank would be allowed to receive public financial support and a potential re-evaluation of conditions regarding the existing EU directive on the reorganization and winding-up of credit institutions to include subsidiaries.

J. THE FINANCIAL CRISIS AND EURO ADOPTION

The Asian crisis of a decade ago made some to talk about a "two corner solution"[31] for exchange rate arrangements in order to forestall major financial tensions. The current, huge, financial crisis has underlined the role of reserve currencies as "shelters" during periods of major distress; it is like we are going toward a "single corner solution" paradigm in exchange rate policy. This role of the single currency has reignited the controversy over euro-adoption for non-euro zone EU member states, new and, interestingly, older ones. For older member states joining the euro zone seems to be more of a political decision, though economic arguments can be highlighted as well. For NMSs euro adoption is more complicated for it involves complying with the Maastricht criteria, however disputed these are in their case.

Let us start with older EM member states, which do not belong to the euro zone. Analysts (Buiter and Sibert, 2008) identify four aspects which make their economies look vulnerable to the current stress in

---

[31] Either a free float or a currency board.

the international financial markets. Namely, countries which are small, possess a large, internationally exposed banking sector, have their own currency and have a limited fiscal spare capacity relative to the possible size of the banking sector solvency gap are in particular vulnerable. In the EU these are Denmark, Sweden and the UK, although the latter is larger compared to the other two and has a legacy of a reserve currency. It can be submitted that both Denmark and Sweden will speed up procedures to adopt the euro. For the UK things seem to be murkier in this regard.

Recent developments in the evolution of financial markets in Europe have made the ECB to step in and guarantee support for some NMSs.[32] This is an unprecedented move. The ECB used, for some time, to provide technical assistance to central banks in countries neighbouring the euro zone. Such dialogue reinforces cooperation between the EU and its neighbours, including countries which are supposed to adopt the euro. However, the ECB never acted as a potential lender of last resort for a non euro zone country so far. The ECB's decision highlights how much the European financial landscape has changed since the creation of the MU. This is now characterized by a growing number and increasing strength of banking groups with significant cross-border activities. And, although in theory each subsidiary of a banking group is a legal entity subject to the legislation of the EU's member state in which it is established, in practice, a deteriorating position in one location could well lead to significant contagion effects. This crisis has brought about a quite paradoxical situation: it is not subsidiaries in NMSs which cause the trouble in the main, but overall practices (such as over-leverage and involvement in the origination and distribution of securities) of banking groups headquartered in countries which belong to the euro zone! Ironically, the ECB is forced to step in because of poor practices in its principal area of concern. From this point of view, the ECB's financial support extended to, for example, to the National Bank of Hungary may be seen as a pre-emptive move attempting to maintain the existing financial stability in a wider euro zone area. But this highlights also the vulnerability of financial systems in NMSs, not necessarily of their own doing.

---

[32] In the case of Hungary, ECB assistance was combined with support from the IMF and the WB in a package of over 20 billion US dollars.

In late 2008, a number of countries in Eastern Europe, such as Poland, Hungary or Romania experienced increased speculation on their currencies. In times of financial distress, small open economies with shallow financial markets and dual monetary systems[33] (with a large volume of euro-denominated credits) are particularly at risk in the face of such events. While the benefits of a weaker currency could be potentially reaped in the short term through higher exports, the medium term effects on the real economy—caused by higher interest rates and lower economic growth—are likely to be more lasting and more damaging. Moreover, a fast depreciating currency could cause a sudden crisis of confidence and trigger an old-fashioned run on the banking system. The search for higher yield by global investors who attempt to improve their earnings position could well destabilise—often unjustifiably—entire financial systems.

The wave of speculative attacks on NMSs currencies and the increasing threats to their financial stability prompts some governments to seek earlier entry into the euro zone. The Polish government has already indicated that it plans such a course of action. Other governments think similarly. Arguably, this will be heavy debated in the period to come in several NMSs. But a major stumbling block for speedier euro accession are the Maastricht criteria—which look more difficult to fulfill in view of the ensuing global economic context. Moreover, a low inflation differential is quite unrealistic for catching up economies. The EC could, in theory, adopt a more permissive approach towards NMS countries willing to adopt the Euro by relaxing/adapting the Maastricht criteria requirements. But not a few influential people in Frankfurt, Berlin, Paris, etc might say that, allowing economies with a rather more "fragile" position to join the euro zone, could weaken the Euro. On the other hand the ECB has both an operational and moral duty to assist central banks in NMSs in case of need. And if this is the case contingent liabilities (involved by swap lines and other arrangements) may be quite significant; they may even be on the rise if NMS are increasingly at pain in coping with the effects of being outside the eurozone. Therefore, it may be that a cost-benefit analysis favours a

---

[33] Euro denominated credits make up a significant share of the total, which indicates the perils of a sharp and sustained depreciation of the domestic currency

faster track of euro zone accession for some NMSs when things are examined for the single currency area as a whole.

It is true that fears of an expanded free riding syndrome when it comes to fiscal rectitude are not groundless. Just keep in mind the examples of Italy, Portugal, Greece after accession in the euro area. But, arguably, some NMSs are more liable to be fiscally sounder, inside the Euroarea, then older member states like those mentioned above. And if this is the case the menace of a weakening euro, because of a precipitate enlargement of its area, loses much of its punch.

NMSs are, seemingly, in a catch-22 situation because of the crisis: if they stay outside the euro zone area they tend to become more vulnerable (speculative attacks against their currencies is a proof of this); if they get inside too quickly they risk not being able to cope with having renounced the flexibility of exchange rate and monetary policy tools. Nonetheless, a decision has to be made in view of the costs and benefits involved. In addition, there are important differences among the NMSs—just think about those countries that have currency boards vs. the floaters and the different magnitude of current account deficits.

V. Concluding Remarks

At the time of writing, the world economy is facing a severe financial crisis which has already started to be felt by the real economy. Financial deleveraging continues to wreak havoc on global financial markets and this leads to increased volatility and uncertainty. At the moment it is rather unclear how long the global recession would be and whether the fall in output would be associated with a period of high inflation— i.e. stagflation. What is seems likely, however, is the fact that economic recovery would take a few years to materialise. The structure of the global financial system is being reshaped with a much lesser role for investment banks, private equity funds, hedge funds, and the like. On the other hand, the increased control of government over financial institutions, through forced bailouts, would change the way the financial sector as a whole will behave.

The intensification of financial turmoil and the impairment of the functioning of credit markets would restrain economic activity in the near future. From the Euro zone economy's point of view two issues stand out. First, the MU needs better mechanisms in place to deal with crises of this magnitude. Second, its goods and services, money and labour markets do not seem to be resilient enough to allow for a speedier economic recovery.

What are then the prospects for NMS to join the euro zone in the not too distant future? In short, things are open. Some Maastricht criteria would be more difficult to achieve by several NMSs in the short and medium term as fiscal policy would be needed to support economic recovery. A possible course of action by the ECB would be to support financially the NMSs which are in need, in effect treating them as *de facto* euro zone members. But there is another argument, too, which would highlight the benefits of a faster track of accession, which would look at dynamic costs and benefits for the countries involved and for the eurozone as a whole.

If the logic of a "single corner solution" would get more in shape in the years to come, that would be illustrated by three monetary blocs in the world: a US dollar-based one, a euro-based one, and an Asian currency-based one.

REFERENCES

Blanchard, Olivier (2006) "Adjustment within the euro. The difficult case of Portugal" Available at: *http://econ-www.mit.edu/files/740.*

Buiter Willem, H. and Sibert, Anne (2008), "The Icelandic Banking Crisis and What to Do about It: The Lender of Last Resort Theory of Optimal Currency Areas" CEPR Policy Insight No. 26.

Corsetti, Giancarlo and Pesenti, Paolo (2004), "Endogenous Pass-Through and Optimal Monetary Policy: A Model of Self-Validating Exchange Rate Regimes" CEPR WP 8737.

ECB (2004) "Measuring Financial Integration in the Euro Area" Occasional paper series No. 14, April 2004.

Égert, B., Halpern, L. and McDonald, R. (2006), "Equilibrium Exchange Rates in Transition Economies: Taking Stock of the Issues" *Journal of Economic Surveys*, Vol. 20, No. 2, pp. 257–324.

"EMU@10—Successes and challenges after 10 years of Economic and Monetary Union" European Commission, 2008.

European Commission (2006) "Public Finances in EMU" European Economy No. 3.

Frankel, Jeffrey A. and Rose, Andrew K. (1996), "The Endogeneity of the Optimum Currency Area Criteria" NBER Working Paper W5700.

IMF Country Report No. 07/259 Euro Area Policies: Selected Issues, July 2007.

McKinnon, R.I. (1963) "Optimum Currency Areas" *American Economic Review* Vol. 53, No. 4, pp. 717–25.

Mundell, R.A. (1961) "A Theory of Optimum Currency Areas" *American Economic Review*, Vol. 51, No. 4, pp. 657-65.

Sibert, Anne (2007) Diverging Competitiveness in the Euro area. Briefing paper for the Committee on Economic and Monetary Affairs (ECON) of the European Parliament for the quarterly dialogue with the President of the European Central Bank.

Wyplosz, Charles (2007) "The Maastricht Criteria" Briefing notes to the Econ Committee of the Europea Parliament, Third Quarter, 2007.

CHAPTER 7

The EU Budget Review: Managing Diversity for a Growing EU[1]

I. Introduction[2]

After over half a century, Europe has emerged as a fairly integrated union of Member States. If initially much of the integration process was inward looking, aimed at ensuring well-being within the Union's borders and extinguishing political rivalries of long vintage, the reality of the 21st century compels the EU to re-examine itself. An inward looking approach is no longer sufficient. Globalisation, security of energy supply, the rise in food and energy prices, global warming, and the enormous progress of Asian economies are just some of the new challenges that the EU needs to deal with in order to maintain and further develop the well-being of its citizens.

The review and reform of its budget are essential steps that the Union must take in order to increase its capacity to face the major challenges of the 21st century. The European Commission's Consultation Paper on reviewing the EU budget is more than welcome. A review on principles and content without taboos, where everything is examined, is a suitable approach for fostering debate. The results of the consulta-

---

[1] This chapter relies on a report on the EU Budgetary Review which was presented at a seminar held in Brussels in March 2008. This report was prepared by Daniel Dăianu (as coordinator), Cătălin Păuna, Alina-Stefania Ujupan and Liviu Voinea.

[2] At the 2006 December Summit the European Council asked the Commission to carry out a review of the budget of the European Union by 2008/2009, paying particular attention to the Common Agricultural Policy and the own resources system.

In September 2007, the European Commission launched a Consultation Paper, which started the debate on the EU budget review. This document presents a non-governmental view, which aims to contribute to this debate.

tion process will most likely be the basis for an eventual reform of the EU budget.

This is an opinion on the EU budgetary review. It does not represent any government position nor is it an in-depth analysis of the minutia of the debate. It is rather a reflection on how the EU budget could better serve the interests of the Union's citizens in the years to come, focused on the current main budget items in relation to both internal and external challenges of the Union. Its aim is to think in European terms while not overlooking the peculiar challenges which emerging economies within the Union are facing.

The first section addresses the evolutionary process of the EU budget into what is now the lowest common denominator between the interests of Member States and those of the European Institutions. The second section refers to major challenges that beset the Union and their implications for its budget. The third part tackles the principles upon which the budget review and eventual reform should be based. The fourth section regards what actually could be reformed on both the expenditure and the revenue sides of the budget, while the last section discusses issues related to the implementation of this reform.

II. The History of the EU Budget: A Small Economic Instrument of Great Political Clout

Compared to federal or national budgets, the EU budget is small and cannot be used as a macroeconomic tool. Initially, the Community budget was a mere fund of less than 0.01% of the average Community GNP,[3] which covered only administrative expenditures (see Fig. 12). It was the creation of the Common Agricultural Policy (CAP) that boosted the budget to ceilings close to 0.5% of the average Community GNI[4] in the 1970s. The accession of new Member States in 1973 (Ireland, Denmark and the UK), 1981 (Greece) and 1985 (Portugal and Spain), some of which were less interested in the CAP and were facing structural problems posed by industrial re-conversion and poor infrastructural development, along with the need to support the internal

---

[3] Gross National Product.
[4] Gross National Income.

market project, led to the emergence and development of the Cohesion Policy. This soon became the second largest item of the budget expenditure.

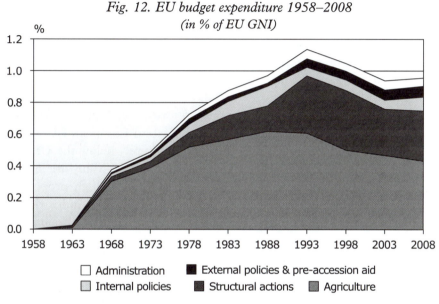

Fig. 12. EU budget expenditure 1958–2008 (in % of EU GNI)

Administration   External policies & pre-accession aid
Internal policies   Structural actions   Agriculture

Source: European Commission.
Available at: http://ec.europe.eu/budget/reform/history/history1957_en.htm

Despite the ascending trend of Community budget and expenditure diversification, it became increasingly hard to reach agreement on the budget among the Member States on the one hand, and among the European institutions, on the other hand. The classic conflict between net-contributors and net-beneficiaries was supplemented by the socioeconomic specificities of each Member State. These specificities materialised in numerous additional provisions, policy orientations, and side-deals in the budget expenditure, and in new emergence of correction mechanisms in the budget revenue.[5] The increase in the European Parliament's legitimacy and power over the budget, and its disagreements with the European Commission and the Council almost led to

---

[5] The first correction mechanism was the UK rebate, introduced at the 1984 Fontaindeblue Summit.

a decision-making deadlock in the 1980, when the Parliament twice rejected the Community budget. The introduction of the Inter-institutional Agreements (1982) and of the Financial Perspectives (1988) was meant to minimise these issues by setting binding multi-annual expenditure ceilings and limiting agriculture expenditure, and by capping the own resources at a maximum of 1.2% of the Community GNP. The Inter-institutional Agreement between the Commission, the Council and the Parliament guarantees the cooperation among these institutions for the annual budgets, according to the framework set by the Financial Perspectives.

The Eastern Enlargement has posed further challenges for the setting of the EU budget. The Central and Eastern European EU candidate countries have economies with GDPs severely below the Union's average (as low as 35% of the EU-15 average GDP). Many are in serious need of infrastructural development and have a high proportion of their labour force occupied in agriculture and older industries. A continuation of the financial assistance under CAP and Cohesion Policy without alterations would have led the EU budget expenditure way above the own resources limit of 1.27% of the EU GNP.[6] A new approach had to be found.

An increase of the EU budget revenue was not an option that the net-contributors were willing to take given the strains already being posed by the implementing the Economic and Monetary Union (EMU) and the decreasing public support for European integration. Furthermore, globalisation and increasing world competition, on the back of slowed economic growth in Western Europe have driven net contributors to a situation wherein solidarity with one's citizens may come at the expense of solidarity with other European states. Consequently, the 2000–2006 Financial Perspectives for the first time established a cap for European financial assistance at 4% of Member States' own GDP and the own resources correction mechanisms were extended to Sweden, Germany and the Netherlands. The 2007–2013 Financial Perspectives, were agreed with more additional provisions

---

[6] The 1.27% ceiling was established by the 1992–1999 Financial Perspectives. This was changed in 2002 with the GNP/GNI change on National Accounts and recalculated at 1.24% GNI.

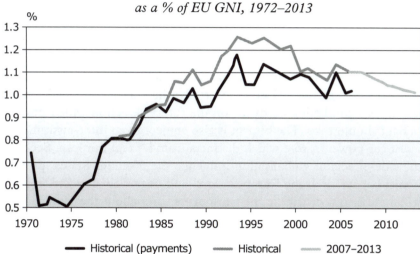

Fig. 13. Evolution of EU budget commitments as a % of EU GNI, 1972–2013

Source: The UK Foreign and Commonwealth Office.

than previous frameworks[7] and maintained the correction mechanisms for the four net-contributors (the UK, Sweden, The Netherlands and Germany). Furthermore, although the own resources cap was established at 1.24% EU GNI average for the first time, the budget of the Union decreased to 1.045% of the average EU GNI, out of which less than 1% will be used in real terms. This decrease is quite telling as to the propensity of donors to raise the EU budget.

This section has examined the evolution of the EU budget, from inception, when its primary role was to provide the Union with administrative pocket change, to its current key position as the lowest common denominator between the interests of the Member States and the EU Institutions. As the purse strings of Europe tighten, we are forced to face serious questions. A fundamental condition for having an operational EU budget is solidarity among Member States. I contest that a more effective EU budget should not be capped at merely 1% EU GNI average, as a matter of principle, and should not have special provisions or correction mechanisms.

---

[7] Only Cohesion Policy contains 17 additional provisions, out of which just four concern the new Member States.

Related to the challenges currently facing the EU budget, it is clear that three key obstacles stand in the way of the Union's continued budgetary development. First, the Community budget must meet the challenges of responding to different and sometimes incompatible national interests and to different integration paradigms. The ongoing dispute between those who favour deeper integration and those who would rather see the EU in a looser form has raged for decades now, and places conflicting demands on the future direction which the EU budget should take. The budget is also subject to an inter-institutional quest for power, a role which distracts from its real purpose. Second, the side-effects of globalisation influence the Member States' protectionist behaviour at the European level and negatively impacts on their willingness to redistribute their resources throughout the Union. And finally, the mismanagement of EU funds triggers more support for subsidiarity and increased national competences in EU policy-making. There is, therefore, an increasing reluctance to transfer competences, responsibility and resources to a European level.

Although politically the EU budget is a unique joint effort of a large number of countries, which chose to put together their resources for common goals, due to these obstacles, it remains an economic tool of low impact.

The challenges that the Union is facing externally and internally call for a deeper reflection concerning the purpose, the structure and the size of the EU budget. I will now proceed to examine these challenges, and their implications for EU budgetary reform in greater detail.

III. The European Union in the New Global Context: Challenges and Opportunities

The European Union is the most successful peace project that humankind has created so far. The post-war period was a rough test for the European nations in terms of political and economic recovery. Poverty, scarcity of food and avoiding another destructive war were then the main challenges to which the founding fathers tried to meet by putting in place the European project. At a time when state intervention was needed to sustain and develop food production, the creation of a

Common Agricultural Policy (CAP) was an appropriate tool to solve the needs of then six Member States. Moreover, the increased interdependence among the European states led to the creation of the Single Market, a significant economic block at the world level. This initial leap of faith by the founding fathers has proved a resounding success. Europe recovered economically and has enjoyed the longest peace period in its history.

Nonetheless, the global context has fundamentally changed during the past decades. The Union has deepened and widened and currently faces powerful exogenous as well as endogenous pressures. In a dynamic world, the Union is required to prove its own ability to act and maintain itself as a major actor on the global scene. At the same time, a big internal challenge is to manage its own ever increasing complexity. This section addresses the challenges facing the European Union and explores the means by which they can be tackled. These challenges cannot leave the EU budget unaffected.

A. EXOGENOUS CHALLENGES—THE CHALLENGES OF GLOBALISATION

Globalisation *per se* is the overarching exogenous challenge to the Union. It is a phenomenon that embeds a range of variables. Globalisation creates winners and losers. It stimulates development, economic growth and technological progress, but not evenly and ubiquitously. At the same time, its less benign effects take their toll on the labour force, the environment, and security concerns. Interdependence leads to greater difficulties in tackling global and environmental issues and can make international financial markets more fragile. The dangers of re-location and stiff competition cause protectionist attitudes in the wealthier countries of the world, which in turn increase poverty in developing areas and lead to massive illegal immigration to prosperous regions. For the European Union globalisation has materialised in challenges, these challenges are as follows.

1 Defining Ourselves among the Newly Emerging Global Powers

If the 19th century was the century of European leadership and the 20th century was that of American leadership, the 21st century will, probably, belong to the booming Asian economies. The challenge for the European Union is to speed up its economic growth and enhance its vigour in order to face its competitors. The European Union responded to global competitive pressures by launching the Lisbon Strategy, aiming to become the most competitive and dynamic knowledge-based economic area in the world by 2010.[8] This overall goal is an ambitious and potentially presumptuous one. In addition, some would argue that one-sided emphasis on competitiveness can strain "the European Social Model." But the goal reflects a *prise de conscience* as to the rapidly and dramatically changing global environment.

A refocus of EU and Member States' actions on increasing competitiveness by fostering innovation and technological development and investing in education is a sensible approach. However, the implementation of such measures in practice is not straightforward and there is a common agreement among policy-makers and academics that much more needs to be done.[9] The increasing complexity of the Union limits the extent to which a comprehensive strategy can be designed at the European level.

The approach to achieving the Lisbon goals taken by several EU Member States already provides us with highly valuable experience. In particular, the reform experience of the Scandinavian countries over the past decade, which should act as a major lesson for the rest of the EU. Regardless of how different national circumstances may be these experiences provide valuable lessons about the potency of national policy-making. Increasing EU competitiveness translates into more adaptive social structures, more R&D and more flexible markets.

EU Member States have different internal characteristics and may design different strategies to tackle the tension between fostering economic growth and reforming their social systems. However, in order to optimize outcomes, Member States should prioritise their actions and learn from each other's experiences. There should be more cross-border dialogue when designing strategies. The EU budget can act as a lever and foster better results if more resources are allocated for enhancing competitiveness, for raising R&D.

---

[8] European Council Conclusions, March 2000.
[9] Please see Sapir (2003), Kok (2004) and the strategic report on the Lisbon Strategy for launching the new cycle (2008–2010).

2 Dealing with Immigration and Security Challenges Posed by Globalisation

One of the hallmarks of globalisation is an increase in migration. Among the challenges facing the Union as a result of this mass migration will be dealing with the inevitable increase in illegal immigration, and potentially heightened security threats, including terrorism. Despite enlargement fatigue, the Union is still subject to a process of territorial enlargement, with the pending accession of other Balkan countries. The Consultation Paper of the Commission rightly indicates that the Union's borders are extending ever closer to less developed countries, areas which are increasingly adversely affected by globalisation. Massive illegal immigration, a clash of civilisations[10] and heightened terrorist threats are major issues which must be addressed. These issues demand a two-fold focus of EU action. Internally, the priorities are to strengthen the Union borders, to design comprehensive and common European immigration and asylum policies, to facilitate intercultural dialogue, and to ease the integration of immigrants within European societies. The EU budget is part of the instrument-mix to use as a response to the needs in this area.

Externally, the EU's goal to be a global actor asks for an active approach and joint actions with other world powers to tackle problems in the less developed areas of the world, and not only of a financial kind. Currently the EU is the largest world donor of external aid. Still, greater efforts are required. Issues such as containing and combating diseases in the third world, securing drinkable water, fighting poverty around the world, and reviewing the Doha Trade Round make up an urgent agenda to be addressed in a more structural way.

3 How to Strike a Balance between Protectionism and Trade Liberalisation?

A reduction in the protectionist measures of the wealthier countries would allow more fair trade and easier market access for non-subsidised agricultural products from less developed areas. Yet, this would lead to significant harm in the European agricultural sector, in the short run, and would increase dependence on other areas of the world,

---

[10] To use Samuel Huntington's terminology.

making Europe more vulnerable. One cannot oppose globalisation; that is certain. However, one can find more appropriate strategies to benefit from it and minimise its side-effects. Protectionism is not the solution, nor is unconstrained liberalisation.

The Union and its budget face the challenge of finding an appropriate balance between enhancing openness in order to fostering growth, and ensuring that its citizens are not paying unfair costs. We must resist the temptations of policy oversimplification and fundamentalism.[11] Finding an appropriate balance brings to the fore an ethical dimension of EU policies. This dimension regards both the people of the developing world and EU's own citizens. The role of the EU budget in this context is to sustain phasing-out mechanisms and re-orientation programmes for those whose subsidies are cut, and at the same time, to sustain together with the Member States, developing programmes in the third world and crisis management actions in conflict areas. Excessive dependence on third parties leads to insecurity and losses of bargaining power and should be avoided, particularly when strategic commodities, like energy are at stake.

Currently half of the energy needs of the European Union are ensured via imports. By 2030, the proportion of imports will reach 65% of total consumption.[12] Most imports come from Russia and the Middle East. The latter is an area which is subject to instability and the quality of EU-Russia relations has been fluctuating over time. Oil and gas are and will be highly strategic commodities. The competition for oil and gas fields will intensify in the years to come, due to both supply and demand side dynamics; the latter being influenced mainly by the rapid development of Asian economies. How this competition would evolve in the future is a reason of concern for all Member States, as is nuclear proliferation, which may develop intensely under the guise of the quest for more renewable energy. These challenges demand a carefully tailored joint approach, due to the implications they may have for the Member States' and Union's external relations. Ensuring energy security is a fundamental prerequisite for the Union to sustain its growth targets and to remain a global actor in the long run. More

---

[11] One example of fundamentalism is the inability to distinguish between liberalisation and deregulation.

[12] Belkin (2007).

efficient and ecological energy supply capabilities must be developed in order to minimise dependence on third parties.

4 Environmental Challenges Posed by Globalisation and How to Tackle Them Through the EU Budget

The effects of global warming are becoming increasingly visible and worrying. The need for growth and development will strongly collide with ecological concerns unless a new development paradigm is implemented. By signing the Kyoto Protocol and setting ambitious targets for the reduction of CO2 emissions,[13] the EU has assumed a leading role and sets an example for increasing environmental protection standards. The economic costs of such measures are not fully visible yet, but are a factor which must be considered when designing future policy approaches. A balance must be struck between protecting the environment and making sure that economic growth is not excessively hindered.

Climate change and the economic rise of Asia give salience to food resources as future strategic commodities. This would, logically, impart to CAP reform a strategic component which does not seem to be taken into account sufficiently at present.

5 An Overview of the Budget's Role in Meeting the Exogenous Challenges Posed by Globalisation

The key to effectively dealing with the challenges of Globalisation is to ensure a set of policies which are sustainable. As some cogently argue the combination of low growth and high public expenditure is not viable in the long run.[14] The pressure for intense competition strains the welfare state and frustrates trade unions and citizens. The result materialises in policy trade-offs, such as those outlined above. These contradictions and the magnitude of the emerging challenges lead to the creation of an international policy agenda defined by issues such as: fair versus free trade, protecting the environment as a global public good, tackling abject poverty, combating security threats, and dealing

---

[13] On 23 January, the European Commission proposed a legislative package, which will enable the Union to achieve its ambitious targets in CO2 emissions and the development of renewable energy.

[14] Sapir *et al.* (2003).

with massive illegal migration. The dramatic changes under way open up the possibility for co-operative relationships, but also for new tensions. One may consider, in this regard, the growing need for energy and basic commodities in Asia, with China and India as the prime consumers, the unresolved geopolitical crises in various parts of the world, nuclear proliferation, and the struggle against terrorism.

It is noteworthy that there is a growing awareness that these are issues that need to be addressed at an international level, in a multilateral context, using collaborative approaches. The Davos Forum this year talked about innovative partnerships. In this context the role of the Union is important as it is the most integrated geo-political region of the world and can be a model of cooperation among countries. There is a need for international public goods, which can provide an alternative to national governments', whose initial impulse in response to increasing pressure from foreign markets and globalisation threats is to adopt protectionist policies. The EU Member States can benefit from the synergy of being more integrated and from experience of working together. The budget is one of the tools that the Union has and must be geared towards providing European public goods as an answer to the major challenges posed by globalisation. A solid answer is based on the sustainability of European actions, which can be ensured, provided that the unique character of the Union is considered. But this character also brings about sources of internal pressure.

B. Endogenous Challenges—Internal Challenges and the Conflicting Priorities of EU Member States

In varietate concordia[15] is Europe's current demos. It fully reflects the key characteristics of the European Union: complex and united. The degree of unity is fundamental to the means by which complexity is addressed within the Union. Managing complexity is the greatest inner challenge that the EU has to face. There is a series of common internal EU challenges which originate in a sort of institutional sclerosis, ageing population and demographics, cross-border cooperation, preserving/developing welfare standards, the functioning of the internal market

---

[15] United in diversity.

and further deepening and widening the Union. These challenges test the Member States' ability to tackle complex issues in a unified way.

There are too, among others, internal issues that place Member States on opposite sides or specific clusters; these issues refer to re-location, economic and institutional reforms, and absorption of EU funds.

1 Contradictory Opinions on the Role of the EU Budget in an Enlargement Union

The Eastern Enlargement has increased the complexity of the Union, posing greater challenges for its management as an integrated system. Complexity is embedded in political, economic, social and cultural dimensions. The integration process is shaped by conflicting paradigms: Advocates of federalist approaches to integration clash with those defending the intergovernmental view. President Barroso states in the Consultation Paper that the review is about a "vision for Europe." This is very hard to reach when on the federalist–intergovernmental axis; Member States are divided in several constellations and have different visions for Europe. These visions are mirrored in the various and sometimes opposing national interests, and in the clashes of different interpretations of challenges and opportunities for the Union.

From the political perspective, the size of the EU budget is paramount, particularly for those who reject transfers of national sovereignty to the European level. From the economic point of view, the EU budget is, basically, a redistribution tool, and its impact is far from what federalists would have envisaged. The very size and structure of the EU budget is a result of the EU complexity and illustrates the Union's metabolism.

The successive waves of enlargement have increased further the variable geometry within the Union, particularly concerning social and economic variety. The European Union reveals several forms of its arch-typical model. One can distinguish between a Scandinavian, a so-called "continental capitalism," a Mediterranean model, and an Anglo-Saxon model. In between are sub-models characteristic of the New Member States. All of them share basic features of the European Social Model. The Union is strained by an apparent contradiction between well entrenched welfare models which it wants to preserve and the need to make markets more flexible in order to strengthen economic growth and diminish unemployment. The rising variety of economic and social conditions, particularly with the Eastern Enlargement, and the broadening range of divergent policy needs and views among member countries concerning the challenges they face and the appropriate means to tackle them risk bringing policy coordination and EU policy-making to a standstill. The adoption of the Lisbon Treaty can be judged in this context as well. This tension will affect the review process and the future reform of the budget, hindering objective decisions on budget and policy design.

2 The Difficulties Posed by an Archaic Institutional Structure

The Union is hampered by its own institutional structure, which has not evolved according to the needs imposed by its growing complexity. Reforms are essential in order to tackle the challenges posed by globalisation. The current institutional set-up impedes these reforms. If the Lisbon Agenda was the EU answer to globalisation challenges, the Lisbon Treaty is an attempt to streamline the malfunctioning institutions that slow down and sometimes block policy reform and successful implementation. The Lisbon Treaty extends the powers of the European Parliament to the entire budget. This constitutes a major step forward in tackling the democratic deficit within the Union. An eventual reform of the budget itself should streamline further decision-making, particularly concerning the Financial Perspectives, by re-focusing the budget on providing European public goods that are in all Member States' interest.

3 Dealing with the Fall-Out of Changing European Demographics

Ageing population and falling birth rates endanger the welfare state systems. Social protection by the state is no longer feasible, as it used to be, with continuous early retirement and a decreasingly active labour force. European policy-makers showed a unified will to tackle these challenges through the Lisbon and Gothenburg Agendas. Nonetheless, employment and training targets have not been fully reached yet, particularly in the New Member States, and the life-long learning process has not been implemented adequately.[16] The EU budget ought

---

[16] See and the strategic report on the Lisbon Strategy for launching the new cycle (2008–2010).

to and can contribute to tackling Europe's demographic problem by supporting further development of life-long learning initiatives and facilitating the education and integration of immigrants. However, given the size and the salience of these issues, it is ever more important for national governments to coordinate their policies, possessing as they do, of more powerful instruments than the Union does.

Relocation within the Union can raise unemployment in old Member States and increase foreign investment and create jobs in the new ones. It stirs dissatisfaction and rivalry among EU citizens and challenges the solidarity between European nations.

Surges in migration may have a trigger function and add to already emerging tensions between the residents of Central and Eastern Europe and some of the EU-15 Member States.[17] The functioning of the labour markets opposes insiders to outsiders. This division is symptomatic of the erosion of social cohesion. A proper harmonisation of the European space can lead to balanced development, avoiding shocks. This requires differentiated policy measures adapted to the economic and geographical specificities of the Union. A better instrumental mix can address this challenge. The EU budget is not meant to have the main role in this case. Regulatory tools are more suitable. Nonetheless, the EU budget can contribute to improving the circulation of services and knowledge by investing in high-tech communication facilities and networks.

4 Disparate Economic Conditions across the Internal Market and the Challenges They Pose

The functionality of the single market implies the existence of the four liberties and the free circulation of knowledge.[18] Questions still exist as to whether these five conditions have yet been properly implemented.

Many voices have expressed their fears over the consequences of the increased outsourcing and off-shoring of activities by the private sector.[19] New Member States were blamed for allegedly prac-

---

[17] See, for instance, the "Polish plumber" issue in the UK, and the tensions in Italy and Spain related to Romanian workers.
[18] The European Commission refers to knowledge as the "fifth freedom" of the Single Market (COM[2007] 803 final).
[19] See, for instance, the recent Nokia decision to move a plant out of Germany to Cluj, Romania.

ticing unfair competition by offering lower taxes, which would further attract jobs to Eastern Europe. This assessment of EU policies is misleading and misjudged. Structural Funds, for instance, should be seen as an overall subsidy provided by the EU to its least developed Member States, a policy which results from a sense of solidarity among EU countries and a practical means by which to foster cohesion across frontiers. The consequence is that advanced economies, which have been supporters of free trade and open markets, return to economic nationalism. Cohesion in the Union could be enhanced if policies were designed for the West and the East in order to bring them closer together. These policies would help achieve real convergence.

The EU budget can play an identity-enhancing role and develop a sense of ownership of and belonging to the Union. More involvement of the EU citizens in understanding and responding to change will increase support for European public policies and goods.

5 Harmonisation and Growth: An EU Budget for an Ever-Expanding Europe?

The process of EU deepening and widening has to evolve in conjunction and as a response to external challenges, despite claims of integration stagnation as a result of the new provisions of the Lisbon Treaty.[20] Some of the New Member States still need to integrate into the Schengen Area and eventually adopt the euro, as part of their accession obligations. The pressure of implementing the Maastricht criteria can hinder their faster economic development. There are, too, serious issues to address related to increasing absorption capacity. Further enlargement to include the Western Balkans is a must, and a condition for preserving security within the continent. Moreover, were it to take place, the accession of Turkey to the Union would increase Europe's geo-political reach and control over energy sources and transportation routes. Nonetheless, the accession of Turkey would add several other dimensions to the Union's complexity and pose economic and cultural challenges.

---

[20] The Treaty clarifies that the European Union is a union of Member States (see in particular Art.1-6, Reform Treaty).

Given the endogenous and exogenous challenges mentioned above it is obvious that the Union needs to achieve a higher economic growth. At the same time, it is clear that the traditional European welfare state is no longer feasible anymore. Reforms are needed in this regard. In consequence, the social contract between citizens and their nation states and between citizens and the Union must be redefined in such a way that sustainable economic growth does not impair social cohesion, this growth must be complimented by an adequate production of European public goods. The EU budget review is part of the redefinition of the social contract with the citizens of the Union. The budget must act as a lever for the development of a self-assured EU, confident of its internal cohesion and its place in the world.

IV. Principles of the Reform

There is a general agreement that the EU budget needs reform. The budget review is the first step in this direction. The issue is however, where we want the EU to be and how much we are prepared to pay for it. In order to ensure that it is feasible, the budget review and the future reform of the budget need to take into account several principles. They should have as a starting point the complexity of the Union, thus the realities in all the Member States. They must consider the Treaty provisions, as well as the principle of solidarity and public opinion. And finally, they must lead to a better coordination of EU policies. In consequence, all policy items must be dealt with at the same time.

A. The Complexity of the Union and Widely Different Realities in Member States Must be Borne in Mind

Earlier, it has been stated that managing its complexity is the biggest challenge that the Union has, because complexity is intrinsically linked to the Union's existence in diversity. A discussion over the EU budget should lead to a budgetary structure that better answers the current EU priorities. This implies considering the Union's complexity, and in particular the variety of economic and social circumstances. The inferior economic situation of the New Member States, some with GDPs of one or two thirds of the Union average, should be considered. In addition to this, sensitivities of older Member States in relation to budgetary spending should not be ignored. This is one of the reasons why the transition to a newly shaped budget should be gradual, and phasing-out/in strategies should be designed.

B. EU Budgetary Action Must be Better Targeted and More Coherent

No budget item should be dealt with separately, as policies are interdependent and one should avoid the possibility of developing overlapping and/or contradictory policy measures.

C. Solidarity Must Apply

Thus a newly designed budget needs to be advantageous for all the Member States and for the Union as a whole. This should not be understood as a new reading of the *juste retour* approach. On the contrary, any change in the budget structure should lead to an increase in the added-value of European intervention, which would benefit the entire European Union, by improving resource allocation.

D. The Lisbon Treaty May Be the New Regulatory Framework for Any Budgetary Reform

The Lisbon Treaty, if ratified, will be the new basis for EU primary law, and therefore, will set the framework of the any review or reform of the budget. For the first time, the Treaty defines the types of competences that the EU may have in policy making and allocates policies according to this classification. It sets new provisions for the area of freedom, security and justice, for energy policy, which is upgraded to shared competences, and for external relations, reflecting increased political will to jointly manage these issues. Old policies still have an important basis in the Treaty. Their objectives are maintained, as is the case with the CAP, and in some cases even strengthened, as is the case with the Cohesion Policy. The latter is targeted not only at economic and social cohesion, but also at territorial cohesion and there is a stronger emphasis on solidarity among Member States.

The Treaty clarifies that any EU action must respect three fundamental principles: conferral,[21] subsidiarity[22] and proportionality.[23] The application of the principles of subsidiarity and proportionality should establish the added-value of EU intervention. Consequently, current EU policies should be subject to a value-added test, according to these principles. Any policy, which is not a Union exclusive competence, which has a Treaty basis and passes the tests posed by the principles of subsidiarity and proportionality should be reflected in the budget, where financial means is considered to be the most appropriate instrument of implementation.

As for the own resources of the EU budget, the Lisbon Treaty has new provisions in this regard and explicitly specifies the possibility of introducing new resources, as well as the possibility of eliminating old ones. This indicates that for the first time there is awareness at the political level that a better response to the challenges of the 21st century also entails a reform of the own resources system of the Union and opens the way to overtly debate this issue.

E. Public Opinion Must be Considered

Although previous reforms have been carried out without particular attention to the public opinion, the French and the Dutch "no" to the Constitutional Treaty revealed the size of the democratic deficit and the necessity to consider public opinion in European deliberations. This fact has been further underlined by "the Irish No" to the Lisbon Treaty, and mounting opposition in a number of other Member States to the competition of the ratification process. A simple survey of the Eurobarometer publications on European public opinion

---

[21] The principle of conferral states that the Union shall act only within the limits of the competences conferred upon it by the Member States.

[22] The principle of subsidiarity applies for the areas that do not fall under exclusive competences of the Union and states that the Union shall act only in so far as the objectives of the proposed action cannot be sufficiently achieved by the Member States, either at central, regional or local level, but can rather by reason of scale and effects of the proposed action, be better achieved at the Union level.

[23] Art. 5 of the Reform Treaty. The principle of proportionality establishes that the content and form of the Union action shall not exceed what is necessary to achieve the objectives of the Treaties.

indicates that there is great support for European level decision-making concerning research and technology, environmental protection, energy policy, foreign affairs, immigration and security, and cooperation with the third world. Some of these issues are priorities already reflected in the Lisbon Agenda. Consequently, a refocus of the budgetary expenditure towards these areas seems to be fully justified. It is noteworthy also that the same Eurobarometer results indicate constant and fairly high support for EU competences in agriculture and cohesion policies, despite these being blamed, by some, as "old policies," which are unable to respond to today's challenges. A sudden cut in the allocations for these policies would not be welcome by a considerable part of the European public in both new and old Member States.

F. EU Budgetary Review Must Coincide with a Review of National Budgets

The review and reform of the EU budget should lead to a reform of the national budgets of Member States. This is essential in order to ensure the compatibility and synergy of EU and national policy-making instruments. Regardless of the issues that the EU budget would tackle, it would be impossible for EU action alone to provide solutions. One needs coherent actions at all policy-making levels.

The Commission's consultation paper raises the issue of EU budget's capacity to respond to changing needs. Both public opinion and political will indicate that there is scope for more concentration on forward-looking challenges and the promotion of the European values and standards to the out-side world. Evidence of this can be seen in the Lisbon Agenda and its strong external dimension. Moreover, the same indicators show that old policies are still on the agenda, thus equilibrium must be found between continuity and change. The question is not necessarily about what policies should suffer cuts in the budgetary expenditure, it is also about whether new implementation means can be designed to improve policy effectiveness, and to increase the budget's capacity of better answering to new challenges.

V. Reviewing and Reforming the Budget: Concrete Measures to Take

Previous sections address the exogenous and endogenous challenges to the Union and the principles that the review/reform should consider. These challenges and principles establish, in our opinion, the context for analysing concrete measures to take for updating the European budget. This section approaches both expenditure and revenue related issues. It tackles the issue of what constitutes a European public good, and how these public goods may be financed. It also provides an in-depth analysis of the CAP, and Cohesion Funds of the European Union, and prospects for improvement through budgetary reform. Finally, this chapter examines the role of R&D funding in the future of the budget, and of the budget as a tool of the European Union on the World Stage. The section ends with an examination of possible future sources of revenue to augment the already overloaded EU budget.

A. EUROPEAN PUBLIC GOODS

1 A Definition of European Public Goods

An adequate supply of European public goods is one of the ways to address the challenges facing the EU and the budget should contribute to that. One needs clear criteria, first to establish what qualifies as a European public good and second, to decide on the most appropriate instrument mix to ensure its supply; hence the extent to which the EU budget can and should contribute to this objective. Expenditure should be determined by looking at the added-value of EU action and what may constitute a European public good. Key policy cases are also addressed.

The issue of European public goods is a dynamic concept. What constitutes a European public good is a function of the priorities that exist at the EU level. These priorities hinge on the state of economies and societies and change according to inner and outer challenges.

There is a set of criteria that may apply in order to establish what would constitute public goods, and consequently areas where intervention at the EU level is justified, bringing added-value to Member States' cooperation.

First, fiscal federalism offers standard economic criteria to assess the added-value of EU action. According to an economic interpretation, EU action is justified only in cases of market failure, i.e., the existence of economies of scale or scope, and of spillovers caused by externalities. Nonetheless, EU added-value is a complex concept and cannot be captured only through economic criteria. It has several political connotations including: the advancement of EU aims and the promotion of EU values outside the European Union, the maintenance and development of the international salience of the EU block, and ultimately, the establishment of stable geo-political state of affairs in the European region. In addition, cost-benefit analysis, while useful to a point cannot provide the whole picture. An example of this is the fact that one cannot internalise all imaginable effects of climate change and future generations cannot vote when we decide about their future.

Second, the Treaty establishes that subsidiarity and proportionality are the essential criteria against which to assess the necessity of EU intervention, and the added-value therein. The principle of subsidiarity clearly states that EU intervention should take place only if "the objectives of the proposed action cannot be sufficiently achieved by the Member States, either at the central level or at regional and local level, but can rather, by reason of scale or effects … be better achieved at Union level."[24] The principle of proportionality limits the content and form of EU action solely to what is necessary to achieve the objectives set out in the Treaties.

Member States themselves have already agreed on strengthening their joint action in a series of areas. In that sense, European public goods are considered to be energy security, environmental protection, security cross-border cooperation, and Lisbon Agenda targets. Besides these, there are European public goods which tend to be overlooked by current debates, but whose importance is rapidly increasing. For example, in the context of climate change and the necessity of increasing internal energy supply, fertile soils are a powerful asset, which needs to be strategically rated and used. Central and Eastern Europe is rich in such soils. A new focus of the CAP towards better management of

---

[24] Art. 5, Reform Treaty.

agricultural assets is the appropriate way forward, and should make use of all suitable tools.

Furthermore, there is the added-value of the EU budget itself, which is frequently ignored by some. Although economically speaking, it is small and does not have the necessary power to act as a milieu-shaping and regulatory tool, as it is the case with national budgets, the EU budget has so far been a political asset for the Union. It does have a compensation function in the decision-making process.[25] It has acted as a consensus instrument, enabling the EU to deepen and widen, ensuring at the same time that each Member State benefits somehow from the process. This is regarded by some as a negative function of the budget, supporting the *juste retours* principle. This is not necessarily the case. It has been stated earlier that the greatest internal challenge of the EU is to manage its own complexity. The budget currently is a tool that helps tackle this complexity by answering the different needs of Member States and supporting a win–win approach to decision-making. It is questionable whether this character of the EU budget will ever disappear. A radical change is needed in the way Member States perceive their Union membership. Nonetheless, efforts should be made in order to improve the capacity of the Union to better respond to internal and external pressures. A reform that increases the sense of ownership and develops the European identity through fostering the creation of European public goods would be a formidable step forward in this respect.

2 How to Establish the Added Value of a European Public Good?

The starting point is the Treaty, and in it the principles of conferral, proportionality and subsidiarity, as defined in Art. 5. Thus the case for EU action is made when, by the scale and the effects of the proposed action, best results can be obtained at the EU level. Pelkmans proposes a test for subsidiarity, having the Treaty as a starting point.[26] However, he admits that his test is a functional one and should be of use to policy-makers as a cost-benefit analysis rather than as a set of criteria, that would establish which actions should take place at the EU level. The interpretation of the Treaty conditions should be broad, and not reduced to economic reasoning alone.

---

[25] Enderlein *et al.* (2007).
[26] See Pelkmans (2006).

The effects are not only about spillovers and economies of scale or scope. They are also about enforcing cohesion in the Union, developing the European identity and strengthening its position in the outside world. One should not forget that the European project was originally implemented because the Member States alone could not adequately deal with various challenges. In the 1950s these challenges related to achieving peace and re-building Europe. In the 21st century they relate, principally, to coping with globalisation pressures in a successful way. Those who think that Member State coordination alone can solve these issues see only one side of the story. Coordination among nations does not ensure sufficient commitment and European nations, on their own, are often not strong enough to perform individually at the global level. The European Union must act together, in a united and timely manner. European public goods are those which help Europe to better tackle inner and outer challenges. They are of a wide variety and range from joint R&D projects, centres of scientific excellence throughout the Union, and skilled labour forces to a socially, economically and territorially cohesive Europe which can better perform at the world scale; Europe can count among its assets good quality and well managed agricultural resources, together with numerous environmental friendly energy sources, and the power to deliver support to developing countries and aid crisis management around world. These in turn can reduce threats posed by migration and terrorism in Europe and help dealing with global governance.

3 Which Policies Provide European Public Goods?

EU policies provide European public goods when they respond to challenges that affect the Union as a whole. Policy objectives should be adjusted and all the instruments available to the Union should be considered when designing EU level interventions. This section addresses the way in which EU policies can tackle challenges and the role that financial assistance should have in the current context. There is little a future budget reform can do concerning policy objectives. These are already established by the Treaty. It is highly unlikely that there will be another Treaty reform in the near future. In consequence, should it not be possible to alter policy objectives, one should improve delivery mechanisms. All the policy-making instruments of the Union should be considered in order to assign the most appropriate instrument mix for every policy. It is well-known that the EU is a regulatory giant and a budgetary dwarf. Spending is just one of the three instruments it can use. The other two are legislation and guidelines. It is not always the case that an important policy objective can be reached solely through financial means, and should therefore be reflected in the budget. The obvious example is competition policy, which is one of the exclusive EU competences. Competition policy is implemented mainly by using the EU's regulatory power and benefits from reduced financial assistance. A similar case could be environmental protection. The budget should reflect only those policy objectives that require financial intervention.

The exogenous and endogenous challenges highlighted earlier in this document pose specific challenges for every EU policy. On the one hand, there is broad consensus that the EU needs to improve its competitiveness and prevent the erosion of its position at the global level. There is also consensus that environmental protection and global warming are issues that cannot wait and immediate action is needed. On the other hand, traditional policies are still important, particularly for the New Member States. The Cohesion Policy has undergone several changes and is increasingly focusing on Lisbon targets. The Common Agricultural Policy needs reform, but this reform does not mean it should be disposed off completely. These two policies, as well as competitiveness and the EU actions at the global level are examined below.

B. The Common Agricultural Policy

The mission for the Common Agricultural Policy is twofold. On the one hand, its objectives, as stated by the Treaty, should continue to be met by the future reform. On the other hand, CAP, as is the case with all EU policies, must adapt to the challenges posed by globalisation and to new internal EU pressures.

The global context is affecting agriculture dramatically. There is increasing pressure on the demand for agricultural products due to the formidable progress of Asian economies. This rise puts upward pressure on the price of basic commodities, including cereals.[27]

---

[27] The current international financial crisis, and an eventual recession in large areas of the world economy, may dampen this tendency for a while. But over the longer term the trend seems to be quite clear.

Likewise, there is considerable pressure on food supply due to the side-effects of global warming on agricultural plots and sources of water.

Both supply- and demand-side dynamics on food world markets will dramatically reduce the need for agricultural subsidies in the Union. However, the impact of global dynamics on the efficiency of farms varies widely and any reform of the CAP must take this into account. The CAP has to be re-examined against this new background. While the volume of subsidies should diminish decisively over time, the EU needs to develop intervention mechanisms to tackle risk and allow for crisis management. At the same tine, the large variation in farm efficiency throughout the EU should be considered. More importance needs to be placed on the value of good land, which constitutes the EU's main agricultural asset (measurements via narrowly constructed cost-benefit analyses are, arguably, misleading). Good quality land and water are European public goods of growing importance and should be managed accordingly, at both national and EU levels. The CAP should be designed in such a way as to better answer to these new challenges. The allocation of resources should reflect this.

1 Current Imbalances in the Distribution of CAP Funds

An image of the EU complexity is illustrated by the very large structural differences among the EU members in the agricultural sector. Romania and Poland account for 48.5% of the total number of agricultural holdings in the EU27, and for 53.4% of the total number of small agricultural holdings (less than 5 ha). The CAP budget for these two countries, however, represents a much lower share in the total CAP expenditures (it will grow, nevertheless, up to 2013); the indicative ratio between the share in the CAP expenditures and the share in EU number of agricultural holdings is 1:10 for these countries, while the same ratio is 6:1 for Germany and 5:1 for the Great Britain. Italy and Spain also have a large share of EU agricultural holdings and of EU family farm labour force, but they too have an even larger share in EU agricultural gross value added (GVA)—which means that, in these countries, the agricultural labour force is more efficient, and the crops are oriented towards more value-added products.

France, Spain and Italy, which are among the top beneficiaries of the CAP, have also some of the highest shares of agricultural GVA

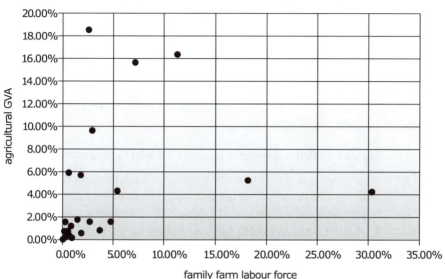

Fig. 14. *Labour force and value added, total agriculture, EU-27=100*

Source: based on Eurostat.
Note: the axes cross at non-weighted EU-27 average values.

of the EU27. This might be interpreted as the result of long-time support through CAP—something that is now in doubt for some of the New Member States, requisite of this type of assistance. Romania and Poland are the likely candidates for more funds, but Slovakia and Hungary also have small land plots; with about 90% of their agricultural holdings amounting to less than 5 ha. Moreover, Greece, Italy and Portugal have a high share of agricultural holdings of less than 5 ha, with ceilings above 70% of total in each case. All these countries would be in fact exposed to severe losses if the decoupled direct aids system is abandoned or if agricultural financing is severely reduced.

Previous reforms attempted to reduce market distortions which resulted from the implementation of the CAP; the results of these reforms are, however, questionable. Regarding the assessment of the 2003 reform, Roberts and Gunning-Trant conclude that moving toward single farm payments is likely to result in less distorted markets for agricultural products, but that there is still a large use of market distorting forms of support (tariffs, quotas, export subsidies) and that the decoupled "payments could maintain established distortions to production patterns."[28] The authors identify at least two reasons for this: expectations (farmers believe they are expected to continue production, and they also expect that a review of the CAP might change the emphasis again on production), and the cost of transfer (from a subsidised product to a non-subsidised one). Hennessy and Thorne, based on survey results in Ireland, hold that a considerable number of farmers would opt for using their decoupled payments in order to subsidise unprofitable production.[29]

2 Direct Payments: Problems with the Present CAP Framework

The first problem is that the distribution of direct payments is questionable from the point of view of social cohesion—as the Commission has stressed on a number of occasions (European Commission, 2007).In the EU-15, in 2005, 50% of beneficiaries received only 3% of total direct aids, while 2% of beneficiaries received 30% of total direct aids. In the ten New Member States that joined the Union in 2004 (NMSs-10), 93.1% of beneficiaries received 39% of total direct aids in 2005 (less than 1250 Euro per beneficiary farm), and 1.3% of beneficiaries received 45% of total direct aids. The higher share of beneficiaries receiving minimum amounts in NMSs-10 reflects the predominance of small farms in the region. But the problem of highly unfair distribution is valid all around the European Union, in the new states and in the old as well.

Secondly, given their stated objectives, the current distribution of direct payments does not achieve optimal results. The answer to both problems, however, is not further decoupling, because decoupling has already proven largely ineffective in this regard. Since the largest farms get most money, and since the largest farms also have the largest production potential, we could in fact expect that decoupling will lead to the same result—the subsidisation of production, for large farms. The solution is neither to reduce the support level while overall payments to big farms increase, nor increasing the amount of land per farmer to qualify for direct aid (both proposals are presented on the consultation's website). Both these proposals would only increase

---

[28] Roberts and Gunning-Trant (2007).
[29] Hennessy and Thorne (2005).

the inequality of payment distribution. The new situation of world food markets should lead to a reassessment of direct payments mechanisms. The reduction of the need for agricultural subsidies should be mirrored in the quantity of direct payments which large, efficient farms receive.

The payments for market interventions and direct aids are foreseen to decrease by 5.74% between 2007 and 2013.[30] The new state of world food markets further highlights the rationale for reducing the volume of direct payments required. However, the persistent unbalance between the two pillars of the CAP; the beneficiary countries and the beneficiary citizens,[31] on the one hand and, significant market distortions induced by the CAP on the other hand, urgently require reform. This would lead to reconsideration of the differing realities in the different Member States and of the significant differences in their agricultural assets, which shall remain substantial for the foreseeable future.

The Treaty (Art. 33 TEU) sets five objectives for the CAP: to increase agricultural productivity by developing technical progress, to ensure a good quality of life for the agricultural population, to stabilise markets, to guarantee the security of supply, and to ensure reasonable prices for food products. The CAP reform should not abdicate from these objectives; in contrast, it should better ensure that these objectives are clearly identified when resources are allocated.

There is no one way street for reform; and we should not assume that reform necessarily means a severe cut in expenditures, in the short run at least. There is an additional moral implication to the issue of reform: if, for example, the CAP is abandoned altogether, funds are cut across the board, or funds are redirected only based on performance, then the efficiency gaps between New Member States and other EU members (which benefited from the CAP for 40 years) will become of a chronic nature. There are several issues that need to be considered when deciding over CAP reform.

---

[30] *http://ec.europa.eu/agriculture/healthcheck/index_en.htm.*
[31] According to the Interinstitutional Agreement of 2006. See also Boulanger (2007).

3 Four Key Issues which Must Be Considered When Reforming the CAP

3a Migration of Farm Labourers

The first issue to consider is that farmers are a particular category of society; many of them have been increasingly threatened by the side effects of globalisation, and a new "ballgame" in world food markets does not automatically change the lot of small farms. In the New Member States agricultural land plots are severely fragmented. The retraining of agricultural labour force requires high investments and the creation of training programmes. An immediate side-effect of a failure to reskill these workers will be migration to urban areas, or abroad, unless appropriate alternatives for rural development are found. Here too, the New Member States have to face a greater challenge due to higher proportions of farmers in the total active labour force and infrastructural shortcomings.

There may also be a trade-off between subsidising agriculture and accepting emigration[32] in countries where the GDP/CAP is low. One could assume that maintaining CAP could potentially diminish the propensity to migrate. Less money to agriculture may translate, in poorer EU states, into higher incentives to leave in search of a higher income. Furthermore, as national governments in transition economies are generally unable to finance agriculture adequately, the CAP transfers may provide the incentive for some migrant workers to return home to rural areas. It is fair to say, however, that the propensity to migrate is mostly due to high wage differentials between East and West and it is not up to the CAP to solve this issue.

3b Limiting the Union's Dependence on Food Imports

Second, despite trade liberalisation, European capacity for food production must be valued and used so that dependence on external sources of food supply does not become excessive. This is a necessity, particularly in the case of imports from countries where veterinary and hygiene standards fall well below EU standards, and eventual pandemics could have serious effects on food supply in Europe. Food supply

---

[32] For example, half of the Romanian emigration to EU 2002–2006 (49%) comes from the rural area—see Sandu (2007).

to the European food market should be ensured where possible from internal sources.

3c Reform of the CAP—Its Effect on Other EU Policies

Third, when addressing the reform of the CAP, one should keep in mind that there are other related sectors and policies which will be implicitly affected by the reform. Environment, food safety, rural economy, competitiveness and trade are usually referred to in connection with the CAP. These issues are largely addressed by the CAP itself: the cross-compliance requirement helps protecting the environment; rural development is implied by the 2nd pillar of the CAP, while trade distortions have been diminished (at least in principle) by downsizing the intervention mechanisms in agricultural markets.[33] Therefore, any reform of the CAP should take account of the context in which it takes place, and of other EU policies which may be affected. Direct cost-based analysis in the form currently suggested,[34] is necessary, but it does not suffice to understand and analyse the CAP efficiency; opportunity costs should also be taken into consideration, and reform should take place with due regard to the wider framework of EU policies.

3d Agricultural Assets as European Public Goods of the 21st Century

The fourth issue meriting attention when considering reform of the CAP is how agricultural assets are defined in the 21st century and which of these are European public goods. Assets such as soil and water have increased in importance in the context of climate change. The preservation of the agricultural habitats should be a priority of CAP, so should be the good management of fertile soils. An excessive reduction of farming activities would lead to a considerable reduction in the

---

[33] Gros and Micosi (2005) say that the CAP, by pushing relative prices and incomes in favour of agriculture, discourages investment in industry and services. Moreover, they say that the new member states have a much larger potential in the latter sectors, and should therefore be less interested in supporting the CAP. Their assertion, however, is not substantiated by facts; on the contrary, the prices of production means grew faster than the prices of agricultural production, over the last 10 years.

[34] See European Parliament DG Internal Policies of the Union, Policy Department on Budgetary Affairs (2007) "The EU Added Value of Agricultural Expenditure—From Market to Multifunctionality—Gathering Criticism and Success Stories of the CAP" Brussels.

number of animals in Europe and to a loss in soil quality. Encouraging the production of organic food products is a must.[35] Energy security is an issue that touches upon agriculture too, given the possibility of developing biofuel crops, and wind powered stations, in cases where the landscape allows.

4 A Vision for the Future of the CAP

In consequence, a reform of the CAP should focus on a redistribution of expenditure with the possibility of co-financing by Member States. Targeting of funds must be improved. Re-orientation and the development of new skills among the current agricultural workforce demands that, more money be allocated to the second pillar of CAP, focused on rural development. NMSs in particular need to modernise agriculture, to develop rural infrastructure and diversify rural activities. Most of these resources should be generated by the reduction of payments to large farms, which represent the bulk of the financial resources allocated from CAP.

The sums allocated for the income-support objective for farms of less than 5 ha should continue as long as job alternatives are not available, while the sums allocated to large farms should be phased-out in accordance with the dynamics of world food markets.

Only by doing this can an effective decoupling of direct payments from production be achieved. Farms with large turnovers should therefore be excluded from direct payments except in exceptional circumstances. This proposal contrasts with the current modulation system being proposed, which envisages, by 2013, marginal cuts for large farms and no increases for small farms. Targeting can be improved by moving from multifunctional purposes to a more specific method of funding allocation. A part of direct aids should be allocated to income-support for farms less than 5 ha, this too could be co-financed by Member States. The other part of direct aids should be allocated for improving the cross-compliance of standards, soil and water management, and preservation of agricultural habitats.

---

[35] The increase of public health problems due to diabetes, coronary heart diseases and obesity, particularly among children, as a result of bad alimentation is worrying. It is important for Europe to have a healthy population in the context of speeding up economic growth, ageing population, and pressures of reform on the social welfare systems.

It is important, however, to agree on the direction which reform should take. This chapter argues that reform should focus on the redistribution of expenditure within the CAP, and on an improved targeting of these funds. While liberalisation of agricultural markets may currently be feasible for those large farms whose turnovers are robust enough to deal with significantly increased levels of competition, until the above measures are implemented to the benefit of smaller farms, such liberalisation will remain an impossibility. As indicated above, there are essential European public goods, which should be managed at the European level through balanced instrumental mix. This analysis focused on the role of financial assistance in agriculture, but legislative measures and guidelines should also be considered.

C. THE COHESION POLICY

The Cohesion Policy faces many challenges; amongst them are high expectations on the part of stakeholders, the threat of "re-nationalisation," and also, what is, in our opinion, a misguided criticism of the policy—namely; that it is responsible for re-location. There have been claims in previous negotiation rounds that Cohesion Policy does not deliver at a European level; and that particularly in the case of wealthier Member States, national governments could tackle regional disparities on their own. There have also been claims that Cohesion Policy favours re-location by simply transferring wealth from West to East, rather than reducing the gaps of development and advancing cohesion among EU regions. The recent decision by Nokia to close down a factory in Germany and to open a new one in Romania was interpreted by some EU politicians as a Cohesion Policy side-effect. The effects of the Cohesion Policy must not be confused with the effects of globalisation, which take place all over the world. The issue is not to avoid re-location within the EU. It is much more important to avoid, where possible, re-location taking place from the EU to third countries. This section addresses Cohesion Policy by first assessing its current situation, second, by identifying the problems it should tackle and its added-value and third, by proposing some direct measures to improve its impact.

1 The Current Health of the Cohesion Policy

The challenge to manage EU complexity could not be better reflected than in the case of Cohesion Policy. The shape of the policy itself is a result of conflicting paradigms brought to bear in negotiation rounds carried out over the years between sympathisers of neo-liberal capitalism and those favouring a regulated approach.[36] The debates between the Friends of Cohesion and the Cambridge Circus, the two groups into which Member States were polarised throughout Cohesion Policy negotiations, always concerned the size of the policy budget, its redistribution function, and its focus on traditional objectives such as infrastructure, sound financial management, competitiveness, and absorption capacity.

Cohesion Policy is often thought to be a "pork barrel" policy.[37] Its broadly defined objectives target numerous measures and include additional provisions for several Member States with special status, in an attempt to ensure that every Member State benefits from the policy. Although the political implications are not contested, the side effects of globalisation have caused problems across Europe. The Union is varied and disparities materialise in different ways across the regions and Member States, each demanding a different type of intervention. This "one size fits all" approach to the Cohesion Policy has drawn criticism; and has called into question the impact and added value of this policy for the Union.

2 Aspects of the Cohesion Policy Requiring Attention

2a The Challenge of Assessing the Real Success of Cohesion Policies

Let us approach Cohesion Policy by returning to idea of spillovers and "the scale and effects of EU action," as mentioned in Art. 5 of the Treaty. There have been numerous attempts to asses the impact of Structural and Cohesion Funds (SCF).[38] Most indicate that

---

[36] Hooghe (1998).

[37] De Rynck and McAleavey (2001).

[38] See for example Bachtler and Taylor (2003), Begg (2004), Boldrin and Canova (2001), Bradley and Morgenroth (2004).

convergence has improved, particularly in the case of Objective 1 regions (those with a GDP/cap of less than 75% of EU average). With the exception of the optimistic cohesion reports regularly published by the European Commission, little or no convergence appears to have taken place in regions other than those falling within the Objective 1 category. It is, however, important to bear in mind the limitations of this type of evaluation.

In the first place, it may be difficult to isolate the impact of SCF from other factors. The lack of real convergence in Objective 2 regions could, for example, result either from a lack of added value, or may indeed be the result of a lack of resources allocated at the EU level. One must recall that Objective 1 regions, where some convergence was reached, have always received more than two thirds of Cohesion Policy allocations, and the involvement of the EU has always been greater, providing over 75% of the total assistance and having more clout in the management and targeting of the funds in these areas. On the contrary, the Objective 2 regions were allocated considerably less funds,[39] all of which were implemented in a less coordinated way. Thus the question of impact and added-value should not be isolated to questions pertaining to resources and implementation.

Second, assessing real convergence does not mean assessing the overall impact of Cohesion Policy. The latter does not concern only economic cohesion, but also social and territorial cohesion. Added-value should have a broader definition in order to try to capture these aspects. A testament to this is the fact that studies[40] which considered other variables in addition to economic indicators consistently found more favourable results. These variables included the positive effects of cross-border cooperation, the exchange of knowledge and best practices, and the effects which the Cohesion Policy has had on the implementation of national policies with which it has interacted. It is worthwhile noting that social and territorial cohesion is difficult to evaluate empirically. Like economic cohesion, social and territorial cohesion is reached in the long term. A simple evaluation of a Financial Perspective span cannot lead to conclusive results. In light of the fact that

---

[39] Currently they benefit from 16% of the total allocations.
[40] See for example Bachtler and Taylor (2003).

Eastern Enlargement has just taken place, it is clear that new Member States are still in the process of learning how best to use and develop their absorption capacity.

Third, performance differences throughout the EU, are often due to issues of national policy-making, rather than the capacity of SCF to deliver results. There are countries and regions that have progressed rapidly in terms of living standards and productivity, while others continue to lag behind in spite of benefiting from substantial transfers. What has made the difference between these two sets of SCF beneficiaries? Evidence indicates that there is a broad array of factors which may explain this divergence in performance. These can be grouped into three major sets. The first set attributes the failure to difficulties in integrating national development plans, the umbrella for SCF deployment, into the country development agenda. The second set points the finger of blame at a failure to plan at strategic level and develop a coherent policy framework, backed by a solid budget formulation and execution process. The third and final set of factors identifies poor administrative capacity in the beneficiary institutions as a cause of poor performance despite the receipt of SCF funds.

Some argue that the best approach in this case is to concentrate Cohesion Policy Assistance towards those who did not manage to make the most of it previously due to the kind of shortcomings indicated above. Others contend that the SCF should focus more on the less developed Member States who are likely to face these difficulties in the future. For the successful cases, re-nationalisation would be the right option. A policy targeted only at the poorer Member States of the Union would reinforce the rapidly increasing feeling of division between the rich and the poor Member States, and would serve only to antagonise citizens in the Western States. This would contravene to the very purpose of the policy, which is to foster cohesion in Europe and not to divide it. Furthermore, globalisation brings challenges that can and should be tackled together, such as the effects of re-location, increasing the flexibility of the European labour force, and tackling migration within the EU. Besides building infrastructure, Cohesion Policy facilitates changes of best practices and speeds up the circulation of knowledge, which are essential for fostering growth.

2b Prioritising the Objectives of the Cohesion Policy

The Treaty[41] sets a clear objective for the Cohesion Policy: to reduce the gaps in development which exist between European regions, and to promote the Union's "overall harmonious development." According to the Treaty, this can be achieved through economic, social and territorial cohesion and through solidarity among Member States. Cohesion Policy has shown a great capacity to adapt to new challenges over time in order to meet these objectives. Currently, a part of its expenditure is allocated to the achievement of the Lisbon Strategy objectives. The second objective of the Cohesion Policy, Regional competitiveness for growth and employment, allocates three quarters of its ceiling to this purpose, in addition, 60% of the sums allocated to the Convergence objective in the EU-15 areas are earmarked for Lisbon Strategy priorities. Nonetheless, most of the areas eligible for the Convergence objective are in the new Member States. It must not be forgotten, however, that these areas are still in need of traditional Cohesion Policy actions, such as improvements in infrastructure to enable them to connect with the poles of development in Europe. Actions of this kind are not old-fashioned. The purpose of Cohesion Policy is primarily to reduce gaps in development and if this can help implement the Lisbon Agenda so much the better. If one agrees that globalisation presses for faster economic growth and increased competitiveness in Europe, then the Cohesion Policy should help tackle these issues too. However, investing in R&D is not the only way to meet these challenges. Regions, which lack basic infrastructure and institutional capacities, will not be able to become competitive until issues surrounding their underdevelopment are tackled first.

2c Finding a Road-Map for the Future of SCF

In light of the above, this section contends that the budget allocation for Cohesion Policy should be maintained or even increased. Given the current global context and the need to support the Lisbon objectives, the three policy objectives addressing convergence, regional competitiveness, and territorial cooperation are well designed and resources are proportionately allocated. The objectives capture at the same time the

---

[41] Art. 158, the Reform Treaty.

need for traditional structural investments, the need for fulfilling the objectives of the Lisbon Agenda, and the need for territorial cooperation. Nonetheless, there is much scope for improvement; particularly in the area of implementation. In addition, much work remains to be done in improving the absorption capacity of new Member States and need to speed-up their progress in order to catch up with the rest of the Union. This, in turn, will require a more pro-active approach on the part of the EU institutions, national governments and the regions *vis-à-vis* the efficient use of the SCF and the establishment of a solid, performance-oriented monitoring system at all levels. To achieve this, a review of the allocation of responsibilities between the EU, national and regional institutions in the management of the SCF is justified. Enhancing the institutional capacity of the SCF beneficiaries, at both local and central levels in order to design and implement projects must be made a priority.

The resources allocated to the Structural and Cohesion Funds have constantly increased—moving from around 17.2% of the EU budget in 1988 to an estimated 35.7% in 2013. There are countries and regions which have made significant progressions in the field of competitiveness, while in others progress has been limited at best. Similarly, there are countries and regions that are catching up with the front-runners in terms of incomes, while others seem to be trapped, in spite of substantial funding support from both the SCFs and national budgets. Coinciding with significant increases in SCF resources, increased flexibility has been introduced into the rules governing their use. Decision making has been decentralised and more of the funds now go towards boosting competitiveness, growth and jobs. Evidence suggests that challenges manifest along two dimensions: a) generic problems, in relation to the development objectives to which SCF funds are being deployed; and b) specific problems, that have to do more with programme implementation.

Against this background of mixed outcomes, two questions appear to demand immediate attention: a) are there tensions between boosting competitiveness and the redistribution of resources which are affecting the performance of the SCF? and b) is enhanced flexibility in allocation, which not only puts the national governments in the driving seat in terms of deciding where resources go, but also gives practically unlimited choices to them *vis-à-vis* where to direct the funds, a problem rather than a solution? Some lessons, which illustrate these tensions, are drawn below on the basis of implementation experiences, including some from the new Central and Eastern European members.

2d The Challenge of Learning from the Past: Lessons Taken from Observing SCF in Practice

Improvements in allocation, efficiency and effectiveness of the SCF require both a better alignment of the national development plans with the EU policy priorities, and a better integration of the EU-wide strategic policy agenda into national development programs. Experience suggests that countries where the national policy framework has placed global competitiveness at the forefront, within an EU context, such as Ireland and Spain, have been most successful in mobilising SCF for development. Among the apparent prerequisites for the successful deployment of SCF are a stable macroeconomic environment, outward-orientated productivity, and a competitiveness which is driven by industrial strategy. Additional factors which have been identified include improvements in human capital and physical infrastructure, better competition, market liberalisation regulatory reform and, critically, improvements in governance. In these countries the SCF has not only become an instrument for attaining national development objectives, but has also shaped the whole resource allocation framework, including the prioritisation and management spending. It is noteworthy that much of this progress has taken place against the background of very loosely-defined EU policy agendas, prior to the implementation of the Lisbon strategy.

The Cohesion Policy context could, therefore, serve as a framework in which to anchor national policy-making, especially among the new Member States.

It is generally accepted that most of the fundamental reforms needed, which often concern the functioning of the public sector, must take place at the initiative of member states themselves, rather than at the EU level. The experiences of Ireland and Spain, for example, suggest that the EU SCF processes have enhanced oversight, benchmarking and knowledge sharing, which have shaped, to different degrees, the public sector processes in the beneficiary countries. The introduction of ex-ante program analyses, multi-annual planning and budgeting for SCFs, and the system of *ex-post* evaluation were subsequently extended in Ireland to the whole public sector, with remarkable results in terms of increasing the efficiency of public spending. These past experiences clearly show that SCFs should have a strong national development dimension. This is particularly true with regard to the new Member States, in light of the large income and productivity gaps which exist between the new and old members of the Union. This means, other words that the SCFs should aid new members in exploiting the opportunities offered by the EU common market by playing the role of an all-inclusive, integrative framework for national development.

3 Direct Measures to Improve the Future Impact of SCF

3a Improving Transparency and Efficiency of Public Sector Allocation and Spending of SCFs at a National Level

The SCF represent, in our opinion, an important instrument for accelerating real convergence within Europe, but the need to improve the allocation and efficiency of public spending, in general, remains an outstanding and sizeable challenge for many members.

The degree of success in achieving convergence varies considerably across countries and regions in spite of substantial SCF funding support, of which some benefited for long periods. Important public resources, including SCF, still go to unproductive policy actions, or what is even worse, are misused in a fraudulent way. There is significant scope for enhancing the quality of public investment in infrastructure and human capital. Evidence points to the fact that the countries with better state of governance seem to spend more efficiently and effectively. At national level, there is a need to improve consistency and clarify the strategic direction across policy products and processes.

Policy products may include government programs, plans for the implementation of the acquis, convergence plans, reform plans, or national development plans (NDP). These various strategic documents often derive from distinct processes involving a number of different players all with opposing purposes. These purposes may focus on political issues, may have as their priority the deepening of EU integration, or may be focused primarily on SCF access. In reality, not all these projects entail sufficient strategic government-wide frameworks that give unequivocal direction to the people and the public sector regarding what the government intends to achieve. While the enhanced flexibility in the allocation of the SCF across sectors in order to better respond to priorities is welcome, parallelisms in planning prevent these fund having the optimum effect on the ground.

Vulnerabilities at the strategic planning stage, which generally takes place at the centre of the government, bringing decision making into the nexus of politics and administration, manifest primarily in two areas. The first of these is the absence or the insufficient development of a broad government-wide policy framework that should define government goals clearly and allow the articulation of more detailed central and local government programs, roles and responsibilities. The second area relates to basic policymaking capacity constraints in sectors and ministries, and the specification of medium-term expenditure, preparation ceilings for government budget entities etc. This should take place for ministries, other government agencies, and for local government entities. It entails revenue forecasting capacity matched with realistic and prioritised sectoral policy planning, and the decision to use such information to discipline budgetary preparation. Having such policies in place would ensure a link between policy thinking and government fiscal realities. Without this tie, policy products and budget proposals often become undisciplined "wish lists" that are difficult to connect to the resources framework.

Integrating policy, planning and budgeting across the government is therefore central to sustaining growth and achieving the strategic objectives of convergence. Institutional, policy and process weaknesses of the public financial management systems are central obstacles to strengthening aggregate fiscal discipline, improving the effectiveness of public resource allocation and aligning these resources with the strategic priorities of the country in question. These issues also affect the absorption of the SCF. Evidence shows that the relationship between policy, planning and budgeting is one of the most important factors contributing to poor budgeting outcomes at macro, strategic and operational levels in the Member States. Key limitations come from the fragmentation of public finance management systems and vulnerabilities visible at all stages of the public expenditure management cycle.

3b The Improvement of Medium-Term Expenditure Frameworks

More emphasis should be placed on developing medium term expenditure frameworks (MTEF) and budgets on programs, to which the SCF should be an integral part and treated similarly to other financial resources.

Faced with conflicting objectives and constrained resources, some Member States have attempted to establish MTEF as a means of balancing the aggregate affordable resources with the policy priorities of their country. However, rarely have the MTEF fulfilled their intended role of enhancing the clarity of policy objectives, improving the predictability of budget allocations, and increasing comprehensiveness of coverage and transparency in the use of resources. Instead, the MTEF are more of an annual exercise, projecting revenues and expenditures several years ahead, rather than a multi-year budgeting initiative to guide annual budgets, together with substantive multi-year programming content. The MTEF are often substantially altered from year to year and lack a thorough connection with other processes, such as the NDP. In some countries, budgets are organised by programme after the line-item allocations are decided upon, indicating the use of programmatic concepts as an ex-post rather than an ex-ante tool to ensure policy orientation in allocations.

3c A Reform of the Annual Budget Cycle in Member States

Improving absorption and effectiveness of SCF requires a review and reform of the annual budget cycle in a number of Member States. Frequent shortcomings among national annual budgets include insufficient strategic and policy guidance fund allocation, weak linkages between funding and performance and frequent budget rectifications. Other difficulties include the reallocation of important resources within the year, delays in the effective start of the budget cycle, and limited cooperation between finance departments and credit holders both in the formulation and execution of the budget. These deficiencies are sometimes augmented by an inadequate macroeconomic revenue analysis and forecasting framework.

3d An Improvement in the Administrative Capacity of SCF Recipients

There is a need to pay significantly more attention to upgrading the administrative capacity of SCF beneficiaries, especially at sub- national level, and at the level of the managing authorities. The capacity to design and implement complex projects in order to access SCF is often very limited. As a consequence, SCF absorption is low and resources invested sometimes do not correspond with the outcomes achieved.

This situation occurs in spite of the fact that new EU members, for example, have received for long periods of time substantial pre-accession funding and expertise support for capacity building. In many cases, however, interaction between those who were involved in the management of the pre-accession funds and those charged with budget planning and policy departments after accession has been limited. This highlights a lack of experience and competence in fund administration which exists in many states at the national level. In order for SCFs to have more of an impact on the ground the administrative management of these funds in both new and old Member States must be addressed.

3e Enhanced Support for Project Design

While there have been improvements in clarifying and simplifying the SCF framework, along with a simplification of the guidelines for project preparation, the standards remain high and would-be beneficiaries often do not have the skills to meet them fully during the project design stage. As a result, project-designers often cut corners leading them to run into problems later on. A frequent issue which arises is that absorption and impact are often decoupled, and the internal rate of return of projects does not ensure their long term sustainability ("building cathedrals in the desert"). There are numerous examples where current spending resulting from project completion was not taken into account. This has introduced substantial rigidity in national and local budgets, squeezing capital spending. Identifying ways to better incorporate private sector skills should improve the quality of the projects both in terms of SCF absorption and developmental impact.

3f Strengthened Monitoring and Evaluation Systems for SNCFs

In order to improve the linkages between programme performance and resource allocation there needs to be a significant strengthening of monitoring and evaluation systems. These systems should assess in a comprehensive and timely manner the extent to which resources help in achieving the intended outcomes and should feedback into the policy framework, enabling eventual corrections and reallocations. Experiences of some old members, such as Ireland, suggest that the effective use of M&E systems not only improves the overall absorption of the SCF, but also allows for rapid redeployment of resources towards better uses. Appropriate incentive schemes, backed by performance indicators in order to reward the better performers and sanction the laggards should be part of the M&E system, and should, at the same time, take into account the institutional capacity of beneficiaries. While levels of SCF absorption do matter, it is even more important to make sure that resources go where they are most needed and where their impact is maximised.

Unequivocal positions *vis-à-vis* these issues are probably not possible, given the large disparities between Member States and regions in terms of development, policy, and institutional maturity, which in turn translate into a broad array of priorities at national and sub-national level. The stated objectives of the SCFs are broad, and its instruments increasingly flexible, thus allowing member countries to employ resources to a broad array of sectors and activities. This has clear and proven advantages. The downside is whether the funds are not rather too thinly spread in order to make a difference in terms of overarching outcomes.

3g Improved Targeting of Funds

A strategic question *vis-à-vis* SCF use is whether there is a need to better focus them, making a more clear distinction between competitiveness and redistribution. For example, the funds focusing on competitiveness could target a cross-cutting EU-wide set of policy priorities, wherein the role of the EU institutions in resource allocation should be enhanced, and the role of the member state appropriately diminished. Equally, the funds targeting redistribution should focus on narrower, country specific set of issues, in which case more control should be delegated to the Member State and eventually to the beneficiary regions themselves. The EU action, in this situation, could focus on fostering exchange of views and best practices.

4 A Final Word on SCFs

In light of the above, it is clear that the Cohesion Policy is one of the most important EU policies at present. It has the capacity and the potential to contribute to a cohesive development of the Union, and can provide us with tools designed to manage the EU's socio-economic complexity. The policy is designed in such a way that it benefits every Member State. This requirement, however, reduces the overall impact of cohesion actions. Issues such as low absorption capacity among the New Member States must be tackled. A balance must be found between concentrating the funds and ensuring that problems posed by regions which are lagging behind all across the Union are tackled. This section argues that a clearer distinction between competitiveness and redistribution could be a solution to this dilemma. Improving programming along with policy planning, as suggested above, are just two among the ways in which absorption SCFs may be increased and their impact maximised.

D. COMPETITIVENESS UNDER THE LISBON AGENDA

EU spending on R&D and competitiveness is consistent with the higher emphasis put on knowledge and innovation by the Lisbon Agenda. The Competitiveness and Innovation Framework Programme 2007–2013 and the recently established "Lead market initiative" are useful tools to foster competitiveness, promote innovation and unlock market potential. However, according to the European Commission (2004), the Research Framework Programme was able to finance only half of the "very high standard" project proposals which it received, due to limited funding. The EU currently spends, on average, considerably less on the area of R&D than either the US or Japan. The Scandinavian Member States are the only states to invest over 3% of their GDP into R&D, and have greatly improved their economic performance as a result; but this has entailed significant reform of their economic and social security systems and has only been made possible by the high proportion of university graduates within Scandinavian society. Furthermore, Scandinavian countries have successfully carried out industrial policies which relied, to a greater or lesser extent, on public-private partnerships. These are lessons that must be applied all over Europe when dealing with R&D investments.

The R&D and competitiveness policy matters because companies do not innovate in isolation, but within a system, and the particularities of this system and of its instruments are essential to performance innovation.[42]

---

[42] Smits and Kuhlmann (2004). The refocus of EU budget and the need for more efficient mechanisms concentrating on the EU's role as a facilitator were stressed out by the Sapir Report (2003).

A fundamental flaw in public expenditure on R&D, both at national and EU level, is that they do not provide sufficient incentives
for private R&D. The EU performance has been very diverse; but on
average it has been surpassed by the US and some by Asian countries.
A recent study from JRC 2008[43] illustrates that even at company level
business expenditure on R&D in the EU is much lower than business
expenditure on R&D in US companies. An example of this is the fact
that in the ITC industry, R&D intensity[44] is 6.2% in EU-25, compared
to 10.4% in the US, not to mention that the size of the ICT sector, as
a share in GDP, is higher in the US than in the EU-25.[45]

At national level, the ratio between public and private R&D has
remained around 3:4 since the Lisbon Agenda was launched. This is in
spite of the fact that the target set by the Lisbon Agenda was a ratio of
1:2, within the framework of 3% of GDP over all R&D expenditures.
At EU level, much of the EU funds for R&D (the Framework Programmes in particular) go to publicly funded research institutes and
universities. Furthermore, there is a certain (informal) bias in favour of
countries with already established research institutes; very few research
institutes and universities from new Member States are project leaders in EU funded projects. One reason for this could be their lack of
financial resources and experience; another reason could be the use of
R&D as a political tool to compensate for net contributions on other
budgetary items.[46]

1 The Future of R&D and Competitiveness Policy of the EU

1a Increasing the R&D Budget

The EU funding for R&D and competitiveness does provide value
for money. Impact assessments in general have shown a high return
on R&D investments, but there is substantial scope for improved efficiency. Afonso and Gonzales Alegre analyse the impact of budgetary
components on economic growth, at the EU level.[47] Arguably, R&D expenditure is "public expenditure as a separate input into the production

---

[43] Lindmark *et al.* (2008).
[44] Calculated as the share of R&D expenditures in value added.
[45] 6.2%, respectively 5%.
[46] See Wynn and Nunez Ferrer (2007).
[47] Afonso and Gonzales Alegre (2008).

function." This is because R&D expenditure influences technology and this in turn influences total factor productivity, which has a positive impact on GDP growth, and on total factor productivity growth. The expenditure targeted at enhancing competitiveness, especially that which provides support to SMEs is a "capital-enhancing" type of expenditure. It is a subsidy for private capital, which also has a positive impact on GDP growth but no impact on total factor productivity growth.

EU expenditure on R&D and competitiveness falls within the definition of a public good (to the extent that knowledge is free) and do possess an added-value component. R&D expenditure satisfies the requirements of subsidiarity and fulfils value for money principles, while having a mixed performance on the proportionality principle.[48]

An increase in the expenditure on competitiveness and R&D is strongly justified by the challenges that the Union has to face and is supported by the political will and public opinion. Consequently, regardless of the possible scenarios for the future EU budget, fostering an increase in R&D expenditure in order to reach the targeted 3% of EU GDP average should definitely be on the agenda.[49]

1b Expanding the Definition of R&D

There are more forms of R&D, many types of knowledge-based economies, and numerous types of competitiveness across the spectrum of Member States. EU R&D expenditure should not relate exclusively to high value added R&D and high-end product innovation.

R&D is now taking the form of technology absorption; knowledge is taking the form of knowledge diffusion, while innovation is taking the form of process innovation, especially in the new Member States. Supporting these forms of R&D aids the "catching up process" taking place in less developed economies in the EU, thereby increasing its value for

---

[48] See Wynn and Nunez Ferrer (2007).

[49] Mrak et al. (2007) propose four scenarios for the next EU budget (2014–2020); expenditure for R&D and competitiveness increases in all four of them: existing expenditure level scenario—competitiveness expenditure more than double in nominal terms (unless further enlargement), existing policies—same evolution for competitiveness expenditure, restrictive scenario—with a moderate growth of competitiveness expenditure, and community scenario—competitiveness expenditures more than triple, in the context of a large increase in EU budget overall.

money. For emerging economies, in particular those of Member States in Eastern and Central Europe, the assimilation of new technologies is of the utmost importance and acts as a premise for contributing to technological progress in the long run. Moreover, the absorption of new technologies and investments in R&D should be linked with further reforms in the educational system, and the promotion of science-based university studies across Europe, in order to provide the necessary human capital to increase competitiveness and R&D, avoiding an unbalanced concentration of graduates within the humanities field.

There is also a need to foster fundamental research in the EU. Initiatives, such as the creation of centres of scientific excellence should be supported, as a means to slow down the brain drain.[50]

1c Current Problems in the Delivery of R&D Funding

This part argues that before any increase in financing is agreed upon, a number of problems must first be addressed. To start, there is a problem of disproportionate allocation to net contributors in compensation for other EU budget items. R&D funds should not be used as a buffer in this manner, but should be focused more towards applied research and business/industrial applications. Secondly, there is the issue of unfair access, since research institutes and universities which are financed on a permanent basis from national public budgets are more likely to win projects from EU funds, given that they have larger annual budgets and more co-financing capacity. Thirdly, the bureaucratic procedures associated with R&D funds are very complicated, and represent an entry barrier for new applicants. Finally, more training needs to be provided by EU institutions on how to absorb these funds. This training should take place in each of the beneficiary countries.

1d A Final Word on R&D in the Budget

The EU competitiveness and R&D policy has become one of the most important tools at European level for fostering economic growth and helping the EU face the challenges of globalisation, in particular the

---

[50] The Romanian Institute for Advanced Research (RIAS) is an idea which aims at using the expertise of world-class experts who work now abroad. This would be a right approach for emerging economies and should be encouraged by the EU.

emergence of new economic powers at a world level. Consequently, R&D is one of the areas that will require greater financing in the future. Nonetheless, it is important to spend money wisely. The complexity of the Union, especially the socio-economic variety among Member States demands for a differentiated approach. There are Member States which can and should focus on innovation and there are Member States whose focus should be directed to absorbing current high-level technologies. Increases in R&D spending can not take place in isolation, and must take account of related policy areas. Differences in the levels of both educational and technological advancement across the Union cannot be ignored, and a stronger role must be given to investment in Public Private Partnerships.

E. The EU Budget at the Global Level

1 The Budget as a Tool to Tackle Migration

A better coordination between Member States, the Commission and other world donors could lead to more significant results in tackling issues in the developing world, without necessarily increasing financial assistance.

The European Union is currently the largest donor of aid in the world, giving approximately 55% of the total aid provided world-wide. The main instrument used to tackle poverty, combat illiteracy, hunger, discrimination against women and enhance environmental protection in developing areas is the European Development Fund (EDF). The EDF is an instrument which is separate to the EU budget, with its own system of resources, management and programming. For the 2008–2013 period it amounted to 22,682 million Euro. Although the EU-15 nations agreed to double the EU's development aid by 2015, there are still Member States who have thus far failed to increase their contributions. As argued earlier, during the discussion on the external challenges which the Union faces, helping the developing world in this manner reduces the likelihood of massive migration to Europe. This is also important for implementing the external dimension of the Lisbon Strategy.

Ensuring security within and for the European Union is a European public good. Member States should intensify dialogue concerning this issue and the EU budget should contribute to this end. Combating migration and ensuring harmonious growth in the EU are also linked with EU's ability to ensure that wars in the other parts of the world do not affect its development. The failure of Member States to find a joint position on Kosovo, for instance, indicates that the EU is far from having a common voice on foreign affairs. Nonetheless, it is essential to be able to carry out at least peace keeping and crisis management missions, such as those defined by the Petersberg tasks. Moreover, the introduction of the solidarity clause in the Lisbon Treaty calls for more efforts towards a common defence policy. All of these projects carry considerations when considering the future of the EU Budget.

2 Energy Policy and the European Budget

In order to be a global actor, the European Union needs to be able to act coherently and fast at the world level. This implies the necessity of a common external policy which is financed by European resources. Common Foreign and Security Policy (CFSP) is not only about sending troops abroad. It also means managing energy policy, by diversifying sources of supply and strengthening the development of energy and gas transport networks. There are many intentions voiced by Member States and private stakeholders to tackle these issues. Until now however, Nabucco is the only project that has really materialised such intentions. Nabucco should be implemented and should receive funding from the EU budget. In its current form there is a marked discrepancy between the importance of ensuring energy security and the small contribution that the EU budget makes to this end.[51] It is, therefore, imperative that the EU fully integrates energy policy into its external actions and allocates adequate resources from its budget to ensuring energy security.

The EU needs a coherent energy strategy materialised in concrete projects designed at the European level, which are financed from the EU budget. Given the high dependence of the Union on external energy sources, the aim should be to enhance energy security through optimal resource management. The EU budget must be one of the major tools used in this direction.

---

[51] The EU budget finances only feasibility studies. The major costs are financed by the Member States and companies.

F. Sources of Revenue for the EU Budget

The budget of the Union was based in the past only on an own re-sources system (custom duties, agricultural duties, sugar levies). These now account for less than 20% of the European revenues. The creation of the Single Market in 1986 led to a sudden increase of the European budget. This was sustained by GNI-based contributions, which now represent its main source of revenues. The Lisbon Treaty introduces provisions, which encourage the review and the reform of the own resources system, particularly the introduction of new budgetary resources. There are a series of principles and a number of options which should be considered when updating the own resources section of the EU Budget.

The European Commission presented in its Consultation Paper on Budgetary Reform a series of principles that budgetary resources should respect, in acknowledgement of the fact that at the moment none of the EU financial resources fulfil all the criteria. Among these principles are: equity, efficiency, simplicity, visibility, financial autonomy, stability and sufficiency. It is hardly possible to define own resources that would fulfil all these.

Pragmatism is key to a functional system. We need a system that works. Therefore it must be sufficient, stable, simple and equitable. It must be sufficient in order to maintain at least the existing level of revenues. It must be stable in the sense that the revenues must be predictable. It must also be simple, transparent and equitable. Correction mechanisms should be abolished and no special arrangements should be made for any Member State.

A larger budget will be needed if the EU is to adequately tackle the challenges posed by globalisation, migration, global warming and security of energy supply, while simultaneously managing the Union's inner complexity.

All these new challenges create new needs and demands on the part of European citizens. These are challenges which the Union must work to meet, in collaboration with the Member States. Nonetheless, the allocation and application of European funds has often raised eyebrows in the public opinion. There have been numerous cases of mismanagement and fraud, which encourage the spread of Euro-scepticism. In order for the EU tax payers to accept further integration, new taxes and a larger budget, they first must see that their resources are used appropriately and for their own good. Therefore, more transparency, accuracy, and responsibility concerning the management of the European funds is a necessary a pre-condition for enhancing the European identity and paving the way for a larger EU budget of the Union.

This chapter argues, therefore, that in the short run, there is no scope for introducing new taxes to European citizens. Contributions to the EU budget should therefore continue to be GNI based. In the long-term, however, the budget should be increased and new resources should be added to the already existing ones.

Several types of taxes have already been proposed as alternatives to GNI contributions.[52] So far only VAT responds to the criteria of sufficiency and stability. Several other taxes on the provision of European public goods, such as taxes on pollution, corporate activities, energy consumption, and European Central Bank profits should be investigated as potential sources of additional revenues to the EU budget in the future.

VI. Implementation of New Provisions

It is most likely that the review process initiated by the European Commission will lead to a reform of the EU budget. The agreement of the last Financial Perspectives was conditional on the commencement of a process of budgetary review. The net-payers are not willing to sustain a similar budget from 2014 onwards. Their weight in the budgetary decision-making process is unquestionable, and therefore the reform of the budget and EU policies looks inevitable in the near future. Regardless of the shape of the reform, new provisions should be implemented gradually, to allow for a smooth transition. Nonetheless, new challenges reemphasise the need to act in a timely fashion; hence a balance must be found between harmonious transition and fast adaptation to a rapidly changing context.

Any sudden cuts or refocusing of financial assistance can trigger disequilibria. Assistance should be phased-out during the length of a

---

[52] See the European Parliament's Resolution of 29 March 2007 on the Future of European Union's Own Resources and Schüssel (2007).

Financial Perspective to allow those who loose assistance to re-orientate towards other activities. A similar length of time should be applied to phasing-in assistance in new areas. Previous experience with Structural Fund allocations proves that time is needed to explore new absorption capacities in order to avoid fund de-commitment.

For increased accountability and better management, Financial Perspectives should have the same length as the mandates of the European Commission and the Parliament. This would enable every Commission College and Parliament to be part of the entire budget cycle: consultation, debate, proposal, negotiation, agreement and implementation. Such a practice would be a great improvement on the current practice and would allow the budget a formidable seven year span.

There should be more flexibility in Financial Perspectives in order to allow the Union to better respond to new and unforeseen situations. Despite this author's understanding of the reasoning behind the establishment of expenditure headings, one must also consider the need to adjust financial intervention to a rapidly changing context. The budget must be able to rapidly respond to the Union's needs. Consequently, we propose either the possibility of transferring a certain proportion of funds between headings or creating a budget reserve (as all national budgets do have!).

VII. Concluding Remarks

This chapter has attempted to present a balanced, unbiased view on how to approach the budget review given the numerous challenges that Europe is confronted with. It first addresses the reasons behind the current status of the EU budget. It then tackles the exogenous and endogenous pressures affecting the Union, highlighting the new challenges which any revised Budget will have to consider. The chapter then goes on to discuss some of the core principles which should guide this budgetary review and eventual reform. The expenditure section of this review comprised an appraisal of the role of European Public Goods when considering budget allocations, and then proceeded to examine in detail the CAP, SCF and R&D funds within the Budget. This in turn was followed by a review of European Competitiveness within a rapidly globalising economy, and finally an examination of the role of the EU Budget as an instrument of change on the world stage.

The main exogenous challenges of the Union originate in globalisation effects. The EU must speed up its economic growth in order to face increasing competition from newly emerging global powers. At the same time, the EU should equip itself to deal with increasing immigration by improving its approach towards the developing world and by re-defining its protectionist policies. Added to this is the necessity of ensuring energy security for Europe and of tackling global warming.

Internally, the Union faces strains caused by its own growing complexity. The discrepancies in economic development, policy views, national interests, and integration paradigms which characterise different Member States continues to make it increasingly difficult to design EU level policies for all. Further enlargement and deepening of the integration process are commitments that must be fulfilled. Nonetheless, the functionality of the single market continues to pose problems. More needs to be done; knowledge should circulate freely. Finally, re-location within the Union is a major issue, which stirs dissatisfaction and rivalry among EU citizens and challenges the solidarity among the EU nations.

In this context, it is fundamental to re-design the EU budget in order to finance European policies which are fit to tackle these challenges. This must be done in partnership with Member States, by providing European public goods. The added-value of EU action and the interpretation of the Treaty provisions in this respect should be broad, and not assessed solely along economic lines. The promotion of solidarity, exchange of knowledge and best practices, along with the improvement of national policy-making, and stronger action on the part of the Union at the global level are just a few factors which bring added-value at the European level.

Concerning agriculture, it is essential to consider the impact of global warming and increased population on the supply and demand for agricultural products. Consequently, proper management of good quality soil and water should be a fundamental objective of the CAP. Second, the side-effects of the CAP over the last 40 years have been a growth in the size of land plots and farms. New Member States, on the other hand, are characterised by small land plots and a concentration of the work force in the agricultural sector. The reform of the CAP should target the internalisation of these problems, initially by securing income support for small farmers, and secondly by increasingly supporting the diversification of rural activities, and the modernisation and development of the rural infrastructure. These measures would allow for the fair treatment of those farmers who were not able to benefit from CAP, and would also enable a better management of essential agricultural assets in the 21st century.

Cohesion Policy is of great importance for the Union's development because it has the capacity and the tools to improve economic, social and territorial cohesion. Problems relating to the Cohesion Policy are concentrated mostly in the area of implementation. There is a need to improve the absorption capacity and to better target and manage Structural and Cohesion Funds.

It is essential that any review of the budget done with the purpose of bringing added-value to citizens at the European level. It should not serve only the interests of the net contributors nor fulfil the needs only of beneficiaries. Finding a way to reconcile these competing demands will be a formidable task. However the necessity of providing European public goods and properly managing the complexity of the Union cannot be ignored. Despite conflicting views among Member States, a common denominator must be found, and a policy which locates common gains which serve all Member States must be put in place.

The size of the EU budget is unlikely to fundamentally change in the near future, since a reform of the own resources, even if agreed upon, will take time to implement. Thus, it is essential to find a position of equilibrium between the provision of financial support to all the Union and the concentration of financial support only on the areas most in need. When deciding on financial support, the other two instruments of the Union which should be constantly considered are legislation and guidelines. The budget should be assigned to ensure the supply of those public goods which necessitate financial assistance.

It must be stressed that a mix of bottom-up and top-down approaches is necessary for budget implementation. The challenges faced by the Union require both overarching coordination and policy differentiation. Consequently, governance at a national level has a salient role to play.

The review and the reform of the EU budget should carefully consider the democratic deficit in the Union and its causes. The numerous cases of mismanagement and fraud concerning the European financial assistance and scandals which have involved EU officials[53] have led to the emergence of mistrust in the EU and the promotion of Euro-scepticism. These hinder the further development of the integration process and the adoption and implementation of appropriately designed reforms to tackle the challenges of the 21st century. Increased transparency, more responsibility, and improved systems of management and control are a priori conditions for a consistent budget reform.

The EU budget can act only as a lever. It is unrealistic to expect a fundamental and rapid change. In view of the size and importance of the pressures linked to globalisation, the inner complexity of the union, and the necessity of an active response to change, it is essential that national budgets and policies also adapt to the current context and act accordingly. Only through such an approach we can ensure that what we have achieved so far through the process of integration is not lost.

REFERENCES

Afonso, A. and Gonzalez, J.A. (2008) "Economic growth and budgetary components: A panel assessment for the EU" European Central Bank, Working paper No. 848.

Bachtler, J. and Taylor, S. (2003) "The added value of the Structural Funds: a regional perspective" European Policies Research Centre, University of Strathclyde.

Begg, I., et al. (2004) "The impact of Member State Policies on Cohesion" Background study for the 3rd Cohesion Report for DG Regio.

Belkin, P. (2007) "The European Union's energy security challenges" CRS Report for Congress, Congressional Research Service. Available at: http://www.fas.org/sgp/crs/row/RL33636.pdf.

Boldrin, M. and Canova, F. (2001) "Inequality and convergence in Europe's regions: Reconsidering European Regional Policies" Economic Policy, Vol. 32, pp. 205–53.

Boulanger, P. (2007) "Les arbitrages Budgetaires" background paper for the task force meeting, 10 September, 2007, Notre Europe, Project PAC 2013.

Bradley, J., Morgenroth, E., et al. (2004) "A Study of the Macroeconomic Impact of the Reform of EU Cohesion Policy" Dublin, ESRI.

---

[53] See the Santer Commission crisis or the current discussions concerning the misuse of assistance funds by some Members of the European Parliament.

Council of the European Union (2000) Lisbon European Council Conclusions. Available at: *http://www.consilium.europa.eu/ueDocs/cmsData/docs/pressData/en/ec/00100-r1.en0.htm.*

De Rynck, S. and McAleavey, P. (2001) "The Cohesion Deficit in Structural Fund Policy" *Journal of European Public Policy*, Vol. 8, No. 4, pp. 541–57.

Enderlein, H., Linder, J., *et al.* (2005) "The EU budget: how much scope for institutional reform?" Occasional paper Series, European Central Bank, No. 27.

European Commission (2004) "Science and technology, the key to Europe's future—Guidelines for future European Union policy to support research" COM (2004) 353.

European Commission (2007) "Communication from the Commission to the Council: Strategic Report on the Renewed Lisbon Strategy For Growth and Jobs: Launching the New Cycle (2008–2010)" COM (2007) 803 final.

European Commission (2007) "Report on the distribution of direct aids to the producers (financial year 2005)" DG Agriculture and Rural Development. Available at: *http://ec.europa.eu/agriculture/funding/index_en.htm.*

European Parliament (2007) "European Parliament Resolution of the 29th of March 2007 on the Future of European Union's Own Resources."

European Parliament (2007) "The EU Added Value of Agricultural Expenditure—From Market to Multifunctionality—Gathering Criticism and Success Stories of the CAP" Brussels, DG Internal Policies of the Union, Policy Department on Budgetary Affairs.

European Parliament, Council and European Commission (2006) "The Interinstitutional Agreement between the European Parliament, the Council and the Commission on Budgetary Discipline and Sound Financial Management" *Official Journal of the European Union*, 2006/C139/01, pp. 1–17.

Hennessy, T.C. and Thorne, F.S. (2005), "How decoupled are decoupled payments? The evidence from Ireland" *EuroChoices*, Vol. 4, No. 3, The Agricultural Economics Society and the European Association of Agricultural Economists, Whitchurch.

Hooghe, L. (1998) "EU Cohesion Policy and Competing Models of European Capitalism" *Journal of Common Market Studies*, Vol. 36, No. 4, pp. 457–77. Available at: *http://ec.europa.eu/agriculture/healthcheck/index_en.htm.*

Kok, W. (2004) "Facing the Challenge: The Lisbon Strategy for Growth and Employment." Available at: *http://ec.europa.eu/growthandjobs/pdf/kok_report_en.pdf.*

Lindmark, S., Turlea, G. and Ulbrich, M. (2008), "Policy Brief: R&D Business Investment in the EU ICT Sector" European Commission Joint Research Center IPTS Seville.

Mrak, M., *et al.* (2007) "EU Budget Review: An Opportunity for a Thorough Reform or Minor Adjustments" Report of the EU Budget Review Taskforce, Slovenia.

Pelkmans, J. (2006) "Testing for subsidiarity" BEEP Briefing no. 13, College of Europe. Available at: *http://www.coleurop.be/eco/publications.htm.*

Roberts, I. and Gunning-Trant, C. (2007) "The European Union's Common Agricultural Policy: a stocktake of reforms" Abare Research Report 07.13, Canberra. Available at: *www.abareconomics.com*.

Sapir, A., *et al.* (2003) "An Agenda for a Growing Europe: Making the EU Economic System Deliver." Available at: *http://www.euractiv.com/ndbtext/innovation/sapirreport.pdf*

Schui, H. (2008) "Nokia's migration highlights Brussels failure" *Financial Times*, 11 February. Available at: *http://www.ft.com/cms/s/0/2ac6fac8-d844-11dc-98f7-0000779fd2ac.html?nclick_check=1*.

Schüssel, W. (2007) "Europe's Finances—The Old System at Its Limits" *Spotlight Europe*, November.

Smits, R. and Kuhlmann S. (2004), "The rise of systemic instruments in innovation policy" *International Journal Foresight and Innovation Policy*, Vol. 1, Nos. 1–2.

Tresch, R.W. (2002) "Public Finance: a Normative Theory" Amsterdam, Elsevier Academic Press.

Wynn, T. and Nunez Ferrer, J. (2007) "The EU Budget. The UK Rebate and the CAP – Phasing Them Both Out?" CEPS Task Force Report.

CHAPTER 8

A Clash of Capitalisms[1]

A visionary and pragmatic US diplomacy after the Second World War helped the restoration of economic wellbeing in the free part of Europe and, also, it did bring closer nations whose history was fraught by mutual distrust and conflict. The European Union (EU), itself, took off on the wings of a Marshall Plan aided recovery. But Europe's ideological and geopolitical split, in the wake of the Second World War, deprived its Eastern nations of this plan's benefits. EU enlargement can be seen, therefore, in a wider historical perspective.

There was a global perspective that framed US foreign policy well before the end of the Second World War. American and British thinkers worked out plans for an international architecture that should help the world recover economically and politically. Fighting hunger, poverty, desperation and chaos, promoting democracy was the thrust of that policy. The latter aimed at providing a functioning international *regime*, which was focused on economic reconstruction and peace, on necessary *global public goods*. That post-war vision continues to be highly relevant since today's world has to tackle massive deprivation and hunger, failing states and disorder, a huge financial crisis.

The complexity of world affairs at the start of the new century and the implications of a worldwide financial crisis raise the stakes in the attempt to deal with global issues creatively and effectively. The current financial mess, climate change, sustainable development (with its

---

[1] This is a revised version of a paper presented at the 60th Anniversary Symposium, "The Marshall Plan: Lessons Learned for the 21st Century," Hôtel de Talleyrand, Paris, France, 13 June 2007. The proceedings of the symposium were published in the volume with same title, co-edited by Eliot Sorel and Pier Carlo Padoan, OECD, Paris, 2008. Section V of this chapter is based on an article, "Capitalism's Uncertain Future," which I have published in *Europe's World* in Summer 2008.

social underpinnings), aid and trade, and, not least, averting a *clash of civilizations* are to be approached in a pragmatic, wise manner.

I. Public Policy in Today's World: A Plea for Open-Mindedness and Pragmatism

A fundamental lesson of the history of public policy is that this has to be pragmatic and open-minded in order to succeed. Harry Dexter White (the main US negotiator in the set up of the Bretton Woods System) and the famous British economist John Maynard Keynes provide a formidable case study in this regard.[2] I mention these two individuals' work having in mind the need of an international regime, nowadays, that should combine the provision of public goods with the use of incentives so that all parties comply with it. That this is not easy to achieve is another matter for discussion. For the very complexity of today's world and the rising number of actors (states, companies, NGOs), make the achievement of workable solutions, sometimes, quite impossible.

The past two decades have been suffused with claims that economic policy, in the advanced countries, is bring driven by an emerging new consensus on principles and practice. The sources of this apparent "new" consensus are, arguably, several. One origin could be traced to the ever longing desire of Man to control his environment (nature) and be more efficient. Max Weber's "rationalization of life" referred to rational accounting, rational law, rational technology, which by extrapolation, can be extended to "rational economics." Another famous sociologist, Daniel Bell, upheld the primacy of knowledge and theory-related activities in ordering our life, man's technological and economic ascendancy—which would imply that economic wizards can secure a fool-proof policy. Even the clash between main competing economic paradigms can be seen in the vein of searching for the ultimate piece of wisdom. Another origin of policy amalgamation comes out of the death of communism. Francis Fukuyama's *The End of History* was seen by many as a description of a single ideology which was meant to rule the world. Last, but not least, globalisation—when seen

---

[2] B. Eichengreen (chapter 4).

as a fundamentalist incarnation of unfettered markets and downsizing of government, operating worldwide—also provided an impetus to the vision of an "ideal" type of policy.

At the start of the new century facts are disavowing over-simplifications. There are numerous examples which prove that conflicting ideas matter a lot, that economics continues to be softer than some try to make us believe. How should one relate economic growth to a sense of fairness (justice) in society? In this regard I side with the thesis that growth must be socially sustainable. When central bank governors show disquiet to possible effects of income polarisation, our eyes and ears must be pretty open! Free markets are a plus wherever they work well, and property rights should be clearly defined and protected in order to harness entrepreneurship and creativity.[3] But it is also clear that trimming the welfare state and the public sector is not enough in order to achieve expected efficiency gains; this endeavour needs to be accompanied by effective regulations of various markets—financial and energy, primarily. The need for an "optimal design" of regulations is quite obvious.

The pressure of global competition forces governments to streamline public sectors. But rich countries, in the West, remain welfare states, *par excellence*, albeit in an evolving manner. One can detect here returning Keynesian touches in macroeconomic policy-making with a retreat when it comes to social policy. Some of wealthy countries' less inspired policies have given renewed high profile to issues such as: *fair vs. free trade*; dealing with abject poverty in the world; protecting the environment as a public good for mankind; a code of conduct for international corporations, how to manage contagion effects in the world economy; policy coordination among the leading economies of the world; etc.

Global economic growth implies global governance. A legitimate question here is what structures of global governance do we have and what the philosophy which underlies it is. It is increasingly clear that the international financial institutions (IFIs) need to reinvent themselves and involve more the emerging heavyweights (China, India, Brazil) in decision-making; the key players (states) in the world have to see eye to eye when it comes to tackle major global issues.

---

[3] See De Soto (1982), Easterly (2006) for the case of poor countries.

The traditional ongoing battle between left and right, within democratic politics, is being shifted, partially, into the international arena. The debate on *global governance* (which institutions and policies) reflects a growing awareness that there are issues which need to be addressed internationally, in a multilateral context and using collaborative approaches.[4] Arguably, the choice between globalisation and "managed globalisation" is between policy disregard for market failures, where they exist, and their social consequences and trying to construct an *international policy regime*, which should address recurrent coordination failures.[5]

Ideology is not dead, and it does shape social and economic policies—although in subtler forms and following cyclical patterns. It may be less felt nationally to the extent the battlefield of ideas expands increasingly beyond national borders. Globalisation is likely to reflect ever more the battle of ideas, with traditional politics delving increasingly into the international domain.

II. Which Globalisation?

Globalisation has triggered enormous controversies. Some see it as a *deus ex machina* for doing away with misery and conflict in the world. Others see it at the roots of mounting tensions in the world. Facts give conflicting signals. Technological change has reduced transportation and transaction (information) costs and speeded up the transfer of know-how, albeit in a highly skewed manner, among regions of the world; the internet connects hundreds of millions of people instantaneously; world trade has expanded tremendously and broadened the scope of choice for individuals throughout the world. The collapse of communism has expanded the work of market forces and democracy in a large area of the world. And the very dynamic of the EU can be seen as an alter ego of globalisation on a regional scale. At the same time, the distribution of wealth in the world seems to be more unequal than 20 years ago. Corporate scandals in the affluent world show that cronyism and bad governance are a more complex phenomenon than

---

[4] See Sachs (2005).
[5] See Stiglitz (2006).

is usually assumed and ascribed geographically; financial and currency crises have caused economic and social havoc in not a few countries; social fragmentation and exclusion have been rising in both wealthy and poor countries; there is a sense of disorder and a rising tide of discontent and frustration in many parts of the world; non-conventional threats, the use of weapons of mass destruction in particular, are an increasing threat.

Arguably, to make sense of facts is to look at the conceptual underpinnings of globalisation. And here there is an interpretation of globalisation which is pretty much overloaded ideologically. The last couple of decades have been dominated by a paradigm which extols the virtues of unbridled markets, privatization and extreme downsizing of the public sector—this is what some call market fundamentalism. The way emerging economies were pushed into opening their capital accounts during the 1990s is a glamorous illustration of this approach. Another example is the way energy markets were "liberalised" in emerging economies without proper regulations.

But globalisation can be understood in a different vein, which looks at the functioning of actual markets and which takes into account insights of modern economic theory: information asymmetries, increasing returns, agglomeration effects (clusters), multiple (bad) equilibria, etc. Thence inferences can be easily drawn: the need for effective regulation of markets, the role of institutions (structures of governance); the need of public goods in the world economy; the importance of *variety* and policy ownership in policy-making.[6] To some, this interpretation of globalisation may sow seeds of confusion. But, in this way, one can dispel a biased interpretation. Moreover, globalisation would no longer be assigned an ideological mantra and one-sided policy implications. Instead, it becomes an open-ended concept, which purports to define the mutual opening of societies, under the impetus of technological change and the manifold quest for economic progress. Consequently, national public policies should be fairly pragmatic and varied (not succumbing to fundamentalism), and geared towards the traditional goals of economic growth, price stability and social justice. Markets would have to be properly regulated and the state would

---

[6] See Rodrik (1998) on why policy has to be pragmatic and draw on various strands of knowledge.

have to provide essential public goods, which crowd in private output. Good public policies can make a difference.

The international economy indicates problems that need adequate answers. One of Keynes' intellectual legacies, enshrined in the Bretton Woods arrangements (that highly volatile capital flows are inimical to trade and prosperity), has not lost relevance. Those who say that it is hard to fetter capital movements in our times make a very strong point, but do not solve the issue. In addition, financial innovation, the growing use of complex derivatives, has reduced the transparency of global financial markets; this, unavoidably, undermines *trust*—without which financial systems are crippled. Some argue that self-regulation is better than regulation (a hot topic here is the case of hedge funds). But is self-regulation the right answer under any circumstances? I have doubts about it. Global governance relies increasingly on indirect tools, for various reasons. But I wonder whether, the under-supply of essential public goods by national governments would not put pressure on structures of global governance (not an "international government") to step in, one way or another.

Free trade cannot benefit poor countries when rich economies heavily subsidize agriculture and use trade barriers whenever they feel "injured"; double talk and hypocrisy make a mockery of the virtues of free trade. Likewise, diminishing aid to very poor countries is hard to justify when acknowledging the huge asymmetries in the world. One has to fight corruption and improve public governance, but aid has a role to play in assisting poor countries. This is a major lesson of the Marshall Plan—its magnanimity, combined with pragmatism and clairvoyance at a time when Europe was in terrible economic distress.

A keen sense of urgency and a pragmatic vision would demand a different policy in order to deal with the threats of spreading epidemics, massive illegal migration, abject poverty and environmental damage—not to mention the scourge of international terrorism. All these challenges make up an agenda which can be assumed by an enlightened interpretation of globalisation.[7] The US and the EU have a key role to play in setting and implementing this agenda.

---

[7] Frieden (2007) calls for a legitimate political governance of globalisation and appropriate domestic policies.

III. The EU at "Midlife": Cause for Celebration, but with Guarded Optimism

The Union celebrated its 50th anniversary at a time of vastly enhanced significance; it is a time of serious challenges[8] that demand a new policy thrust. The Union faces growing complexity, brought on in part by the successive rounds of enlargement. At the same time, its social model is heavily strained by the need to make markets more flexible and demographics.

Managing increasing complexity means dealing with a number of thorny issues. Should tax and fiscal policies be made more convergent in order to prevent a "race to the bottom"? When factors of production are increasingly mobile, who or what should be taxed? How should the Union deal with economic nationalism? Implementing the Lisbon Agenda requires major reforms in education, energy, R&D and agricultural policy, but how should these changes be brought about? Variable geometry, a rising variety of socioeconomic conditions (with geographic positions leading to different neighbourhood policy inclinations) and diverging views among member countries can bring policy co-ordination to a standstill.

In part because of global competition, the EU is under pressure to become more flexible, loosen its bureaucratic entanglements and reform the welfare state. At the same time, market fundamentalism is on the retreat, and there is a strong impetus to bring social and environmental concerns into mainstream policymaking. Meanwhile, failures in financial and other markets during the past decade have fuelled a demand for more effective regulations. It is not becoming any easier to balance these contradictory forces. One key to doing so lies in education policy. Placing more emphasis on such subjects as engineering, math, physics and computer science would help build a competitive edge based on technological advances, higher value-added products and services. Attaining such an edge would relieve some of the pressures pushing against the European Social Model.

---

[8] For a clear and analytical description of these challenges, see Alesina and Giavazzi (2006).

Certainly, continued efforts to streamline the welfare state will be needed. But the difficulties involved should not be underestimated, as they involve a basic redefinition of the social contract. Would wage earners accept a slower rise in their incomes (or even a cut) and would capital-owners accept lower dividends for the sake of greater public and private productive investment? Such possibilities might be conceivable if all parties were governed by ethical imperatives and a sense of responsibility. However, there is much to suggest this is not the case. Recent years have seen an astonishing rise in the incomes of CEOs at a time of modest or even stagnant wages, when income polarization has increased in almost all western societies and the middle class has frequently lost out. The corporate world has been hit by a succession of scandals, eroding trust in its ability to self-regulate. In such an environment, is it reasonable to expect employees to become altruistic? The need in the EU to cope with the pressures of globalisation, of demography (including the reform of the welfare state) is not a reason to underplay morality and the need for mutual respect. In order for citizens to accept painful reforms, to enter a new social contract nothing would be more counterproductive than telling them that they have to give up what has made their lives more dignified; that they have to accept CEOs' rise in salaries and bonuses while the performances of the companies those individuals run stagnate, or even go down.

In the enlarged Europe we need a capitalism that performs economically and socially. For this to happen the liberty of markets to function has to be accompanied by the rule of law, which should punish those who are careless about and disrespectful of public interest. Market fundamentalism is inimical to a decent capitalism, to capitalism with a soul.[9] I would recall that Adam Smith wrote also *The Theory of Moral Sentiments*, that Max Weber connected hard work and moral values (ethics) with the advance of capitalism in the western world. Public policy has to try to correct malign parts of the functioning of markets; it has to deal with the social fallout of unlimited greed, lack of honesty, cynicism, selfishness, etc. Decent capitalism ("that respects

---

[9] Those who argue that business scandals are caused by "insufficient capitalism" (by too many regulations) are laughable. It is like telling Asians that the financial crises of the past decade were due to a too slow opening of the capital account, which is nonsensical.

the dignity of man," to use Amartya Sen's words) needs an effective public policy, aside from virtues to be found in individual beings' pursuits of happiness and material rewards. Bill Gates' capitalism is clearly superior to the one practiced by a Michael Milken, Ivan Boesky or Kenneth Lay. Balancing social and economic imperatives imply ethical values: honesty and trustworthiness, honour and respect, loyalty, hard work, education, family, community, altruism and compassion. I suggest that the OECD should pay more attention to such aspects.

Ethical questions impact international politics as well. Issues such as environmental protection, securing drinkable water, and combating disease and poverty constitute an urgent agenda. Failures in this area can ultimately have security implications, as global divisions become amplified and militant ideologies find a receptive audience among the excluded. The EU (and the US, too) has been charged, not unfairly, with not practicing what it preaches when it comes to developing economies—the collapse of the Doha trade round is a signature example here. This issue, in turn, is connected to the way the Union operates. EU Commissioners often have a difficult time resisting the pressures exerted by the bloc's heavyweights. This is not necessarily surprising but should not be overlooked.

EU policymaking will have to evolve somehow if it is to meet increasingly complex challenges. The steps ahead may be less so, but this does not diminish their importance. Enlargement fatigue is a reality, but so is the need to show vision and statesmanship. If the *Bloc* hopes to act as a guidance rod and a beacon of hope for the rest of the world (and not be seen as a form of "closed regionalism"), it will need to demonstrate the ability to handle seemingly intractable problems on its own turf—including the western Balkans.

IV. Capitalism vs. Capitalism in the 21st century

Investment by sovereign wealth funds (SWFs) reached a record 50 billion US dollars or so in 2007. In the deepening financial crisis, and after their severe losses in the sub-prime debacle, Citigroup, Morgan Stanley, Merrill Lynch and UBS all sought liquidity injections from SWFs by selling them equity. These transactions took place against the background of the SWFs' growing visibility in the world economy. The

G-7 finance ministers invited international organisations, notably the IMF and OECD, to consider the role of SWFs—and the IMF, in co-operation with fund owners, is now developing an SWFs code of conduct, and the OECD is identifying best practices for recipient countries. The EU, too, has taken up the whole issue seriously.

SWFs are not new. Decades ago, several countries (Kuwait in 1953, Singapore, Norway, the United Arab Emirates) established SWFs to manage their substantial foreign exchange reserves—essentially oil and gas revenues that couldn't be fully invested in their own economies without endangering stability. Investing abroad was therefore the logical way forward. The rapid and durable rise in energy prices of recent years, together with the exceptional performance of the Asian economies, led to significant growth in the number of SWFs. In 2007, SWFs were estimated to control assets worth somewhere between 1.5 trillion to 2.5 trillion US dollars, and with rising commodity prices it is thought that this figure will by 2015 have risen to 12 trillion US dollars.

The rise of the SWFs looks likely to have an increasingly significant impact on international politics. The reason for this is simple—some of the SWFs belong to countries that had since World War II been ideologically opposed to the western world. China's foreign exchange reserves, for example, had reached more than 1,400 billion by late 2007, while those of Russia exceed 400 billion US dollars—and both are nations with large SWFs. It's therefore possible to place the SWF phenomenon in a broader context of global competition and of diverging national interests—indeed, it is possible to consider this issue in terms of a clash of capitalisms.

In the wake of the fall of communism some analysts focused on a form a competition amongst capitalist systems within the wealthy western world. The influential French economist Michel Albert in the early 1990s wrote a book called "Capitalism versus capitalism" in which he viewed global economic competition as essentially a struggle between the Anglo-Saxon economic model and the continental model in France, Germany and elsewhere. Over the past decade, the concept of "Fortress Europe" has also gained currency, and the European economies appeared to be successfully reducing their productivity gap with the US. MIT's Lester Thurow saw a tri-polar world economy emerging, with Japan as the third pole. This vision of economic power in the world shared between America, Europe and Japan was glaringly illustrated by the composition of the Trilateral Commission, whose meetings group leaders from all three.

Nowadays, though, a new global competition between different models of capitalism can also be seen. This reflects momentous changes in the world economy, and underlines their geopolitical implications. China's formidable economic ascent in the last two decades, and India's more recent rise along with that Asia in general, all signal tectonic shifts in the global economy. These economies are characterised by dynamism, and that in turn is reflected in their economic growth, their soaring exports, the size of their foreign exchange reserves and not just their absorption of modern technologies (ICTs) but increasingly their own generation of new technology. China and India each graduate over half a million engineers a year, and the presence of their scientists in top professional journals is more then eye-catching. Both countries are also making big inroads into reshaping the world institutional order that has regulated international affairs since the end of World War II. The debate on reforming International Financial Institutions (IFIs), as well as the causes behind the stalling of the Doha trade round, are examples of this. It is no longer realistic to pursue any real issues of global governance without involving China and India.

Chinese and Indian companies can boast global outreach and are now acquiring significant stakes in companies around the world, including in the west. India's Tata group is to begin production of an extraordinarily cheap car that could be a global phenomenon, and it has bought the two famous brands of Land Rover and Jaguar from Ford, the American giant which, like GM, is going through hard times.

China, along with India and Brazil, is increasingly present in regions of the world where it's strategically important to control scarce, exhaustible resources ranging from industrial minerals to oil and gas. China uses international economic aid as a means of bolstering its credentials in poorer countries, notably in Africa, that have major natural resources. This poses a challenge to both the US and the EU. At the same time, Russia is staging a comeback on the international scene precisely because of the enormous scale of its natural resources. Lukoil and Gazprom have been expanding their operations in Europe by capitalising on EU's high dependence on external supplies of energy, and its lack of a common energy policy.

Asia's remarkable economic progress is re-landscaping competitive hierarchies around the world, and is reducing the west's ability to set the rules of the game. This redistribution of world economic power is also having geo-political effects—these concern regional political and economic dynamics, security alliances, the reform of IFIs, global governance structures and competition for strategic resources.

This geo-political perspective suggests that the title of Michael Albert's 1991 book could perhaps be paraphrased. In Asia, with the exceptions of India and to some extent Japan, the prevailing form of capitalism has an authoritarian shade and relies on state structures. This type of capitalism hinges on corporatist structures, on industrial policies and selective protectionism. It operates in Russia too, where the state controls the major energy groups. Clearly, economic rationality has to be reconciled with other factors when the state's wider interests have to be taken into account. That's especially true in a world increasingly worried about the scarcity of non-renewable energy resources and in which global warming is creating very complicated trade-offs for policy-making, and where food looks like becoming less plentiful because of climate change pressures.

Not even India, the world's largest democracy, sees eye to eye at a geo-political level with either the US or the EU. That India and the US have come to an agreement on energy and on the major issue of nuclear weapons does not radically change the scope for competition between these different types of capitalism, even if it is possible to argue that a growing rivalry is developing between China and India on which the US could capitalise. In any case, when it comes to reforming IFIs and international trade, India would clearly side with the other emerging economies.

The western world is and will remain the most powerful bloc, economically and militarily, for the foreseeable future. But the US has been weakened by its external deficits and by military overstretch in Iraq and Afghanistan. Its deepening financial crisis also raises major concerns over business governance, with under-regulation and inadequate supervision and America's blind belief in the self-regulating virtues of markets—market fundamentalism—becoming increasingly problematic. How ironic all this must seem to Asians, given the western world's preaching at the time of the Asian financial crisis a decade ago.

The EU too is struggling to manage its growing organisational complexity while tackling various forms of institutional and policy incoherence. China and the other Asian countries, meanwhile, are progressing economically and technologically at a very fast pace—a trend that's likely to continue in the next two decades or so, even if some of their economic momentum is temporarily eroded by the economic woes of the US and Europe. And Moscow is using the Russian Federation's energy-based financial muscle to play once more at global power politics. All these dynamics look more salient still when placed against the backdrop of the worldwide contest for scarce natural resources, the intricate situation in the Middle East and the rivalries in the Caspian Sea region and in Africa.

Authoritarian techniques like direct state involvement in the economy and society are even finding a degree of favour in liberal democracies. This reflects fears of terrorism, along with the need to cope with global warming while securing energy supplies. The debate in the US on the implications of the Patriot Act, and its echoes in the EU's member states is quite telling, and the rise in economic nationalism should also be seen in this light.

Throughout the world we are witnessing the resurrection of a policy paradigm that sees state intervention as an optimal means of achieving results. Policymaking of a type normally associated with a war economy is therefore likely to proliferate, especially when quick responses and the immediate mobilisation of major resources are needed. The deepening of the current financial crisis is also vindicating those who have long cautioned against market fundamentalism. This is a crisis that is bolstering pragmatism and policies that do not confuse free markets with completely deregulated ones.

Capitalism won the Cold War and defeated the communist system. But it is by no means certain that this guarantees the victory of "liberal democracy"—to use Fareed Zakaria's term for describing the western world. Competition between different types of capitalism has a major geo-political dimension, and, just how the transatlantic relationship in particular, will be managed in the future is a key concern.

Reforms that could bring greater vitality to the western economies are also very important. The EU's Lisbon agenda is a vitally important policy response, yet seems already to have been overtaken by the new focus on global warming and energy security. Now the need is to update the Lisbon agenda, and improve industrial and economic performance.

To sum up, the relative decline of the economic power of the US and EU seems inevitable, in terms of their share of global GDP, industrial production and world trade. But this relative decline, described by the political scientist Nicole Gnesotto in the Summer 2007 issue of Europe's World as "the growing powerlessness of the West," may be accompanied by a rise in its so-called soft power—especially if new countries join the family of liberal democracies. This would be very much in tune with American political scientist Samuel Huntington's idea of the "third wave of democratisation." The expansion of the west's soft power would involve more concern for global issues, such as global warming and international trade, the greater involvement of emerging global powers like China and India in tackling the world's "hot spots" and, not least, a reappraisal of the moral values which have brought economic prosperity and political empowerment to ordinary citizens during modern history. This reappraisal would include paying genuine attention to the concerns of the rest of the world.

V. Final Remarks

The world needs a better (more effective) international institutional architecture, which should deal with global challenges (including the current financial crisis) and take care of global commons. The US and the EU have a key role to play—whether one refers to reinventing the IMF and the World Bank, enhancing the role of the emerging economic giants into the running of IFIs, and not least, in reversing the tendency of erosion of multilateralism of recent years. In this context repairing the transatlantic relationship is urgent in view of the challenges ahead. To paraphrase former secretary of state, Madeleine Albright, this is to be seen as an indispensable relationship.

The evolving global economy, the rise of Asia, bring with them new major competitors and a change of competitive hierarchies. Countries which have skilled people, which invest in education and have forward looking public policies, are more likely to enjoy the fruits of the global dissemination of technology. The talk about a *knowledge-based economy* is not a temporary fashion.

Those who believe that only non-zero games prevail in the world need a "wake up call". The tectonic shifts in the world economy open up the possibility for co-operative relationships, but also for sharpened tensions. Consider, for instance, the growing need for energy and basic commodities in Asia, the unsolved or deepened geopolitical crises in various parts of the world (in the Middle East in particular), nuclear proliferation, and the visible and hidden aspects of the struggle against terrorism. The current deep financial crisis fuels centrifugal forces and highlights the downside of unrestrained globalization.

So, who would formulate and enforce a suitable international regime for the 21st century? The US will not have the capacity do so (as it used to do in the aftermath of the Second World War) any longer. The implications of the current financial crisis play a conspicuous role in this regard. In its current shape, the EU could not take over such a role. And an overhaul of the international architecture of financial institutions hinges on what the main international actors wish to do and on how they relate to each other. If the US, the EU and the emerging global powers can strike a deal on reform, other significant players would eventually come along. Their challenge would be to make "pragmatic" openness work for the world as a whole. That implies shedding a blind belief in the self-healing and self-regulatory virtues of markets. That may be happening.

REFERENCES

Michel, A. (1993) *Capitalism vs. Capitalism*, New York, Four Walls Eight Windows.

Alesina, A. and Giavazzi, F. (2006) *The Future of Europe: Reform or Decline*, Cambridge, MIT Press.

Baverez, N. (2003) *La France Qui Tombe* (France that goes down), Paris, Perrin.

Bebear, C. (2003) *Ils vont tuer le capitalisme* (They are going to kill capitalism), Paris, Plon.

Bell, D. (1973) *The Coming of the Post-industrial State*, Cambridge, MIT Press.

Bofinger, P. (2005) *Wir Sind Besser als Wir Glauben* (We are better than we think), Munich, Pearson.

Brittan, S. (2006) "Globalization depresses western wages" *Financial Times*, 20 October 2006.

Easterly, W. (2006) *The White Man's Burden*, New York, Penguin Press.

Eichengreen, B. (1996) *Globalizing Capital. A History of the International Monetary System*, Princeton, Princeton University Press.

Fitoussi, J.P. (2005) *La Politique de l'Impuissance (The Politics of Impotence)*, Paris, Arlea.

Frieden, J. (2007) "Will Global Capitalism Fall Again?" Brugel essay and lecture series.

Fukuyama, F. (1990) *The End of History*, New York, Free Press.

Giddens, A. (1998) *The Third Way*, New York, Blackwell.

Giddens, A. (2006) *Europe in the Global Age*, London, Polity.

Gnesotto, N. (2007) *Europe's World*, Summer issue.

De Soto, H. (1989) *The Other Path*, New York, Basic Books.

Deepak, L. (1999) *Unintended Consequences: The Impact of Factor Endowments, Culture and Politics on Long-Run Economic Performance*, Cambridge, MIT Press.

Padoan, P.C. (2007), *The Marshall Plan, Lessons Learned: an OECD Perspective*, manuscript.

Rodrik, D. (1996) Understanding economic policy reform, *Journal of Economic Literature*, vol. 34.

Rodrik, D. (1998) *The Global Economy and Developing Countries: Making Openness Work*, Washington D.C., Overseas Development Council.

Sachs, Jeffrey (2005), *The End of Poverty*, New York, The Penguin Press.

Sapir A. (2003) "An Agenda for a Growing Europe. Making the EU Economic System Deliver" Report of an Independent High Level Study group, EC, Brussels.

Sapir, A. (2005) "Globalization and the reform of the European social models" Background document for the presentation at ECOFIN informal meeting in Manchester, September, Bruegel.

Servan Schreiber, J.J. (1968) *Le Defi Americain* (The American Challenge), Paris, Gallimard.

Sen, A. (1999) *Development as Freedom*, New York, Alfred Knopf.

Sinn, H. W. (2004) *Ist Deutschland noch zu retten?* (Can Germany be saved?), Berlin, Ullstein.

Stiglitz, J. (2006) *Making Globalization Work*, New York, Norton.

Summers, L. (2006) "The Global middle cries out for reassurance" *Financial Times*, 30 October.

Thurow, L. (1993) *Head to Head*, Cambridge, MIT Press.

EPILOGUE

Keynes Is Back[1]

The financial crisis is causing anguish and tremors around the world, forcing governments to nationalise large chunks of their banking sectors and central banks to inject huge amounts of liquidity into money markets. Some have hastened to claim this crisis indicates that capitalism does not work; others accuse governments of, *de facto*, ushering in socialism. Both trains of thought are misleading.

Economic freedom and entrepreneurship, which lie at the root of innovation and economic advance, rely on and feed on free markets; that much is indisputable and explains why communist economies collapsed, eventually. In this regard Ludwig von Mises, Friedrich von Hayek and other proponents of classical liberal economics were quite right. But it is misleading to argue that free markets are synonymous with non-regulated markets, with the effective extinction of public sectors and public policies. Modern economies and societies do need regulations and public policies to ensure an adequate supply of public goods and prevent or limit negative externalities, business costs borne by society. That implies the need for a public sector that functions against the backdrop of a free allocation of resources (at market prices) and vibrant economic competition. And there is also need of a moral compass, without which everything else becomes bogged down sooner or later.

Many now accept that the Asian crisis of 1997 was caused, primarily, by a premature opening of the capital account in the region's economies. Similarly, a rush to privatise public utilities is not warranted; indeed, some utilities are better left in public hands. The oversimplification of "good practices" in governance—and, not least, the hypocrisy that has, in more than a few instances, accompanied their

---

[1] This is an article which appeared in *European Voice* on 21 October 2008.

propagation by industrialised countries—is now more than obvious around the world. This deep financial crisis, the failed Doha trade round and the lack of results wherever development policies have been simplistically encapsulated in the ideological mantra of neo-liberalism are quite telling. There are profound structural weaknesses in most poor countries—corruption, opaque property rights, waste, the theft and huge misallocation of public resources—but they do not add up to a convincing argument in favour of accepting, without qualifications, policy remedies that are too general and, sometimes, divorced from local conditions.

The financial crisis that has now struck at the very heart of the world's financial industry is, arguably, a persuasive refutation of the paradigm that glorified total deregulation. The repeal in 1999 of the Glass-Steagall Act that limited ownership of financial companies operating in other market segments, like the decision in 2004 to exempt the brokerage operations of Wall Street investment banks from limits on the amount of debt they could take on, have proved to be historic blunders. The huge bail-outs under way in the financial sectors are going to introduce, or reinforce, elements of state capitalism in numerous industrialised countries, including the US. The impact on national budgets could by tremendous for years to come. In order to mitigate the pain inflicted and to reduce dependency on external borrowings, savings ratios will have to rise in all economies whose banks have been recapitalised in a significant way. A legitimate question arises: Can the societies of rich countries, almost out of the blue, economise and become forward-looking? The answer hinges very much on social cohesion (solidarity) and the capacity of politicians to lead in times of distress.

If one adds here the implications of aging and strained welfare states, climate change, as well as the competitiveness challenges posed by emerging global powers, it is not hard to delineate the contours of a very complicated public-policy agenda that will last for decades to come.

The effects of the current financial crisis have hit the Western world at a time when a decade-long tectonic shift is under way in the global economy. The rise of China, India, Brazil and the resuscitation of a capitalist Russia are ushering in an increasingly multi-polar world, with profounder reverberations economically and geopolitically. The struggle for the control of exhaustible resources (oil and gas in particular) epitomises this phenomenon. The financial crisis has given more salience to the inherent weaknesses of policies that are fundamentalist rather than pragmatic.

The fall of communism, which was equated by some with the "end of history," has immensely favoured the advance of neo-liberal ideas. Needless to say, the overwhelming superiority of the US on all fronts (economic, military, technological) offered a sort of a sui generis Pax Americana and created the prerequisites for an international regime. The latter was supposed to order the world by providing international public goods and resolving or preventing major conflicts. But neo-liberalism—or market fundamentalism—has revealed its serious flaws over time and has currently, willy-nilly, been put on the shelf in order to ensure market economies continue to function. What is happening now is not a dismissal of market forces as an essential mechanism for resource allocation and to stimulate entrepreneurship, but is, rather, an invalidation of a gross misinterpretation of what it takes for a modern economy to perform economically and socially over the long run.

Fragments of state capitalism are being put in place and we will see what will remain of them over time. Probably, substantial portions of the new state sectors in the making will eventually become private once again. Monetary policies are geared now toward achieving financial stability and have acquired a sort of flexibility that is reminiscent of the injunctions of John Maynard Keynes, the great British advocate of the value of government intervention, regarding ways of avoiding bad equilibria (the Great Depression was a terribly bad "equilibrium"). The very concern of governments and central banks with radically overhauling the regulation and supervision of financial markets, so that "Minsky moments"—moments at which, according to the now deceased economist Hyman Minsky, financiers lay waste to the economy—are averted is a strong validation of Keynes' intellectual legacy and of his sense of realism in understanding the functioning of markets in general.

The crux of the matter here is that our reshaped mixed economies have to function in such a way that extravagant policies are avoided for the benefit of democracy and the welfare of most citizens. Cycles cannot be eliminated, and there will be further crises in future. But a financial meltdown, with its very dire effects on the real economy, can be prevented by adopting proper policies and regulations.

The EU and US will come out of this crisis with reshaped economies (with larger public sectors) and will continue to be, fundamentally, liberal democracies. But the financial crisis has already weakened them and will not halt the ascendancy of the new global powers. The future will be driven by a competition between liberal democracy and authoritarian forms of capitalism (principally exemplified by China and Russia). In liberal democracies, war-type economy measures may have to be resorted from time to time; indeed, the operations currently under way to rescue banks fall within that category of policy action.

Western countries will have to come to grips with their weakened relative status in the world economy and shed much of their hubris in dealing with the rest of the world, for their own sake. This would apply to the reform of the International Financial Institutions and a new architecture for tackling global governance issues. As some say, a new Bretton Woods is needed. This marks the return of Keynes and the idea of government stimuli. We need common sense and pragmatism in economic policy-making, not fundamentalism.

Appendix 1

European Parliament Resolution of 9 October 2008 with Recommendations to the Commission on Lamfalussy Follow-Up: Future Structure of Supervision (2008/2148(INI)

The European Parliament,
- having regard to the Fourth Council Directive 78/660/EEC of 25 July 1978 based on Article 54(3)(g) of the Treaty on the annual accounts of certain types of companies(1),
- having regard to the Seventh Council Directive 83/349/EEC of 13 June 1983 based on the Article 54(3)(g) of the Treaty on consolidated accounts(2),
- having regard to Council Directive 86/635/EEC of 8 December 1986 on the annual accounts and consolidated accounts of banks and other financial institutions(3),
- having regard to Council Directive 91/674/EEC of 19 December 1991 on the annual accounts and consolidated accounts of insurance undertakings(4),
- having regard to Directive 94/19/EC of the European Parliament and of the Council of 30 May 1994 on deposit-guarantee schemes(5),
- having regard to Directive 2001/24/EC of the European Parliament and of the Council of 4 April 2001 on the reorganisation and winding up of credit institutions(6),
- having regard to Directive 2002/87/EC of the European Parliament and of the Council of 16 December 2002 on the supplementary supervision of credit institutions, insurance undertakings and investment firms in a financial conglomerate(7),
- having regard to Directive 2004/39/EC of the European Parliament and of the Council of 21 April 2004 on markets in financial instruments(8),
- having regard to Directive 2004/109/EC of the European Parliament and of the Council of 15 December 2004 on the harmonisation of transparency requirements in relation to information about issuers whose securities are admitted to trading on a regulated market(9),
- having regard to Directive 2006/48/EC of the European Parliament and of the Council of 14 June 2006 relating to the taking up and pursuit of the business of credit institutions (recast)(10),

- having regard to Directive 2006/49/EC of the European Parliament and of the Council of 14 June 2006 on the capital adequacy of investment firms and credit institutions (recast)(11),
- having regard to the amended Commission proposal for a directive of the European Parliament and of the Council on the taking-up and pursuit of the business of Insurance and Reinsurance (Solvency II) (recast) (COM(2008)0119),
- having regard to the Commission Communication of 27 September 2004 on Preventing and Combating Corporate and Financial Malpractice (COM(2004)0611),
- having regard to the Commission Recommendation 2004/913/EC of 14 December 2004 fostering an appropriate regime for the remuneration of directors of listed companies(12),
- having regard to its resolutions of 11 July 2007 on financial services policy (2005–2010)—White Paper(13), of 4 July 2006 on consolidation of financial services industry(14), of 28 April 2005 on the current state of integration of EU financial markets(15) and of 21 November 2002 on prudential supervision rules in the European Union(16),
- having regard to the Report of the Financial Stability Forum on Enhancing Market and Institutional Resilience of 7 April 2008,
- having regard to the Council conclusions on the EU supervisory framework and financial stability arrangements, adopted on 14 May 2008, and Council conclusions on related issues following its meetings of 3 June 2008, 4 December 2007 and 9 October 2007,
- having regard to Article 192, second paragraph, of the EC Treaty,
- having regard to Rules 39 and 45 of its Rules of Procedure,
- having regard to the report of the Committee on Economic and Monetary Affairs (A6-0359/2008),

A. whereas there is an ongoing review of Directives 2006/48/EC and 2006/49/EC and an expected proposal on credit rating agencies,

B. whereas the Commission has not addressed a series of requests from Parliament, including those made in its above-mentioned resolutions and whereas a list of recommendations as to how the functioning of financial markets supervision might be improved is set out in the Annex,

C. whereas financial supervision has not kept pace with market integration and the global evolution of financial markets demanding an update of the existing regulation and supervision systems in order to tackle systemic risks better, provide financial stability, attain the objectives of the European Union and contribute to an improved global financial governance,

D. whereas any suggestion made by Parliament for legislation should be principle-based and the recommendations set out in the Annex should be developed in consultation with the supervisory authorities, financial markets participants and other relevant bodies,

E. whereas there is a growing number of pan-European entities, whose activities span several Member States; whereas the interlocking of many national authorities has increased complexity and blurred the lines of responsibility, especially for macro-prudential supervision and crisis management,

F. whereas the current financial crisis, which was triggered by US subprime mortgages and derived products, has spread worldwide due to the increasingly integrated nature of markets, reinforcing the indication that existing financial market regulation and supervision is not sufficiently convergent at either EU or international level; whereas a reform of financial market regulation and supervision is therefore welcome,

G. whereas the crisis has led to a credit squeeze entailing a higher price of credit for many market players; whereas economic growth and employment are impaired by the current turmoil on the financial markets,

H. whereas capital markets intermediation and new kinds of financial vehicles did bring about benefits, but have also given rise to new sources of systemic risk globally,

I. whereas the "originate-to-distribute" model has enhanced competition and spread risk; whereas that model has, however, weakened incentives to evaluate and monitor risk and led to a breakdown in due diligence in some cases,

J. whereas improper practices such as inadequate risk management, irresponsible lending, excessive debt (leverage), weak due diligence and sudden withdrawal of liquidity pose significant risks to financial institutions and may threaten financial stability,

K. whereas innovative techniques, which were designed to diminish risk at the micro level, and themselves complied with current regulation, could lead to risk concentration and systemic risk,

L. whereas harmful regulatory arbitrage should be prevented,

M. whereas the increasing cross-border nature of banking in Europe and the need to respond in a coordinated way to adverse shocks, as well as the need to deal with systemic risks effectively, require divergences between the national regimes of Member States to be reduced to the greatest extent possible; whereas there is a need to move beyond the studies that the Commission has already carried out in this regard and to amend Directive 94/19/EC as soon as possible to provide the same level of protection for bank deposits across the whole European Union in order to preserve financial stability and depositors' confidence and avoid distortions of competition,

N. whereas adequate levels of transparency towards the public, investors and supervisory authorities must be ensured,

O. whereas compensation schemes which reflect individual and corporate performance should not reward excessive risk-taking for short-term, at the expense of necessary long-term, performance and prudence,

P. whereas conflicts of interest, which may arise from the business model used by financial institutions, credit rating agencies, and audit and law firms, must be addressed and monitored,

Q. whereas failures by credit rating agencies in respect of complex structured products and misconceptions of the meaning of ratings by market participants have generated substantial negative externalities and market uncertainties; whereas credit rating agencies' procedures need reviewing,

R. whereas self-regulatory solutions, proposed by the credit rating agencies are as yet untested and probably insufficient to meet the pivotal role they play in the financial system,

S. whereas market integration, while generally beneficial, should be accompanied by an appropriately integrated approach to supervision, which also avoids unnecessary red tape and is consistent with better regulation policies,

T. whereas the Commission should carry out a comprehensive impact assessment of a legislative proposal,

U. whereas the European Union needs more consistent and effective, properly implemented, but not overly burdensome, regulation and supervision in order to mitigate the risk of future financial crises and ensure a level playing field across borders and among all market participants; whereas the European Union should play a leading international role and should reinforce the consistent implementation and convergence of its own regulation and supervision,

V. whereas a comprehensive review of current EU regulatory and supervisory arrangements is necessary together with measures to improve global supervisory cooperation covering the capital adequacy framework, transparency, and governance as key prerequisites for effective regulatory and supervisory arrangements in a coordinated manner,

W. whereas the supervisory approach should be adapted to specificities of the business and aspects of it that are already regulated; whereas the objectives of financial market supervision and the prudential supervision of particular institutions vary,

X. whereas future proposals should take account of negotiations on the Solvency II proposal and the review of Directives 2006/48/EC and 2006/49/EC,

Y. whereas supervisory cooperation needs to take into account the third-country dimension of supervision of international groups as most, if not all, major financial groups in the European Union have third-country interests,

Z. whereas following the Council conclusions of 3 June 2008, 4 December 2007 and 9 October 2007, a major programme of work is already under way to make targeted improvements to the arrangements for EU supervisory cooperation; whereas extensive work programmes are under way in the European Union and worldwide with a view to understanding the causes of market turmoil and responding appropriately,

AA. whereas a group of wise persons should be set up by autumn 2008, bringing together different stakeholders, such as supervisors, regulators and industry representatives, and elaborating a longer term supervisory vision; whereas that group should be tasked with developing a blueprint and a roadmap for a more radical long-term reform towards full institutional integration; whereas going beyond the architecture of financial supervision, the group could also address issues such as a single rulebook for financial supervision, a deposit guarantee scheme and a common insolvency regime, which are commensurate with an integrated financial and supervisory system,

1. Requests the Commission to submit to Parliament by 31 December 2008, on the basis of Article 44, Article 47(2), Article 55, Article 95, Article 105(6), Article 202, Article 211 or Article 308 of the EC Treaty, a legislative proposal or proposals covering the matters dealt with in the detailed recommendations below;
2. Confirms that the recommendations respect the principle of subsidiarity and the fundamental rights of citizens;
3. Considers that, where appropriate, the financial implications of the requested proposal or proposals should be covered by EU budgetary allocations;
4. Instructs its President to forward this resolution and the accompanying detailed recommendations to the Commission, the Council and the governments and parliaments of the Member States.

(1)	OJ L 222, 14.8.1978, p. 11.	(9)	OJ L 390, 31.12.2004, p. 38.
(2)	OJ L 193, 18.7.1983, p. 1.	(10)	OJ L 177, 30.6.2006, p. 1.
(3)	OJ L 372, 31.12.1986, p. 1.	(11)	OJ L 177, 30.6.2006, p. 201.
(4)	OJ L 374, 31.12.1991, p. 7.	(12)	OJ L 385, 29.12.2004, p. 55.
(5)	OJ L 135, 31.5.1994, p. 5.	(13)	OJ C 175E, 10.7.2008, p. 392.
(6)	OJ L 125, 5.5.2001, p. 15.	(14)	OJ C 303E, 13.12.2006, p.110.
(7)	OJ L 35, 11.2.2003, p. 1.	(15)	OJ C 45E, 23.2.2006, p. 140.
(8)	OJ L 145, 30.4.2004, p. 1.	(16)	OJ C 25E, 29.1.2004, p. 394.

Annex To The Resolution:
Detailed Recommendations on the Content
of the Proposal(s) Requested

1. RECOMMENDATION 1—BASIC PREREQUISITES FOR EFFECTIVE REGULATORY AND SUPERVISORY ARRANGEMENTS

The European Parliament considers that the legislative act(s) to be adopted should aim to regulate:

1.1. Measures to improve the EU financial services regulatory framework

Capital adequacy framework, in particular:
a) revise capital requirements rules by strengthening risk management, liquidity and exposure provisions in a consistent and, where appropriate, counter-cyclical manner for entities operating on financial markets, and ensure appropriate capital requirements for all entities operating on financial markets while taking into account systemic risk;
b) enhance the resilience of the capital adequacy framework to be able to deal with financial market disruption, whilst respecting the responsibilities of national authorities;
c) ensure that the rules are counter-cyclical as far as possible;
d) reform the framework to improve risk management; ensure adequacy of mathematical models, and, as appropriate, expand the range of scenarios and frequency of stress testing;
e) ensure appropriate capital requirements for complex financial products and derivatives;
f) ensure disclosure of off-balance-sheet items, structured investment vehicles (SIVs) and any liquidity assistance facility, and require proper assessment of the risks that they pose, so that market participants are aware of their existence and of how they operate.

1.2. Measures to improve transparency

a) Securitisation: foster transparency, clarity and the provision of data on complex financial products and the securitisation process, taking into account industry-led initiatives in this area; ensure that the securitisation and credit rating process does not result in an unjustified increase in the total value of the securitised product beyond the value of the underlying assets.
b) Complex Financial Products (CFS): ensure that credit rating agencies use consistent and appropriate rating terminology that clarifies how such products differ among themselves especially in terms of volatility, complexity and vulnerability to market stress, while taking account of the need for in-

vestors to develop procedures to assess the quality of structured products without relying solely on ratings.

c) Accounting rules, valuation and pricing:
  i) ensure an appropriate accounting treatment of material securitisation vehicles, so that companies and financial institutions cannot artificially keep material special purpose vehicles or SIVs, etc. off their balance sheets;
  ii) ensure that the rules on valuation and pricing standards for complex financial products are appropriate, in particular in the context of IAS 39, to be elaborated in cooperation with the IASB and other competent international bodies.

d) Unregulated markets: increase transparency of over-the-counter (OTC) markets with regard to their liquidity, address major sources of systemic risk (i.e. counterparty concentration risk), and, where appropriate, encourage market participants to clear OTC trades in clearing houses.

1.3. Governance measures

a) Securitisation: require originators to assess and monitor risk and ensure transparency of the debt or mortgage backed securities in order to allow investors to perform adequate due diligence.

b) Remuneration schemes: ensure financial institutions disclose their remuneration policy, including stock options, in particular the remuneration and compensation packages of directors; ensure that all transactions involving management can be clearly identified in the financial statements; ensure prudential supervisors include in their assessment of risk management the influence of remuneration, bonus schemes and taxation to ensure that they contain balanced incentives and do not encourage extreme risk taking.

c) Corporate liability regime: ensure that liability regimes providing for appropriate fines and other penalties for failure to comply with financial services legislation are established, allowing executives in financial institutions to be suspended or disqualified from working in all or relevant parts of the financial sector in the event of a breach of duty or wrongful trading.

d) Credit rating agencies: measures addressing e.g. conflicts of interests, quality assurance systems and oversight in a manner consistent with the considered recommendations of the Financial Stability Forum, the International Organisation of Securities Commissions, the Committee of European Securities Regulators and the European Securities Markets Expert Group relating to potential enhancement of credit rating processes, drawing lessons where appropriate from the oversight of auditors; give particular consideration to: transparency on rating methodologies, assumptions and stress tests; for supervisors to be able to call for an "audit trail" of the originator/credit rating agency correspondence and to be notified in the event of significant concerns over models; ensure that credit rating agencies provide enhanced information as to the particular characteristics of complex debt products, mortgage related products and traditional debt, and that the rating agencies apply differentiated symbols for the rating of complex debt products, mortgage related products and traditional debt; foster transparency of credit rating agencies, provide enhanced transparency as to the methodology and criteria relevant to particular ratings of complex debt products, mortgage related products and traditional debt.

2. RECOMMENDATION 2—FINANCIAL STABILITY AND SYSTEMIC RISK MEASURES

The European Parliament considers that the legislative act(s) to be adopted should aim to regulate:

a) Financial stability and systemic risks: establish databases, forward-looking scenarios, policies on macro prudential supervision and financial stability, as well as an early-warning system and ensure that the European Central Bank (ECB), the European System of Central Banks (ESCB) and the Banking Supervisory Committee of the ESCB (BSC) take an active role in their initiation, elaboration and operation; ensure that EU supervisors and central banks provide the ECB, via the BSC, with relevant non-public and confidential up-to-date aggregate micro-prudential information/data to allow it to fulfil this function and prevent systemic risk;

b) EU crisis prevention, management and resolution arrangements: In particular:

  i) enhancing crisis prevention and management arrangements at EU level, where necessary, including:

  – monitoring and assessing systemic financial risks at EU level;

  – setting up an EU early-warning system and early-intervention mechanism for dealing with weak and failing entities, when an EU cross-border financial group is concerned or when the EU financial stability is threatened; such a mechanism should be well-defined, clear, able to prompt action and comply with EU State aid rules;

  – facilitating the cross-border transfer of funds within a group in extreme situations by taking into account the interests of the creditors of the group's individual entities and having regard to Directive 2001/24/EC;

  – cross-border crisis management and clarifying State aid rules in cases of cross-border crisis;

  ii) enhancing crisis resolution arrangements by improving the EU rules on winding up and setting up arrangements of burden sharing among relevant Member States in cases of insolvency within cross-border financial groups;

c) Ensure that EU rules on deposit guarantees are urgently revised to avoid arbitrage between guarantee levels in Member States that may further increase volatility and undermine financial stability instead of increasing security and depositors' confidence; they should also guarantee a level playing field for financial institutions; EU rules on deposit guarantees should be amended to support further development of ex-ante schemes financed by contributions from financial institutions; the level of refund should be significantly increased and the availability of refunds to retail clients in case of failing financial institution should be ensured within a reasonable timeframe including in cases of cross-border situations;

d) Promote similar rules for insurance guarantees, whilst recognising the different nature of insurance and banking;

e) Ensure market diversity and encourage institutions that have long-term funding or liabilities to diversify market and liquidity risks.

3. RECOMMENDATION 3—SUPERVISORY FRAMEWORK

The European Parliament considers that the legislative act(s) to be adopted should aim to regulate, streamline, integrate and complete the present supervisory system by means of the following:

3.1. Supervision of large cross-border financial groups

a) By 31 December 2008, a regulation will require colleges of supervisors for the largest cross-border financial groups or holdings operating in the EU. The regulation should contain clear criteria for identifying the cross-border financial groups or holdings for which such colleges will be mandatory. In cases of substantial third-country involvement, separate parallel structures should be avoided, and third country supervisors could be invited to be involved as far as reasonable and practicable;

b) The colleges will be composed of representatives of the national supervisory authorities dealing with prudential supervision. The regulation should contain clear principles for the national supervisors that have to be represented in the mandatory colleges, taking into account the group's market size in a Member State, the volume of cross-border operations, the volume and value of assets to reflect the importance of the group activities, ensuring that all Member States in which the parent undertaking, subsidiaries and significant branches are operating will be represented, and also taking into account the need to involve third-country supervisors where reasonable and practicable. Special attention should be given to the challenges with which supervisors in rapidly catching up economies are faced. To achieve operational integration, the consolidating supervisor must have full process-leadership within the college, i.e. the consolidating supervisor must be the central point of contact for the financial group, ensuring appropriate delegation of tasks and responsibilities within the college;

c) The colleges will normally be chaired by the consolidating supervisor from the Member State where the central administration or the main EU office of the cross-border financial groups or holdings is established. The consolidating supervisor will host and primarily staff the secretariat;

d) Ensure collection, exchange and access to relevant information among the members of the college and among all supervisors involved within the EU and stimulate arrangements for maximising exchange of information with third-country supervisors;

e) The colleges will decide, where appropriate, on the basis of a qualified majority voting (QMV) system based on principles and objectives that will ensure consistency, fair and appropriate treatment and a level playing field.

3.2. Configuration of EU supervision: Lamfalussy Level 3 Committees

a) By 31 December 2008 a regulation will strengthen and clarify the status and accountability of the Lamfalussy Level 3 Committees, giving the Level 3 Committees legal status commensurate with their duties, and coordinate and streamline the action of the different sector supervisory authorities, reinforce their tasks and ensure appropriate staffing and resources;

b) In addition to advisory tasks, the Lamfalussy Level 3 Committees will be given the task (and the tools and resources) to ensure and actively promote supervisory convergence and a level playing field in the implementation and enforcement of EU legislation. National supervisors should be committed to the execution of the tasks and decisions of the Lamfalussy Level 3 Committees. This should be included in the mandates of the national supervisors and their mandates must be brought better in line with each other;

c) The Lamfalussy Level 3 Committees should present an annual work plan. Parliament, the Council and the Commission should approve the Committees' annual work plans and reports;

d) The Lamfalussy Level 3 Committees can take decisions on the basis of a fair and appropriate QMV system that takes into account the relative size of the financial sector and the GDP of each Member State, as well as the systemic importance of the financial sector for the Member State; such a procedure should be elaborated both for decisions on supervisory convergence issues and for the advice to the Commission on legislation and regulation;

e) The Lamfalussy Level 3 Committees should:
   i)   develop procedures for data provision in cross-border situations;
   ii) issue recommendations on specific (macro) supervisory practice issues;
   iii) issue guidelines to ensure coherence and streamline the supervisory practices of the colleges;
   iv) develop procedures to mediate conflicts that may arise between members of a college;
   v)   design common reporting standards and data provision requirements for groups, preferably in a multi purpose format such as Extensible Business Reporting Language (XBRL);
   vi) represent the EU in international sector bodies of supervisors such as the International Organisation of Securities Commissions;
   vii) establish a periodical panel review process for each of the colleges to ensure convergence on college processes. The review panel should be set up as a joint group of the Lamfalussy Level 3 Committees and the BSC,

the latter bringing in the macro-prudential perspective which is crucial to ensure close cooperation between supervisors and central banks and to effectively manage crisis situations;

f) The chairs of the Lamfalussy Level 3 Committees should meet on a regular basis to reinforce cross-sector cooperation and coherence between the three Lamfalussy Level 3 Committees. Where possible, mediation should be used to resolve disputes in the first instance with the mediator(s) agreed by the parties to the dispute in issue. Failing that, a group, made up of the chairs of the Lamfalussy Level 3 Committees, together with an independent chair and vice chair, should be given the legal powers to mediate and, where necessary, intervene to resolve conflicts between supervisors within the structure of colleges and sectoral Lamfalussy Level 3 Committees. The chair and vice chair for that Lamfalussy Level 3 Committee coordinating group should be nominated by the Commission and approved by the Parliament for a five year term;

g) Together they should:
   i) coordinate between the Lamfalussy Level 3 Committees;
   ii) provide for common data and statistics;
   iii) cooperate with the BSC and the ECB for the purpose of coordinating financial stability issues;
   iv) where necessary, establish appropriate arrangements for dealing with conflicts that may arise between the national and/or sectoral supervisors that participate in colleges, or between the Lamfalussy Level 3 Committees;
   v) promote a European supervisory culture for the future that is solid and sustainable and provides for a better cross-sector and cross-border integration and coordination;

h) Elaborate a supervisory architecture that is solid and sustainable and which provides for a better cross-sector and cross-border integration and coordination.

3.3. EU financial stability arrangements

a) By 31 December 2008, a proposal will require arrangements for financial stability oversight at EU level. Those arrangements should ensure the efficient collection and analysis of micro and macro prudential information for the early identification of potential risks to financial stability, integrated with global work on financial stability. Those arrangements should enable EU supervisors and central banks to react promptly and develop a rapid reaction force for crisis situations with a systemic impact for the European Union;

b) The oversight arrangements should, most importantly, aim to strengthen horizontal links between macro-economic and financial market supervision. Strengthening the ECB's role in this respect is necessary. Procedures for cooperation and information-sharing between the Lamfalussy Level 3 Committees and ESCB/BSC should be developed;

c) Specific issues to be addressed should include:
  i) establishing a proper system of supervisory data collection and exchange;
  ii) analysing and elaborate those data;
  iii) developing procedures for the provision and collection of confidential data;
  iv) providing early-warning signals about dynamics that can endanger the stability of the financial system;
  v) mechanisms for rapid reaction force in case of a threat to financial stability;
  vi) representing the European Union in international bodies of supervisors such as the Financial Stability Forum and identify an EU counterpart for supervisors in other parts of the world.

APPENDIX 2

Financial Markets Cannot Govern Us[1]

The current crisis is a heavy indictment of "market fundamentalism." This crisis points the finger at major weaknesses of a model of economic and business governance, with its under-regulation and inadequate supervision, under-supply of public goods (including healthcare, infrastructure).as well as a blind belief in the self-healing/equilibrating virtues of markets).

Some are tempted to see the ongoing financial crisis as a recurrent accident, albeit more severe, along an economic cycle and following worldwide very cheap credit for years in a row. But a careful reading would go at its structural roots. Globalisation of markets and financial engineering, with precarious and, frequently, missing regulations, highly skewed incentive schemes, and numerous conflicts of interest, have created the milieu for the current crisis.

Financial markets have become increasingly opaque and, identifying those who bear the risk together with evaluating it represents formidable tasks. The size of the so-called "shadow banking sector," which is lightly, or not regulated at all, has been constantly increasing over the last couple of decades. Banks themselves have been in a game of "origination and distribution" of highly complex financial products; banks have engaged in more than questionable packaging and selling of debt tied to high risk mortgages. Inadequate incentive schemes, short-termism and blatant conflicts of interest have increased speculative, casino-type trading.

Dubious mortgage credits, based on the idea that an unlimited increase in housing prices would allow them to pay back their debts, are only the acute symptom of a much broader crisis, which relates to a type of financial governance, to a business model. The top three rating agencies in the world were themselves interested in investing in the securities they were rating, because of the high commissions they could get! And a major investment bank epitomises a loss of any sense of ethics: it earned billions of USD by speculating downwards on subprime securities while selling them to its clients!

Ironically, financial innovation that was designed, purportedly, to diminish risk at the individual/micro level has ended up in exacerbating it at the macro level, thus enhancing systemic risk. In hindsight, episodes such as the LTCM or Enron falls, can be seen as stress tests for the financial system. It is quite surprising to hear officials (central bankers, supervisors, etc.) claiming that the

---

[1] This text was published by the French daily *Le Monde*, 22 May 2008.

magnitude of the current financial crisis could hardly have been imagined not long ago. Alexander Lamfalussy and the Committee of Wise Men, in a report on European securities markets (2001), underlined the trade-off between apparent higher efficiency and financial stability. Paul Krugman, in his "Return of Depression Economics" (1999) warned against the menaces posed by the expanding and hardly regulated shadow banking sector. In 2003 Warren Buffett called derivatives "financial weapons of mass destruction." And a Bank of England report on financial stability, of April last year, by referring to the model of origination and distribution highlighted the catastrophic distance between lenders and the consequences of their decisions. Other down to earth voices rang the same bell!

The scope and nature of this financial crisis refutes glaringly those who have said that the financial industry is capable of self-regulation. There is a need to revise the regulatory frameworks for the operation of investment vehicles; hedge funds, all other investment vehicles, the shadow banking sector, in general, have to be regulated. The use of financial instruments (like CDOs) has to be regulated, so that the transparency of markets be restored and investors be adequately informed. As banks are required to hold minimum reserves a similar rule should apply to all financial institutions. Likewise, the magnitude of leveraging should be capped. Better regulation does not mean a reversal of financial openness; the opposite is true. Financial openness, in order to be sustainable (and not produce irreparable damage), demands proper (enforceable) regulations.

This financial crisis has made more visible the growing income inequalities which have accumulated in the past decades. There is no need to be a left-oriented democratic politician in order to decry such an evolution.

It is worthy to notice that rising income inequality in both the US and Europe has gone in tandem with an ever growing financial sector that seems to have acquired a *raison d'être* of its own. Since all regulation has practically been abolished in the financial area financial assets represent 15 times the total Gross Domestic Product (GDP) of all countries nowadays. The credits granted have reached unprecedented amounts; the accumulated debt of households, financial and non financial companies and of the American public local and regional authorities amounts to more than three times the US GDP, i.e., the double of what it was in 1929. The financial world has accumulated a massive amount of fictitious capital, with hardly an improvement for humanity and the environment owing to it, and it has generated increasing inequalities in favour of those with the power to issue this capital. The salaries of top CEOs, or at least those who have adopted a financial and not an industrial rationale, are between 300 and 900 times higher than the average salaries of those working for them, whereas in the first century and a half of capitalism up until the 1960s, that ratio was at most of 40 to 1. The share of direct and indirect wages in the GDP has been steadily decreasing in the last 25 years by 8% to 11% in the main industrialized countries. Between 1 and 5% of the richest part of the population has benefited almost exclusively from the increase of half of the GDP in 20 years. It is true that technological progress has contributed to rising income inequality (by favouring highly skilled labour); but misguided policies have had their major role, too, in this regard. All of this brings a huge ethical issue to prominence.

Many who talk about free markets seem to ignore that Adam Smith (seen as the father of *laissez faire* economics) wrote also *The Theory of Moral Sentiments*; and that Max Weber, the famous sociologist, connected hard work and moral values (ethics) with the advance of capitalism. Public policy has to deal with the social fallout of unlimited greed, lack of honesty, cynicism, selfishness, etc, which the current financial crisis illustrates conspicuously. Decent capitalism ("that respects the dignity of man", to use Amartya Sen's words) needs an effective public policy, aside from virtues to be found in individual beings' pursuits of happiness and material rewards. Profit seeking is the essence of a market economy and without efficiency progress is unimaginable. But when everything, including one's soul, is for sale, social cohesion melts and the system breaks down.

The current financial crisis casts a long shadow on and diminishes the West's ability to have a more effective dialogue with the rest of the world in dealing with global issues, in managing side-effects of globalisation—in a period when Asia's extraordinary economic progress poses unprecedented new challenges.

If we want to be effective in our global endeavours, including dealing with the global warming, we need to pay genuine attention to the concerns of the rest of the world, whether in trade, development aid, etc. The spectacular rises in energy and food prices compound the effects of the financial turmoil and are ominous for what lies ahead, in the years to come. Quite tellingly, hedge funds have been involved in driving the prices of basic staples (e.g., rice) upwards! Most severely affected are the citizens of the poor countries of this world. This means famine, destitution, a proliferation of failed states, more immigration. —

But things are not rosy in the Union, too. Some EU officials are boasting about "robust European economies," better financial supervision and regulation (than in the US). But is it quite so? Just consider the spreading pains in the real estate markets in the UK, Spain, Ireland; and more is, arguably, going to happen. Think also about economic nationalism and populism, which are both on the rise in Europe. Think about the social fabric of our societies. The implementation of the Lisbon Agenda must consider the implications of the current financial crisis and of the rises in the prices of basic commodities (energy and food). These implications will impact on domestic politics in the EU, on the whole metabolism of the Union.

EU policy-makers, at Union and national level, have to provide a firm response to the current financial crisis, which should be viewed from the wider perspective we have tried to sketch above. This implies an economic and business paradigm which should favour pragmatism and open-mindedness. The age of market fundamentalism has, arguably, come to an end!

✽   ✽   ✽

We believe it is in the highest interest of Europe to take adequate stock of these developments and try to identify the foreseeable consequences in the short and in the longer run as thoroughly as possible, so as to allow the Union to examine the appropriate measures and come up with the adequate proposals for the International Community to try to counter the effects and root causes of this crisis.

It is high time to set up a "European Crisis Committee" gathering high-profile politicians, former Heads of State and Government or Finance Ministers as well as renowned economists and financial experts of all continents. This Committee, if you agree to set it up and finance it, would have the following tasks:

– to make an in-depth analysis of the financial crisis, in the wider context we have tried to outline above;

– to describe and assess the economic and social risks entailed by the financial crisis to the real economy, particularly in Europe;

– to suggest a series of measures to the Council of the European Union in order to avoid or limit these risks and to prevent future repetitions of even more severe financial crisis;

– to present to the Council of Ministers, the Member States of the UN Security Council, the Director-General of the IMF and all authorities and bodies concerned a set of proposals to limit the effects of this crisis and prepare a World Financial Conference in order to redraft the rules of international finance and the governance of global economic issues.

In 2000 we have agreed to make Europe the most competitive economy in world. This was reconfirmed in 2005. We must ensure that Europe's competitiveness is supported and not undermined by the financial markets. We need to act now: in the name of our workers, for more investment and for economic growth, all in all, for more social justice.

Signed by:
Helmut Schmidt, Otto Graf Lambsdorff, Lionel Jospin, Jacques Delors,
Michel Rocard, Romano Prodi, Jacques Santer, Göran Persson, Pär Nuder,
Massimo d'Alema, Hans Eichel, Poul Nyrup Rasmussen, Daniel Dăianu,
Paavo Lipponen, Ruairi Quinn, Laurent Fabius, Anneli Jaatteenmaki

The Recurrence of Financial Crises in Economic History

THE ENRON SCANDAL, 2001

Enron, an American energy company, boasted revenues of more than US 110 billion US dollars in 2000 and was named by *Fortune* "America's Most Innovative Company" for six consecutive years. By November 2001, Enron was undergoing the largest bankruptcy in history. There are many causes of the Enron collapse, most of which could be found at the root of today's sub-prime crisis. Firstly, there was the conflict of interest between the two roles played by Arthur Andersen, as auditor but also as consultant to Enron.[1] Secondly, the company presented false and misleading pictures of its financial health and results of operations. Most of these operations were complex structured finance transactions rolled via through off-books financial entities such as special purpose vehicles (SPVs). Thirdly, the objective of these fraudulent activities was twofold: to convince analysts and credit rating agencies that its reported earnings were real and to achieve its stated profit target which would allow company's employees to receive their bonuses. In some ways, the culture of Enron was in itself the primary cause of the collapse. This seems to become more apparent today when not a few companies are, sometimes, involved in a similar type of activities.

THE DOT-COM CRASH, 2000

The public's increasing interest in the internet-based companies had pushed up their share prices at a very fast rate. People, having no prior knowledge of stock trading, bought technology shares based on expectations of higher returns generated by future profits. But in March 2000, the bubble burst, and the technology-weighted NASDAQ index fell by 78% by October 2002. The crash had wide repercussions, with business investment falling and the US economy slowing in the following year, a process exacerbated later by the 9/11 attacks. Subsequently, these events led to a temporary closure of the financial markets. The response of the Federal Reserve was to gradually lower interest

---

[1] See "SEC Settles Enforcement Proceedings against J.P. Morgan Chase and Citigroup" Press Release, 2003-87. Available at: *http://www.sec.gov/news/press/2003-87.htm*.

rates throughout 2001, from 6.25% to 1%, in order to stimulate economic growth.

THE COLLAPSE OF THE LONG-TERM CAPITAL MANAGEMENT FUND (LTCM) IN 1998

Four years after its inception, the LTCM hedge fund collapsed, precipitating the first in-depth analysis by policymakers of the potential systemic risks posed by the hedge fund industry. Although LTCM had, at the beginning of 1998, a leverage factor of thirty to one,[2] LTCM's partners believed, on the basis of their complex computer models, that the long and short positions were highly correlated thus, yielding a small net risk. While the LTCM problems started to emerge when Russia defaulted on its government obligations, its collapse was precipitated by the "flight to liquidity" across global fixed-income markets, when investors started to shift their assets into more liquid assets. As a consequence LTCM's short positions were priced higher relative to its long positions causing the hedge fund to collapse. However, the LTCM crisis proved to be much deeper, threatening to pose a systemic risk to the financial system. This happened because other large hedge fund managers followed similar strategies as suggested by sophisticated computer models.[3] Other reason was the similarity of positions held by a number of market participants, like investment banks. After the fund had lost substantial amounts of the investors' equity capital, in order to avoid the threat of a systemic crisis in the world financial system, the Federal Reserve co-ordinated a 3.5 billion US dollars rescue package from leading U.S. investment and commercial banks.

The seriousness of the crisis prompted the US President's Working Group on Financial Markets to issue a report on the hedge fund implications for systemic risk in financial markets.[4] As Ben Bernanke put it, "[t]he Working Group's central policy recommendation was that regulators and supervisors should foster an environment in which market discipline—in particular, counterparty risk management—constrains excessive leverage and risk-taking. Effective market discipline requires that counterparties and creditors obtain sufficient information to reliably assess clients' risk profiles and that they have systems to monitor and limit exposures to levels commensurate with each client's riskiness and creditworthiness."[5] Although those recommendations

---

[2] In early 1998 LTCM had equity of 5 billion US dollars and had borrowed over 125 billion US dollars.

[3] Garleanu and Pedersen (2007) suggest that there may has been a multiplier at work.

[4] Hedge Funds, Leverage, and the Lessons of Long-Term Capital Management (1999).

[5] Ben S. Bernanke, "Hedge Funds and Systemic Risk" Speech at the Federal Reserve Bank of Atlanta's 2006 Financial Markets Conference, Sea Island, Georgia May 16, 2006.

seemed to have common economic sense, they have failed to be comprehensively applied. Much of the on-going sub-prime crises stems from excessive leverage and risk-taking by market participants against the background of reckless use of new financial instruments.

ASIAN CRISIS, 1997

This was caused by large private capital flows to emerging markets in the search of higher yields. The resulting large quantities of credit that became available in Asian countries ignored risks and induced a highly-leveraged economic climate that pushed up asset prices at an unsustainable level. Subsequently, asset prices collapsed, generating large credit withdrawals from the crisis countries which caused a credit crunch and widespread bankruptcies.

THE "BLACK MONDAY" CRASH, 1987

The US stockmarket suffered its largest one-day fall, dropping by more than 22% with European and Japanese markets following suit. The crisis was sparked by market participants' conviction that insider trading and company takeovers on borrowed money were dominating the markets. Programme trading strategies for selling stocks indiscriminately, as markets fell, also exacerbating the decline. In order to prevent major commercial banks to fail, the central banks cut interest rates aggressively. In the aftermath of the crisis, regulatory bodies introduced the so-called "circuit-breakers" aimed at limiting programme trading and allowing them to suspend all trades for short periods.

LATIN AMERICAN DEBT DEFAULT, 1982

During the mid 1970s many nations in Latin America, including Chile, Mexico, and Argentina introduced substantial economic reforms, involving the liberalisation of foreign trade, domestic financial markets, and privatisation of public industries. Exchange and capital controls together with other economic barriers were loosening without any increase in regulatory oversight. As a result of financial reforms foreign capital became easily available to domestic banks. The borrowing frenzy led Latin America to quadruple its external debt from 75 billion US dollars in 1975 to more than 314 billion US dollars in 1983, equivalent to 50% of the region's gross domestic product (GDP). As interest rates increased in the US and Europe in 1979, Latin America countries found more difficult to finance their interest payments. As most foreign banks refused to roll over Latin America debt—most of which was short-term—many banks became close to being insolvent until a massive rescue was engineered between the Federal Reserve and the IMF. In this case the traditional banking crisis was compounded by the effects of the subsequent currency crisis. As in the S&L case (see below) irresponsible lending was the prime cause for the crisis.

The Savings and Loan (S&L) Crisis, 1980s

This represented the failure of the savings and loan association in the US when, over 1,000 savings and loan institutions ended up with a position of net equity. However, this did not prevent them from being able to borrow large sums at favourable rates, thanks to deposit insurance. That recklessness in lending was a factor aggravating both the boom and the subsequent bust of the S&L crisis. As in the current sub-prime crisis, the banking problems of the 1980s came primarily—although not exclusively—from unsound real estate lending. The final cost of resolving failed S&Ls was estimated at over 160 billion US dollars, with much of this cost being paid with taxpayer's money. Probably the most important lessons to be taken from this crisis are those pertaining to regulatory issues. The S&L crisis highlighted the need for strong and effective supervision of insured depository institutions. Moreover, it showed that sorting out ailing financial institutions requires that the deposit insurance fund be strongly capitalised with real reserves, not just governmental guarantees.

The Penn Central crisis, 1970

The Penn Central Transportation Company, was, at that time, the largest non-financial company in the United States to go bankrupt. It had massive amounts of short-term commercial paper outstanding when the interest on its loans became an unbearable financial burden. The ensuing collapse of the railroad company led to a panic in the commercial paper market. Although an attempt was made by the government to save the company by guaranteeing its loans, it failed. This episode has striking similarities with the sub-prime crisis. The creditworthiness of the rating agency ensured the issuance of large amounts of commercial paper which, subsequently, could not be rolled over. Then, as today, the Federal Reserve opened the discount window, fearing that the crisis would spill over into the banking system.

The Great Depression, 1929

The Great Depression triggered by the 1929 crash is another benchmark episode in the history of financial crashes. At that time, the bull market prevailing prior to the crash seemed to be fully justified. The post war economic boom spurred by new technologies were promising large increases in sales and corporate profits. The stockmarket fall was massive, by the time it reached bottom in 1932, 90% had been wiped off the value of shares. The effects on the economy were severe, by 1932 the US economy had declined by half, and one-third of the workforce was unemployed.[6] In March 1933 the US

---

[6] But the effects of the US stock-market crush were felt strongly throughout the world. Economic hardship generated by this crisis was in fact sowing the seeds for the World Word II.

President, Franklin Roosevelt took office and launched the New Deal, which addressed landmark changes in regulatory and supervisory rules.

BARINGS CRISES (1890 AND 1995)

In 1980, losses by a leading UK bank, Barings, made on its investments in Argentina forced a massive sale of securities in the United States. These were mainly triggered by the liquidity problems of British banks. In England, the Bank of England acted in its "lender of last resort" role and intervened in financial markets in order to prevent a systemic collapse of the UK banking.

More than a century later, the same bank went bankrupt due to an explosive combination of financial and organisational shortcomings. Fraudulent activities of the bank's management were facilitated by weak internal and external controls. Important supervisory and supervision rules were introduced by central banks in the aftermath of the 1995 Barings crisis.

OVEREND AND GUERNEY, 1866

Overend and Guerney was a discount bank which was supplying cash to London's commercial and retail banks.[7] A large number of these were left without access to funds when Overend and Guerney went bankrupt in 1866. It was then when Walter Bagehot advocated a new role for the Bank of England, namely the "lender of last resort." Its objective would be to avert a systemic crisis by providing liquidity to the financial system during crises.

---

[7] At that time London was the world's financial centre.

Three-Month Inter-bank Spread Rates Over the Base Rate

Fig. 14. % Difference between 3-month interbank rates and base rate

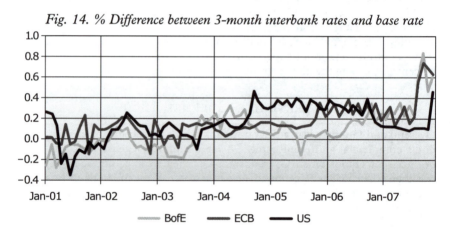

BofE = Bank of England; ECB = European Central Bank; US = The US Federal Reserve.

Index